ROUTLEDGE LIBRARY EDITIONS:
ETHICS

Volume 15

AN ADVENTURE IN MORAL PHILOSOPHY

AN ADVENTURE IN MORAL PHILOSOPHY

WARNER FITE

LONDON AND NEW YORK

First published in 1926 by Methuen & Co Ltd

This edition first published in 2021
by Routledge
2 Park Square, Milton Park, Abingdon, Oxon OX14 4RN

and by Routledge
52 Vanderbilt Avenue, New York, NY 10017

Routledge is an imprint of the Taylor & Francis Group, an informa business

© 1926 Warner Fite

All rights reserved. No part of this book may be reprinted or reproduced or utilised in any form or by any electronic, mechanical, or other means, now known or hereafter invented, including photocopying and recording, or in any information storage or retrieval system, without permission in writing from the publishers.

Trademark notice: Product or corporate names may be trademarks or registered trademarks, and are used only for identification and explanation without intent to infringe.

British Library Cataloguing in Publication Data
A catalogue record for this book is available from the British Library

ISBN: 978-0-367-85624-3 (Set)
ISBN: 978-1-00-305260-9 (Set) (ebk)
ISBN: 978-0-367-46854-5 (Volume 15) (hbk)
ISBN: 978-1-00-303169-7 (Volume 15) (ebk)

Publisher's Note
The publisher has gone to great lengths to ensure the quality of this reprint but points out that some imperfections in the original copies may be apparent.

Disclaimer
The publisher has made every effort to trace copyright holders and would welcome correspondence from those they have been unable to trace.

AN ADVENTURE IN MORAL PHILOSOPHY

BY
WARNER FITE
PROFESSOR IN PRINCETON UNIVERSITY

'Ο δὲ ἀνεξέταστος βίος
οὐ βιωτὸς ἀνθρώπῳ

The unexamined life is not fit
for human living.
Socrates, in "The Apology."

METHUEN & CO. LTD.
36 ESSEX STREET W.C.
LONDON

First Published in Great Britain in 1926

*This Book was first published in America under the title of
"Moral Philosophy : The Critical View of Life."*

PRINTED IN GREAT BRITAIN

PREFACE

THE purpose of this essay is to present a moral philosophy in the form of what may be called a philosophy of life. It is not my purpose to offer a "constructive system", such as to display an increasing conclusiveness as it approaches completion. What I will present is a point of view; which becomes necessarily less distinct, and raises ever deeper questions, as it broadens towards the horizon. And a point of view, because I believe that nothing in philosophy, however truly objective (and it is my purpose to offer something objective), is either intelligent or intelligible except as the expression of a point of view, in the last analysis inevitably personal. For this reason I have not hesitated to speak in the first person, to draw upon personal experience, or to give expression to personal opinion, taste, or feeling, whenever this would best convey my meaning. Somewhat for the same reason the book is not addressed exclusively, or perhaps primarily, to students of philosophy. It has been my hope to speak intelligibly to every cultivated man; to every person curious about the meaning of human life as presented, not in philosophy only, but in literature, art, and science.

To those acquainted with my "Individualism", printed in 1911, I would suggest that the point of view of the present volume is a further development (and therefore, I hope, a juster and more mature expression) of the point of view of the former volume. There I was interested in tracing the consequences of self-consciousness in social and political relations; here in the working of self-consciousness throughout human life. The present volume is an attempt to follow the *motif* of self-consciousness—not to the end, for there is no end—but until I can follow it no further. I take the opportunity of expressing my obligations to the friends who have given me the benefit of their judgment; to Mr. Herbert Agar and Mrs. Agar, whose criticism convinced me of the necessity of re-writing some more important passages; to Professor Charles W. Hendel, jun., of Princeton University, Dr. Laurence Buermeyer, of the Barnes Foundation, and Professor S. McClellan Butt, of the University of North Carolina, former pupils and sometime colleagues, who have helped me by their counsel in matters innumerable.

It will be understood that the author alone is responsible for the views expressed in the essay.

W. F.

PRINCETON UNIVERSITY,
June, 1925.

CONTENTS

	PAGE
PREFACE	v

CHAPTER I
MORALITY—WHAT IS IT?

§ 1. The meaning of " morality". § 2. Obligation *vs.* choice   1

CHAPTER II
THE MORAL PHILOSOPHER

§ 3. The orthodox moralist. § 4. The moralist as a naturalist. § 5. Moral insight   8

CHAPTER III
THE MANY MORAL WORLDS

§ 6. Orthodox morality and the moral standard. § 7. The moralities of race, class, and occupation. § 8. Differing moral tastes. § 9. The good men of the moral philosophies   21

CHAPTER IV
THE LOGIC OF THE STANDARD

§ 10. The odiousness of comparisons. § 11. The moral standard and the business point of view. § 12. Social utility in law and orthodox morality. § 13. " Positive " morality   34

CHAPTER V
THE MOTIVE OF AUTHORITY

§ 14. The categorical imperative. § 15. The basis of authority. § 16. The authoritarian tradition. § 17. Austere morality. § 18. Authority *vs.* morality. § 19. The sentiment of reverence   49

CHAPTER VI
THE ORDERED SOCIETY

§ 20. The order of reverence. § 21. The utility of the reverential order. § 22. The ordered society and the biological species. § 23. Ordered relations *vs.* social relations. § 24. The decay of reverence and the dawn of morality . . . 66

CHAPTER VII
THE UNITY OF THE SPIRIT

§ 25. Morality among the values. § 26. Utility and the system of means and ends 82

CHAPTER VIII
THE PRAGMATIC ATTITUDE

§ 27. The forward-looking attitude. § 28. Anticipation *vs.* retrospection. § 29. Imagination and the specious present. § 30. Reflective intelligence and the flux of life . . . 89

CHAPTER IX
THE WISDOM OF THE SERPENT

§ 31. Intelligence and the serpent. § 32. The moral fault and the intellectual. § 33. The clever rogue and the simple honest man. § 34. The critical life and the question of intelligence. § 35. Intelligence *vs.* intellect, mathematical and logical. § 36. Intelligence personal and critical 103

CHAPTER X
THE BEAUTY OF VIRTUE

§ 37. Aesthetic taste and moral law. § 38. The experience of beauty and virtue. § 39. The beauty of utility. § 40. The moral ground of aesthetic criticism 126

CHAPTER XI
THE BEAUTY OF KNOWLEDGE

§ 41. Aesthetic impressions and scientific facts. § 42. History as a branch of art 141

CONTENTS

CHAPTER XII

JUSTIFICATION BY KNOWLEDGE

§ 43. Judgment *vs.* criticism. § 44. Objectivity and rationality. § 45. The illusion of deliberate wickedness. § 46. "*Tout comprendre*" and "*tout pardonner*". § 47. The moral question and the practical 152

CHAPTER XIII

THE ENJOYMENT OF LIFE

§ 48. The Epicurean attitude. § 49. An Epicurean confession. § 50. Epicurus and Pater. § 51. Enjoyment and imagination. § 52. The enjoyment of friendship and the enjoyment of religion. § 53. Serious enjoyment 170

CHAPTER XIV

THE SUBSTANCE OF LIFE

§ 54. The particular nature of man. § 55. Biological evolution and the experience of thinking. § 56. Thinking and imagination. § 57. Imagination and human life. § 58. Imagination, morality, religion. § 59. Imagination and the metaphysical problem 193

CHAPTER XV

THE EXPERIENCE OF TRUTH

§ 60. The man of science and the man of culture. § 61. "Mere ideas" and the picture-psychology. § 62. "Mere feelings." § 63. Science and anthropomorphic prejudice. § 64. Truth and satisfied imagination. § 65. Error and lack of imagination. § 66. Experience of reality *vs.* coherence and correspondence 214

CHAPTER XVI

THE PRESENCE OF THE DIVINE

§ 67. Knowledge and "communion with the divine". § 68. The motive of knowledge and the motive of love. § 69. The idea of God and the presence of God 237

CHAPTER XVII

POETIC ILLUSION AND POETIC TRUTH

§ 70. Poetry and religious experience. § 71. Experience as experience of the real. § 72. Man as an animal and man as a human being 260

INDEX OF NAMES 275

AN ADVENTURE IN MORAL PHILOSOPHY

CHAPTER I

MORALITY—WHAT IS IT?

§ 1. The meaning of "morality". § 2. Obligation *vs.* choice.

§ 1

WHAT is it to be moral? In the following pages I shall give my answer to this question and endeavour to make its meaning clear. I shall assume that it is the reader's aim as well as mine to be moral. I shall assume also that he will agree with me, in the end if not in the beginning, in using the term "morality" to cover all that is important in human character and personality,—which means, as I aim to show, that morality involves so much more than is commonly supposed. When a man claims to be a better player of bridge or billiards than I am, or a better historian or mathematician, or a more competent man of affairs, I can admit his claim without compunction or feeling of responsibility. These are fields in which I have assumed no special obligation of excellence. But when he claims to be more moral than I am, I must protest—at least if I respect myself. Or if I do make the verbal admission, it means that I am allowing him to use the term "moral" in what is for me a conventional sense. I admit perhaps that he is more *respectable* than I am while saying to myself that there is something better than respectability. Yet this is not precisely what he means by being moral, as little as it is what I can let him mean. If we have found something better than morality it seems that the word has here been misplaced. In the end each of us is standing for something than which nothing can be assumed by him to be better. That something, that most important thing in life, I take to be the only true meaning of "morality".

I make this point at the outset because there are some persons, in no sense immoral persons, for whom "morality" is a term of depreciation; such as the pious Christian who insists that mere morality, further described as "worldly", is of little value for salvation; or the man of sensitive taste who contrasts morality with spiritual insight; or finally, perhaps the etymologist who reminds us that "morality", like the correlative term "ethics", is derived from a term meaning "custom". With all of these distinctions, however described, I am more or less in agreement. But to that against which the discrimination is made I will not give the name of "morality", preferring rather to describe it as a customary and conventional "righteousness". Etymology to the contrary, I shall locate the essence of morality precisely in its contrast to custom; following here the usage of the plain man who says that to appear in public without a collar is doubtless improper but surely not immoral. It may be asked why I have not avoided this danger of ambiguity by describing my subject-matter in other terms, such perhaps as "human nature" or "the meaning of life". My answer would be that in this field there are no unambiguous terms and that it is my purpose to offer what is known as moral philosophy.

What is it, then, to be moral? As a formal definition I offer the following: *morality is the self-conscious living of life*. Stating this more simply and concretely, I say that to be moral is to know what you are doing. The moral man is the man who, so far as he is moral, knows what he is about, and the immoral man is, thus far, he who does not know. But by putting it in this fashion—which, however, states the gist of the matter most clearly to myself—I may be tempting some more fastidious reader to reject the answer once for all as vulgar nonsense. I will then try to put it more acceptably by saying that to be moral is to be thoughtful; to be conscious; which to me means to be self-conscious; to live one's life, if possible, in the clear consciousness of living. And to be thoughtful, intelligent, self-conscious—what is this but to be conscientious and responsible? Surely we seem to be close to morality now. On the other hand, to be thoughtful, always to know what you are doing, is to be critical; to live, not by habit and instinct, but by judgment and choice.

For this conception of morality I might perhaps offer reputable authority by quoting those two famous sayings of Socrates, "Virtue is knowledge" and "Know thyself", and I might then call myself a disciple of Socrates. The trouble here is that there seems to be no moral philosopher who is not "a disciple of Socrates". It is from the Platonic Socrates, however, as he speaks in the "Apology" that I have taken the text for my title-page. Ὁ δὲ ἀνεξέταστος βίος οὐ βιωτὸς ἀνθρώπῳ. "The unexamined life is not fit for human living." The examined life—in other words, the critical life. The moral life, as I conceive it, is the examined life. Given the examined life, I say that nothing else is needed.

But I may also suggest what is meant by referring to the theory of aesthetic of Benedetto Croce. According to Croce, beauty is a question of expression; and not at all a question of what is expressed. Here he contradicts Aristotle, for example, who says that some subjects (*e.g.*, some persons) are suitable for tragedy, others are not. Croce's theory is implied in the remark, by whom I know not, that any man could write an interesting autobiography if only he would give a faithful record of his life. Any man might thus claim for his life a dramatic dignity if only he could express what he has lived through. Well, Croce's conception of beauty is the conception to be offered here of morality. Morality, if you please, is expression. There are no kinds of human nature that are intrinsically moral, others intrinsically immoral. A man is moral or immoral, so far as he expresses his own nature, so far as he lives his life knowingly.

§ 2

Given, then, the examined life, or the life that knows or expresses itself, I say that nothing else is needed. This gives the central point of my position and at the same time the issue with which the discussion will be everywhere confronted. For there will be many to retort by saying, Granting the examined life, something else *is* needed. It is not enough to live your life thoughtfully, you must reach the right conclusions. Otherwise your thinking will be valueless. And morality is not so much a matter of what you think as of what you do. It is a question not of motive, but of act. The road to hell is paved with good intentions. The Grand Inquisitors were doubtless thoroughly conscientious—therefore all the more dangerous. The more intelligent man may be only morally the more corrupt; and to be self-conscious may be only to be self-centred. To know what you are doing, or to act knowingly, is doubtless a necessary *condition* of morality—since morality cannot be predicated of such things as rivers, volcanoes, or motor-cars; but to identify morality with this condition is to define it negatively and insufficiently. Positively defined, it is not enough to act knowingly, one must also do what is *right*.

What is right! This suggests a set of terms wholly foreign to those which I have used in the answer given above. What is it now to be moral ? In this vocabulary the answer would be, to be faithful to your *duty* ; to obey the moral *law*, to conform to the approved *standards;* which are securely based upon fundamental and eternal *principles*. By placing the two sets of terms side by side—on the one side, right, duty, law, standard, principle, and on the other knowledge, intelligence, thoughtfulness—we may see, in the contrast of implications, the general character of the issue.

I may state the issue more formally by distinguishing

two classes of ethical theories: absolutistic, or authoritarian theories, in which morality is based upon authority, or law, assumed to be superior to and binding upon human choice; and what I shall call humanistic or libertarian theories, in which morality is derived from human nature and human choice. Stoicism marks the direction of absolutistic theories, Epicureanism of humanistic. My own view I will describe as humanistic, though I shall also state its implications in other terms. And I shall freely refer to the authoritarian view as the "orthodox" view, not for the sake of the epithet which this term has become, but because, as a matter of sober terminology and of etymology, it is the word best fitted to indicate the view of those who conceive intelligence to consist in "right thinking" and morality to be "a question of right and wrong".

This enables me to add a further point of definition to the motive of the essay. For, as against this orthodox view, I shall deny that morality is "a question of right and wrong" and also that intelligence consists in "right thinking". The word that I shall use as best marking the meaning of both is "criticism". And what I will present is a "critical" philosophy of life. To define this word is of course the task of chapters to come. But the nature of the question may be suggested by pointing to the difference of attitude represented by "the moralist", traditionally conceived as stern, forbidding, and exclusive in his judgments, and by "the critic", *i.e.*, the critic of art and literature, supposed to represent a genial catholicity of taste. The critic may by chance indeed be also a "moralist", intent upon establishing standards of orthodoxy in the field of criticism. The typically "pure" critic, however, is commonly little interested in questions of orthodoxy. His mind is working upon a very different question: not whether the object of his criticism, novel, poem, picture, or symphony, is in any sense "right "or "wrong", orthodox or heterodox, but is it interesting? Is it worth while? Is there anything in it? And what he means is, Is there any meaning in it? This novel, this picture, this poem, this song—is it a merely conventional echo of tones, colours, words, or is it the immediate utterance of individual experience and thought? And if there be a meaning in it, the only thing interesting is to understand that meaning. Such, as I conceive, is the attitude of the critic of literature and art; and such likewise, in opposition to the orthodox distinction of right and wrong, I take to be the attitude of any genuine inquiry concerning morality.

It may also help to define the issue if I point to the difference in theories of the state (where indeed, as Plato truly observes, we find ethics "writ large") corresponding to the divergence of ethical theory; to the difference, namely, between the absolutistic theory, embodied in the popular conception of "the German state", and the theories variously described as liberal, democratic, or individualistic. The latter might be called the humanistic theories of the state. And also the critical theories; as teaching that political life and virtue consist less in obedience to law than in popular criticism.

In the literature of moral philosophy these two classes of theory may be said to represent respectively two *motifs*, corresponding to two traditional elements of the moral problem. On the one hand it seems that morality is the fulfilment of an obligation (in the traditional literature of ethics "moral" and "obligation" are the two words most often conjoined); on the other hand it seems that moral action must be freely chosen action. The difficulty is then to see how it can be both. We seem to be faced with an antinomy. We warn the moral agent that he must fulfil his obligations—just because they are binding; and then we add that he must freely choose to fulfil them—as if they were not binding. Faced with this difficulty, the absolutistic theories tend to stress the obligation and let the freedom come in where and how it can—perhaps only in a Pickwickian sense. The humanistic theories lay stress upon the freedom. They may offer a Pickwickian definition of obligation, or, in anarchistic fashion, repudiate it altogether.

I would not make light of obligation. Rather would I say that he who wants anything is thus far obliged; and that he who loves is in loyalty bound. The conception of obligation that I shall dispute is the following. Authoritarian moralists, seeking a secure anchorage for the conception of obligation, are accustomed to fasten it to some conception of absolute power or supreme authority, such as the will of God, the sovereignty of the state, the paramount interests of society, or possibly, in these latter days, the biological laws of nature. This authority, whatever it be, is assumed to be morally prior to that of the choices and judgments of individual men and to furnish the criterion by which to measure the moral validity of these judgments. My conception of morality rejects all such moral absolutes. A morality thus based upon authority does not differ in principle, I should say, from the old-fashioned morality of hell-fire. This does not require me to deny the existence of God—not any more than to deny the existence of society. Nor does it commit me to an especially "worldly" view of life. What I dispute is the relevance of "authority". If authority be the basis of morality, the latter term might as well be abandoned. For its "right" is no longer distinguishable from might.

CHAPTER II

THE MORAL PHILOSOPHER

§ 3. The orthodox moralist. § 4. The moralist as a naturalist.
§ 5. Moral insight.

DEFINITIONS of ethics, or discussions of the meaning and function of ethics, are supposed to be (as they often are) as remote from a productive analysis of morality as surveying is from farming; the idea being that it is one thing to plot the field of ethics and quite another thing to say what the field will produce. It is upon the contrary assumption, namely, that a conception of ethics is in itself a description of morality, that I venture to open the discussion with a chapter on the study of ethics and the moral philosopher.

As a formal definition of ethics (to stand in the background) I will propose the following. Morality has been defined as the self-conscious living of life. The study of morality, or ethics, may then be defined as *a study of the meaning and value of life*. Or, since the study of morality is ever the discussion of a problem, ethics may be defined as a study of *the problem of life*. Or again—and this is the aspect of the subject to be emphasised here—as a study of the *varieties of life* and their individual significance.

Such a conception of ethics may at first glance seem so broad as to be meaningless. Yet any narrower conception fails, it seems to me, to reveal the full significance of the subject or to explain why the discussion of moral problems should be, as it always is, a matter of absorbing interest to every more thoughtful man. The development of the conception will occupy all of the chapters to come. In this chapter I shall indicate its tendency by contrasting it with the orthodox conception of ethics as represented by the orthodox moralist.

§ 3

What does "the man in the street" understand by ethics ? Or, if I may choose a spokesman nearer home, what is the conception of ethics in the mind of the average undergraduate of an American college[1] who has just registered his name for the next term's course ? Something like this, I venture. Ethics, as he understands it, is "a study of right conduct". The purpose of the course in ethics is to teach the student "what is right". This means, in the first place, that he expects to derive from the course an exposition of the established principles of morality; principles hardly less established than the principles of physics or the principles of law, and hardly less supported by authority. And then from these principles he expects to derive, or to have authoritatively derived for him, a compendium of rules, a guide to life, which will once for all mark out for him the (straight and narrow) path of duty. Further, perhaps, he expects to receive expert solutions of certain nice questions, such as, Is a lie ever justifiable ? though he is not quite prepared to substitute the expert solution for his own common sense.

But what he also expects, perhaps above all, is that the teacher will "exercise a moral influence", and that his teaching will also be preaching. He is to "speak as one having authority". If the tone of authority be missing the pupil will suspect the morality. Nay, I have known pupils who would authoritatively instruct their teacher in this matter. I come here to be influenced, their attitude has

[1] I am reminded that the point of view of the English student is very different; and certainly that of the German student. Even in the United States the attitude I have described in the text is more characteristic of the " college student " than of the student of the larger " university ". Yet the average American undergraduate, even in the larger universities, remains a " college student ".

seemed to say, and now I find the responsibility imposed upon me. I come for sound doctrine, and I get problems. In other words, I come for edification, and I am compelled to think.

There is a curious difference between ethics and other subjects in the college curriculum. The teacher of other subjects is bound to enlighten his pupils but he is under no obligation to convert. The teacher of ethics must not only convert, he appears to be authorised to mould the character of his pupils. And for the matter of that, after the pattern of his own, which is to serve as an example. And what is more, the average pupil, by no means in this respect a refractory pupil, expects his character to be moulded. And further, he will impose this as an obligation, and bestow the authority, upon any other persons, including his fellow-students, who set out to be moral. In their view the moral is inseparable from the didactic. As a further point of difference I may remark that while professors in other subjects are crowned for discoveries, discoveries in the field of ethics are more likely to be damned.

Such are the implications of the definition which makes ethics a study of right conduct. As a study of right conduct the ethics thus defined is what I have called orthodox ethics, in the sense that it conceives of morality in terms of right and wrong. This view of ethics is by no means confined to the man in the street. The man in the street is only adopting the traditional assumption of the schools. For widely as these may differ with regard to the ethical motive and the spiritual quality of the ideally good man (of which something will be said in the next chapter), there seems to be on the part of each school an attempt to show that, in the end, in terms of practical conduct, its own good man will satisfy the requirements of the orthodox standard. As J. S. Mill will show, the utilitarian is in practice as orthodoxly moral as any Kantian rationalist or any intuitionist. Their motives may differ, their practice is the same. So that it seems plausible to say, with Wundt and Leslie Stephen, that men agree generally as to *what* is moral and differ only as to *why* it is so; and therefore that the only function of ethics is to find the reasons for what we already know to be right.

§ 4

As against this orthodox conception, I propose now to offer, not so much a definition of ethics (the ending of the term suggests a "science", and it is my purpose to show that there is no such science) as a conception of moral philosophy; and less perhaps a conception than a picture of the moral philosopher, or the moralist. The moralist I will present as a *naturalist* who studies, not conduct, but *persons*.

To make the *motif* of this clearer I will repeat the query put to me several years ago by a clever and quick-witted woman; a thoroughly humane and cultivated person, who, however, as a trained and zealous student of nature, was disposed to take the point of view of natural science on its own word as the final criterion of wisdom and of truth. From previous conversations I had guessed that she found the profession of philosophy rather amusing if also somewhat mystifying. Finally came the question: in a world so full and various with fascinating things, such as glaciers, sea-anemones, and (I forget her third item, but I will insert) shovel-headed sharks, how could any really live person be interested in the abstractions of philosophy?

I will admit that the question floored me. It was a question which (after twenty years of teaching philosophy) my Freudian sub-conscious self preferred not to have raised. Though never a collector myself, and having only the slightest interest in the difference between one rock, one bird, one leaf, or one tree, and another, I had none the less envied the naturalist, or natural scientist, with his collections and his museums. If he were asked what he was doing in the world he had always something to show for it. He could entertain his friends with items of interest which normal persons could understand and appreciate. I could entertain mine only with—"abstractions". What in the world, then, is the philosopher really studying?

The answer, which came to me only long afterward, I have suggested above: the philosopher studies persons. I am not here proposing an academic definition of philosophy —or at best only one more. It will be sufficient to suggest that all the distinctively philosophical problems—the problems of logic, of psychology, of ethics, of the theory of knowledge, and no less of metaphysics—arise from the fact that there are persons in the world. With no persons in the world there would be no problems for philosophy but only problems for science, to be solved neatly and surely by scientific method. Hence the scientist would prefer to ignore the fact of persons, or at any rate to leave it out of his calculation. As a "modern scientist" in particular, he claims to treat the world impersonally; that is to say, to observe and report the objective facts in the world before him and to say nothing of the fact that it is he who observes them. This, he insists, has nothing to do with the facts observed.

The philosopher suspects the contrary. He, therefore, will study, not only the world, but also, and particularly, the scientist himself, the knowing person. And when he considers the knowing person in connection with the world known, what strikes him most forcibly is that, while the world known is for science supposedly one, the knowing persons are many and various even within the camp of scientists. And the supposedly impersonal and scientific view of the world is only one among others. This variety and multiplicity of personal view is grievous to the scientist, since it lies in the way of a calm acceptance of scientific authority. But the true philosopher delights in it.

Thus it comes about that the more reflective philosopher loves best to study philosophy itself in the form of the history of philosophy; in which the variety of human motive is seen in its most reflective form. For him the history of philosophy is the study of philosophy *par excellence*. The scientist, on the other hand, is comparatively little interested in the history of science. The history of science is not science but only gossip about science—antiquarian and polite. From the scientific point of view the persons composing the scientific world are of no importance. Their personal motives and experiences have nothing to do with the facts which it is their duty to discover What is important is the fact itself; and when the fact is established the discoverer may well be forgotten. Such is the point of view of science in contrast to the point of view of philosophy.

Now ethics, or moral philosophy, is most of all a study of persons. I shall not pause here to specify in what manner or degree ethics differs from psychology and each again from the broader study of philosophy. What I would point out (in answer to the inquiry of my naturalistic friend) is that the moralist is also a naturalist. He too, if you please, is a collector of specimens. Only, his specimens are persons and their points of view. They cannot, unfortunately, be preserved in jars; they must be stored less securely in the mind of the collector. But if it still be suggested that he is "playing with abstractions", then I shall ask to be introduced to something really concrete. And as for the interest of the collection—I do not doubt that glaciers and sea-anemones are stimulating to an intelligent imagination, but what may be claimed for them I claim *a fortiori* for persons. Indeed I cherish the prejudice that the interest in persons stands for a somewhat nicer taste.

The true moralist is collecting whenever he is awake. And not merely such items as the Ten Commandents, the Code of Hammurabi, the Categorical Imperative, and the Golden Sayings of Epicurus. These serve mainly as tags for his collection. His choicest bits are those personal idiosyncracies, tricks of manner and speech, and personal weaknesses (which the moralist, mindful of the code of his profession, will always hesitate to treat as weaknesses) which all unwittingly reveal the personal point of view. When Bishop Butler speaks of God as "the Lord and Proprietor of the universe", I see at once his conception of moral authority: God is for him an English landed-gentleman. Hence the moralist's choicest field is where truly well-bred persons never venture—the field of gossip. When Mrs. Jones tells him what Mrs. Brown said to Mrs. Smith and what Mrs. Smith said in reply, and then adds confidentially her own opinion of both, the moralist notes the presence of three interesting points of view (not forgetting that of Mrs. Jones) whose differences and mutual relations he deems worthy of respectful analysis. And nothing delights him more than a conversation between two persons of whom neither grasps what the other has in mind. One of my most instructive specimens of this kind is a conversation between a Hindoo gentleman and a Christian lady, each of whom found in the other a true type of "heathen". The exasperated Hindoo gentleman guessed very well how he was being regarded, but the Christian lady remained blissfully unconscious. She had no inkling of the horror aroused in her auditor by her frequent references to "the precious blood of Christ". In "India", he assured me very earnestly afterwards, "it has been thousands of years since we have believed in human sacrifice."

Such may be said to constitute the moralist's private collection. For his professional collection he must explore the world. And to some extent literally; for I fancy that only a residence for some time in a foreign country can enable one fully to appreciate how differences of custom and ways of living, apparently superficial, stand for deeper and genuinely moral differences of outlook upon life. As a retired scholar and thinker, however, his chief field of exploration must be the field of culture—of literature and art—made accessible to him through the medium of libraries and museums. Here of course his most important specimens are his fellow-moralists, especially those preserved in the history of moral philosophy—such as

Plato, Aristotle, Epicurus and the Stoics, Spinoza, Hobbes, Shaftesbury and Bishop Butler, Hume, the two Mills and Herbert Spencer, Kant and T. H. Green, Schopenhauer and Nietzsche. For among his points of view these are perhaps the most articulately ethical. Yet it is after all the intensely personal character of these moral philosophies that makes them significant. Had Spinoza really succeeded in demonstrating morality geometrically none of us would take the trouble to read him.

Important again for the moralist are the literatures of history and anthropology, especially of those anthropologists who with sympathetic imagination have not forgotten that they were studying human beings. A rich field for his purpose is the field of literary criticism. There he will find a valuable collection of points of view already "prepared" for him by the literary critic ; whose criticism, as I shall point out later, is fundamentally moral criticism. But an indispensable field of research for the moralist of the present day is the field of serious fiction. Nowhere else will he find such a variety of person and motive or a form of literature which more inevitably reveals the perceptive capacities of its creators—for though the characters be fictitious (I fancy they are never quite so) the writer is sure to be real. I have heard of moralists who never read novels. 1 wonder how they could expect to have much to say on the subject of morality.

Such is the naturalistic moralist. For him it takes all kinds of men to make a moral world, and the more kinds the better. Orthodox morality admits only one kind, and that the right kind.

§ 5

I will now anticipate some of the consequences of this view in the form of answers to a few of the more obvious questions.

The first is more likely to be an accusation. And so, I shall be told, what you mean by morality is "the ethics of naturalism" ! To this I reply that in the common acceptation, in which naturalism is opposed to idealism (and is perhaps a euphemism for materialism), naturalism is just the reverse of what I mean by morality. In this acceptation I prefer to identify morality with supernaturalism. I have drawn the moralist as a naturalist because I wish to insist upon his empirical and naturalistic preoccupation with concrete individuals, *i.e.*, with persons. But I might well have drawn him, after the fashion of Shaftesbury and Butler, as "a student of human nature". In these terms I may best put the answer to the question.

For between the study of nature and the study of *human* nature there lies an important difference. The student of nature may contemplate his specimens lovingly and indulge in curious speculations about the play of forces which has made them what they are, but he hardly ventures—not if he be a strictly scientific student of nature—to ask how it would seem to be a glacier, a sea-anemone, or a shovel-headed shark. The sea-anemone is a living thing; what, then, is its attitude towards life? Orthodox science discourages such questions and he who values his position in scientific society is careful not to suggest them. Let us, says the scientist drily, stick to the facts. Now it is precisely this forbidden kind of question that is uppermost in the mind of the naturalistic moralist; and it is precisely this power of sympathetic imagination—the power of seeing others as they see themselves and ourselves as others see us—that measures one's capacity as a moralist and also constitutes one's own morality. This comprehension of motives is what is commonly, but very accurately and significantly, called "moral insight".

A consideration of the meaning of moral insight will help also to answer our next question. For I may be asked whether the attitude which I have described as "naturalistic" does not involve a cooly supercilious and self-conceited treatment of one's fellows as "specimens", and thus an immoral attitude in the moralist himself. Not, I should reply, in one who studies them with moral insight. The factor of moral insight introduces into the relations between the student of human nature and the object of his study exceedingly perplexing questions. I am inclined to say indeed that he who can explain just how I know my neighbour will have answered the last question in metaphysics. Thus much, however, seems clear : one who studies the ways and points of view of men comprehendingly can hardly be coolly supercilious, much less self-conceited, however naturalistic and critical. There is no incompatibility between the critical attitude and personal interest and affection. It may even be said that each implies the other, and that those whom we question most curiously we love most warmly. Nor between personal affection and a sense of humour. We love the little children just in the fact that they delight and amuse us. And as for the "bitter humour" with which we annihilate an enemy—this seems to contain an element of paradox. For to make it effective, and really annihilating, it seems necessary first to control and cool, perhaps also to conceal, the bitterness ; while if you really loathe the person in question you may fear to condescend to humour. Humour is too compromising.

In any case it seems that the study of man introduces considerations hardly contemplated in the study of nature. The sea-anemone, however curious and beautiful, is disposed of when he is described and named. He has nothing to say in reply. To stamp your fellow's point of view—as "oriental", for example—is only to learn that the oriental view has something to say about the meaning of life for you and me. Hence for those who choose study as a reposeful avocation it is wiser to study sea-anemones than to study men.

The next question is more technical. Naturalistic ethics, it will be asked,—what is this but plain psychology ? In other words, if the moralist is the "student of human nature" why not call him a psychologist ? My instinctive reply would be that I don't care what you name him. For I greatly suspect that these distinctions of disciplines

—between ethics and psychology, ethics and politics, ethics and economics, psychology and logic, psychology and philosophy, logic and epistemology, etc., etc.—without a laborious chapter on which no Teutonic treatise can get under way—are but so many legal fictions, or academic fences, set up by each professor to prevent a neighbouring professor from borrowing his chair. But since a failure to answer might leave an ambiguity I will put it thus: I am quite ready to abandon the distinction between psychology and moral philosophy (but not to allow moral philosophy to be "reduced" to psychology), if only the psychologist will assume the responsibility of cultivating moral insight and undertake to use it as a method of psychology. The offer is not likely to be accepted.

Stated more formally, the issue is as follows. The traditional distinction between psychology and ethics is that, while both are (say) studies of men, psychology studies a man for what he is, ethics for what he ought to be. But now, what do you mean by what a man *is*? What a sea-anemone *is*, it seems that we can state clearly enough; since we are careful not to endow the sea-anemone with imagination. Hence it *is* just what it is, a determinate present fact and nothing more. But when we ask what a man *is* we discover (if we use moral insight) that he never *is* just what he is as a present determinate fact. Every man not absolutely dead is endowed with some imagination; and this means that what he does now and what he is now, is guided more or less by what he judges it worth while to do and worth while to be, *i.e.*, by what he is trying to be and ought to be. And thus the "is" and the "ought to be", the psychological and the moral, are so vitally connected that neither can even be stated apart from the other.

I may put the point differently by saying that, in contrast to the sea-anemone, the man more or less knows what he is; and this knowing ought to be a vital part of the man for any study that calls itself "psychology." Say, then, that A is a liar; and add to this that A knows that he is a liar. What *is* A now? What is a liar who knows that he is a liar? Or (in terms of "fact") what can you predict of him when he finds out and "comes to himself"? This is precisely what no one knows, least of all the scientific psychologist. And this is precisely the moral fact, an indeterminate sort of fact which does not readily meet the requirements of fact.

In the light of this we can see perhaps why what is now called psychology was numbered a few generations ago among "the moral sciences", and why this phrase was used then to cover all those studies of man, or of human nature, which we now call, less aptly, as it seems to me, "the social sciences". And on the other hand it is doubtless a realization of the indeterminately "moral" quality of the conscious fact that has led the more advanced of scientific psychologists to abandon "psychology" and content themselves with a description of human "behaviour". The new science of behaviourism will treat the man precisely as we treat the sea-anemone, the assumption being that there is as little imagination, or of "trying to be", in one case as in the other.

Finally it may be objected that the naturalistic preoccupation with the variety of human nature tends to blur the distinction of good and bad and to make any man as good as any other. But hardly, I might reply, if morality is to be identified with the intelligent, or critical, life—unless indeed we are to assume that all men are equally intelligent. Yet this will still mean that the intelligence of each is to be judged according to what he in particular is trying to do, according to his particular conception of life, or kind of human nature; and as for the kinds of human nature, none is better than another. Such is my answer. But I must confess that the question of who is the better man does not now strongly appeal to me and I even suspect it to be immoral. Why should one wish to know? I doubt if my reader would care to admit even to himself that it is any part of his interest in morality to learn to which and to how many of his fellows he is entitled to say, "I am holier than thou." Nor could he feel it less incumbent upon him to be all that he ought to be because he is already better than some of his fellows. It may be very important from a practical standpoint to ask who is the better carpenter, the better physician, the better man of business, but this is not to ask who is morally the better man.

CHAPTER III

THE MANY MORAL WORLDS

§ 6. Orthodox morality and the moral standard. § 7. The moralities of race, class, and occupation. § 8. Differing moral tastes. § 9. The good men of the moral philosophies.

§ 6

THE orthodox moralist is commonly to be identified in social intercourse by the extent to which he talks about standards; in moral philosophy by his extended discussion of "the moral standard". He is the man very frequently to be found among academic men, who refuses to listen to any moral observation of yours without first asking you, "What is your standard?" who insists that, as the primary condition of morality, "what we need is standards"; who deplores "the decay of standards"; and whose definitive moral condemnation is, "They have no standards." It is not always easy to make out whether this attitude is one of conviction or of scepticism since at times it seems that any standard will do provided it be a standard. But the usual implication is that there is but one standard of morality for all right-thinking men, the nature of which will be obvious to all who sincerely look for it.

This attitude sat attractively enough upon the resident of a small community of a few generations ago, when most communities were small and travel was difficult. In that setting it may be regarded as picturesque. This old-fashioned citizen had little consciousness, or at least little comprehension, of any culture but his own; and from the point of view of his own experience of the world the distinction between the heathen and the people of God seemed obvious and rational; as deeply grounded in the nature of things as for Plato and Aristotle the superiority of Greek to barbarian, of man to woman, and of freeman to slave. The situation is different to-day. The confluence of peoples and of ideas may very well be a confusion of tongues. Even so we meet face to face, and thought to thought, too many different kinds of men to rest comfortably in the conviction that our own is the right kind. And too many standards are suggested for the integrity of "the moral standard". All, it seems, are moral standards. It is then no longer picturesque to assume a common standard for all "right-thinking men".

§ 7

What we learn, however, from the difference of standard, and precisely from each one's belief in the exclusive validity of his own, is that the differences are moral differences. This is very obviously true of the differences of nation and race. Instinctively we tend to look upon the foreigner as immoral. "An immoral foreigner" seems a natural conjunction of terms. It is not merely that he is strange; an important part of his strangeness is that, to us, he is lacking in moral perception. An elderly and kind-hearted English lady once said to me, quite without arrogance, that in her opinion God had created the British people for the special task of bringing Christianity and salvation to the world—this was said, by the way, in Germany many years before the War. Mr. Punch may classify her with his other old lady who complained that daylight-saving deprived her begonias of the morning sun. But in point of fact few Englishmen, perhaps few Americans, can believe that a Frenchman is quite able to grasp the meaning of "sound morality". Few Anglo-Saxons can attribute full moral perception to a Jew—except as he is allowed to be different from other Jews. The Anglo-Saxon cultivates an ideal of dignity and reserve. To him the Jew seems ingratiating and expansive. The Jew, it might be said, seeks to be on terms of personal confidence with his fellows, and thus he desires to please. It hardly occurs to the Anglo-Saxon to ask whether this desire to please may not be the expression of a moral ideal; nor, on the other hand, does he very carefully examine the moral quality of his own cherished attitude of "reserve". He is content to attribute the Semitic attitude to the want of a proper—in the last analysis, morally proper—dignity.

The Russians present a nice problem for right-thinking moralists. In a few generations past they have contributed most of what is great to European music and fiction. In the presence of Tschaikowsky, Tourgenieff, Tolstoi, and Dostoievsky, it is not easy to dismiss them as simple barbarians. Yet as depicted by their novelists, even excluding such as Dostoievsky, they are a strange people. At one moment they astonish us by the depth and tenderness of their spiritual insight; at the next by the profundity of their reflections upon life; in the next moment we find them in a whirl of violence and dissipation or else prostrate with a devastating cynicism. They seem to be both more sophisticated than we are and more naïve. Is there a key to their inconsequentiality? To any naturalistic moralist they present a fascinating problem. The orthodox moralist prefers to set them down as sentimentalists and romanticists, *i.e.*, as morally defective.

Yet the Russians present a problem because we are in contact with their literature. There are other races, such as the Chinese, which apparently present none. Their bland indifference to western ideals of progress is easily set down to ignorance and "backwardness". We know indeed, vaguely and abstractly, that the Chinese is an ancient civilization, which is marked by a coherent social order, by a high development of the fine arts and a marvellous skill in the mechanical arts, and by an elaborate tradition of manners and morals. But only a few are in a position to know this concretely. Hence we cheerfully take up "the white man's burden" of teaching the Chinese our civilization, and possibly of enforcing it upon them. "The white man's burden" is perhaps the most naïve expression of orthodox morality and for that reason the most instructive. What it presupposes is a classification of all races and peoples as morally superior or inferior according to one conception of morality and one scheme of civilization, namely, our own.

Such of course are only the commonplaces of the traditional moralist. It is worth noting, by the way, that "the moralist" of the older tradition, as distinct from the more modern teacher of scientific ethics, was inclined to be mildly sceptical about the final rightness of any accepted standard. Yet I wonder if we have fully grasped the questions raised by his naturalistic survey. If the Chinese are to advance in civilization does it mean that they are to adopt western ideas? Has the Japanese adoption of western ideas been truly and purely an advance in civilization? It may be that we have much to teach the Chinese but would a Chinaman be better or worse if he became an Englishman or an American? And coming nearer home, if our American negro-labourer, or waiter, became a gentleman, and the cultural equal of the white gentleman whom he serves, would this mean that in becoming a gentleman (assuming that the ideal of the gentleman is a moral ideal) he also became white? If so it seems that we ought to commend him for "aping the whites".

Besides the race-moralities there are class-moralities, and these class-moralities, unobservant of the class-element, will then purport each to stand for morality as such. Our European moral code is supposed to be mainly Christian, but our moral philosophy—the traditional ethics of the schools—is clearly an inheritance from the Greeks, Plato's "Republic" and Aristotle's "Ethics" constituting its most classical documents. Now the Greek ethics, of whatever school, was an aristocratic ethics. The Greek conception of the good man and the good life was derived from the point of view of a leisure class, the point of view of the working population remaining inarticulate. Plato, the best Greek representative, by the way, of the principle of rightness, treats his artisans as if they were hardly worth consulting. Aristotle tells us unhesitatingly that one cannot realize the moral ideal without an independent income and he also upholds slavery as a natural institution.

To modern ideas this limitation of virtue to a favoured class is both repellent and absurd. Yet we are not ready to abandon the Greek conception of the best and most virtuous life. To us as to Aristotle it seems that the life of a gentleman, with its implications of leisure and culture, is the best life; only we should like to interpret it liberally, without the invidious class-distinction, and without reference to a qualification based upon property. It is along this line that T. H. Green conceives the social ideal to be a society in which all men are gentlemen, in which, however, the mark of a gentleman is not a matter of externals. But this is only to raise the question, Can the idea of a gentleman be made independent of external conditions? When we admit that the one-room tenement of the poorest classes makes decency of living almost impossible (including specifically moral decency) it seems that we have admitted Aristotle's view. And if we carry the notion of decency further to the point where it issues in the conception of culture and refinement (and if this be not a moral conception, what is it?), we shall find it difficult to disentangle our idea of the good life from an order of things which involves class-distinctions and servants. For my own part, although I dislike the institution of servants, and find no one more amusing than him who bases his claims to gentility upon knowing "the proper tone" in which to address a servant, yet I find it difficult to see just how that man or woman of spiritual refinement who most appeals to me could be bred without some measure of this background of service and leisure. And leisure not based upon service seems at least remote.

The class-element in this conception of the good life is pointed out by Georges Sorel, the French syndicalist, in his book on *"Les Illusions du Progrès"*. Sorel makes it indeed a ground for complaint that all ideas of progress, those of social reformers among others, have implied that the proletariat was to take on the culture and the manners of the leisure classes. To the claim that this leisure-class culture stands for superior intelligence he replies by showing that in France, at any rate, philosophy and literature have been designed for the diversion of an idle and restless court society and have therefore carefully avoided coming to terms with existing social conditions.[1] Of such intelligence the eighteenth-century *abbé*, clever, witty, and sceptical, is the representative type. But with this in mind it may then occur to us to ask whether the moral philosophy of the schools is not the product of a leisure-loving class of academicians whose leisure requires the support of wealth and power. This indeed is inevitably true even though we attach the best significance to "leisure"—and to my mind leisure is indispensable to any true life. And then we may go further and point out that not only our moral philosophy but the greater part of our science and scholarship is the work of men whose profession is teaching and whose conception of the intelligible is therefore likely to be influenced by what may be practically taught and in particular by what is available for examination. My belief is that this will prove to be a fruitful consideration for the student of logic. Its bearing upon the logic of orthodox ethics I will point out in the next chapter. Sorel, however, will have none of this leisure class culture. It is the task of his syndicalism to destroy not only the leisure class but the class-ideal; and the proletariat is then to set up its own conception of the good life. What the proletarian good life will be like, we are not told. It seems that, even more resolutely than other class ideals, it is to be enforced upon the unwilling; only it will not pretend to be other than a class-ideal.

---

[1] According to Jodl, *Geschichte der Ethik*, Vol. I, Chapter XII, it is this motive that marks the difference between Helvetius and Bentham, whose ethical theories are virtually identical. Bentham, however, was a social reformer; Helvetius a social satirist.

Those who believe that virtue is eternally one should reflect further that, quite apart from the social and economic distinctions of class, moral ideals vary with the special conditions of life, and especially with occupation. The qualities of character demanded of a locomotive engineer or of the captain of a ship we hardly expect of the poet and scholar. These qualities are not in the poet's line. The parsimony, or meanness, which Aristotle rightly excludes from his magnanimous man may rank as a virtue in the poor clerk or labourer with a family to support. Yet each is disposed to set up his own standard of virtue as a universal moral ideal. The man in easy circumstances tends to be disgusted by the meticulous economy of his less fortunate neighbour and to call it sordid. On the other hand the man to whom the great problem of life is the problem of economic respectability—the problem of paying his own way and owing no man anything—is disposed to look upon all the more liberal forms of life as somewhat frivolous, incompatible with genuine moral seriousness; just as for the man who works with his hands it requires some imagination to conceive that those whose work is chiefly mental render any real service to society.

Consider, again, the virtue of courage. This we are likely to prescribe as an indispensable virtue—at least for the male sex—without reflecting that it is mainly of military origin. Even "moral courage" betrays militant implications when we reflect that its effective exercise calls for a certain aggressiveness, a certain delight in conflict, and a corresponding indifference to giving offence. In the last generation or two this originally chivalrous tradition has been reinforced by the biological view of life, with its doctrine of the struggle for existence and the survival of the fittest, with the result that athleticism has become the dominant type of virtue, and praise is bestowed upon the "red-blooded man"; while a corresponding stigma rests upon the man of gentler tastes, or the "effeminate" man, now demonstrated to be a moral defective. For my own part, I find it somewhat difficult to conceive how a red-blooded man can be capable of appreciating the finer and more humane sides of life; while I find a willing admiration of "moral" courage embarrassed by the fact that moral courage is so much easier for him who can see only one side of the case. And I seem to have known one or two effeminate men who could justly be described as the salt of the earth. But the fact that the courageous virtues are described as "virile" (and we remember that etymologically "virtue" itself signifies "manliness") suggests that virtue may differ according to sex—unless we are to assume, as some sound moralists do, that men stand for a higher moral type than women.

§ 8

A little reflection upon current morality will show that in morality as elsewhere there are also differences of personal taste. Our own national taste is indicated by the fact that the phrase "an immoral man" means, unless expressly qualified, that the man is sexually immoral—so that it becomes intelligible to say, "This man is a liar and a thief, but he is not immoral". In view of this prevailing taste no political party cares to risk a candidate whose "private life" is open to attack though they will risk one who is known to have made a fortune out of public funds. In a candidate for public office it might seem that purity of motive in public life is more important than sexual purity; and as a matter of fact there are those, including myself, who would emphasize the former. Yet if the candidate for office must first of all be congenial to the public I do not know that either is more "right" than the other.

The older moralists embodied their "systems" of morality in tables of the cardinal, or fundamental virtues. Each of us tends to emphasize some one virtue as *the* cardinal virtue, which is fundamental to all of the others. One man prefers courage: for him everything is pardonable but cowardice. Another, like myself, prefers honesty —honour, truthfulness, and sincerity. In his view the one

THE MANY MORAL WORLDS

really unpardonable sin is hypocrisy, and the one condition to be exacted of a friend is openness and sincerity. A third will pardon a good deal of falsehood, disloyal weakness, or pecuniary irresponsibility in the man who is kindly and generous, always ready to do a good turn for his neighbour. A fourth consigns to outer darkness all who are not sober and prudent citizens. It seems indeed that most men specialize in a certain "line" of virtue as the standard by which they both judge others and demand to be judged themselves.

Yet in judging others there are few, even among the believers in orthodoxy, who make no concessions to personality, or to temperament, or to special conditions. We always make some allowance for "foreign ideas". We do not so severely condemn sexual irregularity in a Frenchman or a French woman, for whom marriage is a matter of arrangement and requires the consent of parents, as we should among ourselves. And I dare say we should be ready to excuse polygamy in one who could show that polygamy was the custom of his country. Those who condemn a marriage of convenience in the young may approve of such a marriage in the middle-aged. On the other hand we look for more evidence of spirituality in a clergyman than in a layman. We do not despise the householder who quietly yields his goods to an armed burglar—we are more likely to praise him for his good sense—but we have only contempt for the similar cowardice of a policeman. And even though we assert it to be the solemn duty of every citizen to interest himself in public affairs we admit some excuse for those who are temperamentally retiring. Finally, it seems that we all make concessions to men of genius, hardly expecting from them that fidelity as husband and father, or that promptitude in the payment of bills, which we exact of lesser men. It seems that we judge them as we judge the great men of history, more by the claims that they make for themselves than by any that we would impose upon them. The universal moral standard applies only to the common run of men.

§ 9

Nor will it help the argument for a moral standard to attribute this variable personal element in our moral estimations to the unscientific character of popular judgments—on the assumption that academic ethical theory will reveal a unity of criterion and of method. There is indeed a certain unity of character in academic ethics, but a rather dismal unity constituted by the fact that the literature of ethics consists so largely of the discussion of some half dozen stock questions : such as, whether virtue is one or many, whether the good is perfection or happiness, whether the idea of obligation is analysable, whether benevolence can be derived from self-love, whether conduct is to be judged by motive or by intention. I will not say that these questions are meaningless, but to my mind their chiefly important meaning is what they mean for the moralist who is dealing with them, and the chiefly creative result is what his discussion reveals of his personality, point of view, and attitude towards life. This revelation is the moralist's truly important contribution to the subject-matter of morality. In these terms the history of ethics, now far from enlivening, would be a fascinating chronicle and a series of the nicest literary and critical problems. It would best be presented, not as so many "systems", nor yet as so many moralists, but rather as so many ideal pictures, painted by the many varieties of human imagination, each entitled, "The Good Man".

And after contemplating them carefully I fancy that we should pronounce them all good men. I have pointed out that all of the good men of Greek ethics were aristocrats but they were not all of one type. Plato's good man is unworldly, or other-worldly ; he is the poet's ideal, the man of transcendent purity and refinement, partly hero and partly saint. Aristotle's good man is the man of the world, yet the man of the world who is also a gentleman ; the "magnanimous", or "high-minded" man, always liberal and generous, and therefore a man of property, but too high-souled to make it a matter of calculation. The good men of the Stoics and Epicureans were neither worldly nor other-worldly. Neither Stoic nor Epicurean found much to stimulate his imagination in this world or the next. Hence for both the good man was the sage, who by achieving an independence of desire had attained tranquillity of mind. But while the Stoic would embody in his sage the idea of dignity and greatness, the Epicurean sought to make him genial and humane. And thus the Epicurean sage bent gracefully to the adverse winds of life, finding tranquillity of mind in letting them take him where they would. The Stoic held rigidly to his course, the course laid by reason, and found his tranquillity of mind in a scornful contempt for what he suffered.

The modern Stoic is Immanuel Kant. At first glance one wonders whether this rigid formalist of moral laws and imperatives was interested in anything human whatever. Note, however, this alternative reading of his "categorical imperative": "act as if the maxim of thy action were to become through thy will a universal law of nature." Now in these days the notion of personifying a law of nature seems hardly stimulating. But Kant lived in the century thrilled by the mathematical physics of Newton; the century in which one could sing with fervour Addison's hymn beginning with, "The spacious firmament on high". All of the perplexing difficulties of Kant's "Critique of Pure Reason" may be said to lie in the attempt to vindicate Newton while questioning the metaphysical finality of natural science. And for Kant the eternal and magnificent regularity of the astronomical system (of "the starry heavens above me") was a new revelation to the human imagination of the infinite greatness of God. But the potentiality of this divine greatness was then also to be found in the constitution of human nature, in that faculty of reason, that power of controlling desire by the conception of law, by which men are marked off from the lower animals. And the specific contrast to this divine attribute was to be found in desire, variable and uncertain, which is common to men and animals. Accordingly, when Kant makes morality to consist in the suppression of desire on behalf of a single-minded regard for universal law, he will give us, not a bare formula devoid of human meaning, but an inspired vision of a transcendently noble ideal of human life. Kant's good man is the man who in dignity and greatness is most akin to God.

Very sordid by comparison seems the good man of the utilitarians—as represented, say, by Bentham and the elder Mill. Yet in spite of the seeming purpose of the utilitarian to dissolve morality into utility, his good man stands for an ideal genuinely moral. John Stuart Mill would describe the utilitarian view as an Epicurean view of life—because for both the end of life was "pleasure". But no two attitudes toward life could be much less alike. The Epicurean was weary and disillusioned, and wondered whether life was worth living. The utilitarian moralist may have the same doubts, but his good man never asks the question: life is here, the only question is then how to realize its cash-value. And no abstract discussion of the conception of "pleasure" will give us the utilitarian's meaning, for that meaning was of all ethical meanings the most concrete. Utilitarianism is morality as viewed from the point of view of modern commerce and modern industry—from the point of view of a commerce and industry which has become *organized*, and of a social class, or class of activities, which has been marked off and segregated, all as the result of the steam-engine. Utilitarianism stands, then, for a point of view hardly definable in terms of Greek, or perhaps of mediaeval culture, and for a class not previously articulate. The utilitarian logic is the logic of modern economics. It seeks to evaluate life as goods are evaluated in the market, and its standard "pleasure" is only the monetary standard (with all of its accompanying perplexities) in other terms.

The utilitarian good man is then, whether worker or employer, the man whose moral ideal is economic respectability and independence—the man who pays his way and owes no man anything. For him the important virtues are common honesty (*i.e.*, a special sensitiveness to the demands of honesty where money is handled), industry, thrift, and sobriety. How these virtues may stand for moral heroism and for spiritual achievement will best be understood by those (not usually, by the way, persons who have leisure for moral philosophy) for whom the possibility of holding an insecure "job" is the lifelong alternative to destitution. These virtues are hardly to be found in Aristotle's leisure-class ethics or in idealistic ethics generally. And it is as against this leisure-class ideal that we must understand the utilitarian's special (and of course exclusive) claim to stand for true morality. The utilitarian good man recognizes his economic responsibility Against this the claim of the cultivated classes would be that out of their leisure they have created most of what makes life worth living. Economically, however, they have been a supported class; the Greek culture in particular rested upon a basis of slave-labour. Indirectly indeed it is conceivable that even in economic terms they have far more than paid their way. But this is a question in which idealistic moralists appear to be not greatly interested. The sense of economic responsibility is the utilitarian contribution to the conception of morality.

These are but a few of the good men seen in the visions of moral philosophers. It will be admitted, I think, that they are all good men though not all equally pleasing to each individual taste. Every moral philosophy is *moral* if once you grasp the point of view. Yet to resolve them into a system of good men based upon a universal standard of classification, seems quite hopeless.

CHAPTER IV

THE LOGIC OF THE STANDARD

§ 10. The odiousness of comparisons. § 11. The moral standard and the business point of view. § 12. Social utility in law and orthodox morality. § 13. "Positive" morality.

MANY an orthodox moralist will admit that the facts with regard to moral judgments make the common standard at least difficult to verify. But he will then probably appeal to a logical necessity in the form of the following dilemma: either a common standard or no morality. In other words, we *must* have a standard if there is to be a moral life.

This states the question for the present chapter: why *must* you have a standard? What is the nature of the necessity? It is my purpose to show that the necessity in question is not so much a moral necessity as a business necessity.

§ 10

And I wonder why, to begin with, in a specifically moral relation, it is necessary to make any definitive judgment whatever. Suppose that I form a new acquaintance and that the acquaintance ripens into friendship; why is not the fact of the friendship enough for me? That fact means that my friend "grows upon acquaintance". I find in him more background, a more engaging personal character, a larger possibility of sympathy and understanding, than I had expected; and though we understand one another, he does not cease to stimulate my imagination. I may not state to myself in any final fashion what it is that attracts, but something of all this must be true if there is any real friendship, if the friendship is any moral fact whatever. In the face of this achieved fact, it seems to me that I should be the veriest prig to ask, Yes but is he moral? That is, where does he stand in the common moral scale? Not that I will refrain from judging him or from analysing his character. Quite the contrary, the moral process is, I should say, analysis without end. My point is that the growing friendship is itself the process of analysis and that so far as it satisfies there is no further appeal. It would be a very different matter if I were swallowing a mass of revolting obscenity, or closing my eyes to a taste for sharp practice, for the sake of the introductions he could offer me or for his tips on the stock-market.

It is a maxim of polite manners that comparisons are odious. This is one of the cases where the maxims of manners are so much more moral than the maxims of orthodox morality. At an afternoon tea Mrs. Jones, a professionally moral person, begins to question me about my friend Brown, of whom she disapproves. Aware of this I take the opportunity to explain to Mrs. Jones unobtrusively some of the nicer points about the personality of Brown which are not evident to the world at large. But Mrs. Jones is not satisfied, and presently she challenges me with (referring to another friend of mine of whom she approves), "But surely you will admit that Mr. Smith is a finer moral character." "My dear Mrs. Jones," is my crushing reply, "*that* is the kind of question I never ask." "Is it not the question you ought to ask?" retorts Mrs. Jones severely, inwardly putting me down as a moral sceptic and a suspicious person; while I marvel at the stupidity of so many of the persons who adopt morality as their profession.

Such a question may be excusable in the small child who presses you to declare that he is a better boy than his brother; or possibly in the fifteen-year-old girl who rejects any friendship which will not admit that she is more loved and more admired than any other. Perhaps we may also pardon the youth of the undergraduate who is "working for marks". But our refusal to answer the child, and our haste to assure him that our love for him can never be a matter of comparison—our anxiety to eradicate the disposition that lies behind the question—make clear enough our conviction that all such questions are morally false.

§ 11

Yet we do make comparisons between persons and many such comparisons seem to be unavoidable. What, then, is their meaning and motive? In the answer to this question I shall venture to draw upon my experience as a college teacher; a kind of experience which tends, I suspect, to bring out rather clearly the outstanding features of any system of grading persons, its necessity from the administrative point of view, its irrelevance from the point of view of truth. The college teacher is called upon at the end of each term, first to classify his pupils as "passed" or "failed", and then among the "passed" to distinguish some four or five grades of excellence. In a very large class the task is not personally embarrassing, since one's relations to one's pupils are then of necessity more or less impersonal. But to a small class, say of fifteen or twenty, with whom individually I have arrived at personal and friendly relations and each of whom has perhaps come to stand in my mind for a personality, I feel almost tempted to apologize for a violation of the rules of courtesy. In theory these grades stand for intellectual attainment, in practice they are also moral estimates. But from either point of view they appear to be far from decisive and no one thinks of taking a student's grade as more than a very partial indication of his qualities of mind or character.

These indeed could not be expressed in terms of any system of grades. Whenever I read a set of examination papers what chiefly impresses me is that the merits, or demerits, so far as they are evident, are all different. One man distinguishes himself by reach of imagination; another, naturally slow-minded, delights me by the certainty of his final attainment; a third displays his unusual intelligence by squarely answering the questions that have been asked and not some others; while a fourth, whose blundering paper would have to rank low in any scientific scale, nevertheless gives evidence that for him the course of study has been a moral and intellectual awakening. And possibly the best material for a moral or intellectual valuation would consist in a group of papers in which each student had seriously set himself the task of explaining what the course had meant to him as a matter of personal experience. But such exhibits would hardly serve the purpose of the college administration.

For the purpose of these reports is not moral but utilitarian. What is wanted is not so much a true appreciation of the student's merits as an appreciation that will be intelligible to the public—in other words, a negotiable appreciation. The college is not a person, seeking personal satisfaction, but an institution, depending more or less upon the favour of the public. At the very least it must have students. But it is not enough for the student that he is satisfied with what he gets—as it would be if he were attending a symphony concert. Partly on behalf of personal and social prestige, but mainly in these latter days as a recommendation to business or professional opportunity, he wants a certified statement, and of course a statement that will appeal to the business man or the administrator. Neither the personal appreciations of his teachers nor his own record of experience would serve this purpose; for though individually more significant they would call for attention and discernment on the part of those to whom they were addressed. They would doubtless be edifying, but the business man or the administrator has no time for edification. What he wants is to get things done, and his question is therefore, What to do? Shall

I take this man or reject him? The simplest answer to this question from the college is the degree, preferably the same degree for all.

The college degree involves as a rule only the question of passed or failed. The distinctions of excellence among the passed are the outcome of somewhat different motives; no less utilitarian, however, and no less irrelevant to the distinctively moral valuation. The truly moral incentive to good work, we are all agreed, is the value of the work itself. What does *that* mean to you? But experience seems to suggest that better results will be attained by appealing to the competitive instinct and the desire for invidious distinctions (*i.e.*, by enlisting the immoral on behalf of the moral). Whether the result achieved is truly moral—in other words, whether it is truly cultural—may perhaps be doubted.

But surely, I shall hear, it is nonsense to suppose that the motive embodied in examinations and grades and standards of conduct is solely competitive. For is it not clear that objective standards will be no less necessary if I am to satisfy the truly moral desire of measuring, for my own self-satisfaction, my own progress—this, if you please, as a part of the critical life? To this I will reply by asking, What is the relevance of this so-called objective standard to my *self*-satisfaction? For example—for some time past my leisure hours have been consumed by the reading of a long and somewhat ponderous volume in the German language on a subject related to philosophy. Owing to the circumstances of my own thinking, few books have aroused in me a more deeply questioning interest. Few have been read with such close attention. This book has been for me an experience. Yet how well I could stand an examination on the book of the academic sort, I hardly know—I have not read it with this in mind. Am I to admit, then, that this experience which I have *erlebt*, or lived through, may have been all an illusion, a mere nothing? Or, if I must speak in terms of "progress", may I entertain the possibility that I am now just what

I was before I read the book, not having lived meanwhile? If so it will be well to close our discussion at this point, once for all, with the conclusion that morality is moonshine; for if you must have a "test" for morality, I can think of none so real as this.

I will carry the illustration a step further. The college student of the present generation, full of practical wisdom beyond his years, is disposed to greet each subject of study proposed to him with the question, What's the use of it? What do I get out of it? The question is put more insistently, of course, to the studies of literature and philosophy; and addressed to philosophy (say at the close of a course in philosophy) it is likely to mean, Well, what is the conclusion? What is the right answer? I forgive the question in the student because he is unconsciously reflecting the spirit of the age. But I am tempted to suggest as the "right answer" (recalling a similar inquiry), An evil and adulterous generation seeketh after a conclusion, and there shall no conclusion be given it.

Seriously, however, I might ask this: If your motive be practical wisdom, do you think it any part of practical wisdom to study the literature of philosophy? Come, let us reason together. One of the more practical problems of philosophy is the problem of an ideal order of society. This problem has perplexed and absorbed the best minds of every thinking generation since it was proposed by Plato in his "Republic". The literature of the subject is enormous and ever increasing. Assuming the possibility of a "right" answer, how high would you estimate the probability that this or that teacher of philosophy has found it? In the true language of practical wisdom, What could you bet on it? Would it not be wiser to put your money on a sure cure for cancer or tuberculosis? You have doubtless the right to expect from your teacher a frank statement of his attitude towards the problem, of his personal feeling and opinion, but what would be your secret opinion of the teacher who advertises his own as the finally "right" answer?

And meanwhile you ask what you have got out of it, out of the study of the problem. But this question, which is indeed a real question, you can answer for yourself. Has the study of social philosophy been a dull and meaningless affair, or has it given you food for the imagination—has it been a stimulus to reflection? If so, you have surely got something very important, if life be important. You are now, as a person, not just what you were before, and the world before you is not quite the same world. Nor could it again be made the same world by any process of reversal. You have got "progress", if you please—not indeed the progress which you can see in a building rising higher day by day, nor the progress that can be exhibited in a balance-sheet, but progress in experience and thus in life, which is the only moral progress.

I have introduced this question of academic standards because to my mind it suggests very neatly the true logic of standardized morality. It has no less a bearing upon the logic of science. To those who would uncover the scientific *motif* I will recommend the now popular "intelligence-tests," as representing at once the logical development of the system of academic grades and of the application of science to life. But my present purpose is moral. Those who conceive morality to consist in devotion to a standard are likely to cherish the impression that they have surpassed all others in setting up an ideal spiritually lofty and austere. To them I would point out that, on the contrary, they are importing into morality something closely resembling the pragmatic point of view of the man of business.

For if I apply the moral standard to my friends it is not because I am in any doubt about their worth or about what is due from me in the way of loyalty. I am thinking of how they will be estimated by others and of the attendant advantages or difficulties; of how my other friends will take them, of how far my reputation may suffer, and of the possible effects upon business or profession. If a man loves a woman and wishes to make her his wife he may indeed desire to know whether his love is genuine, whether it rests upon a firm basis of understanding. But no reference to a standard will help him here. And if he comes to the point of asking whether she is the proper person for him to marry, it means in plain words that he is asking whether she is a socially marketable commodity. It is the same kind of question as that which might arise concerning the home that one owns, to which, say, I am much attached and which has therefore for me a moral value. It is worth fifteen thousand on the market, but a persistent bidder, superior to market-valuations, offers me thirty thousand. Am I morally justified in rejecting the offer? This is a real question; but it is answered if after due reflection I am content to let the offer go. To refer the question to a standard is to adopt the business man's point of view; then of course I am bound to accept the offer. The appraisal by standard means that what I have in mind is not so much what is good as what is current and marketable; not so much what is true as what is statable; and not so much what will yield satisfaction as what can be easily managed.

§ 12

The utilitarian *motif* implied in the moral standard will again be evident if we view the orthodox morality in the light of the analogy of law. It is no mere epithet to call this point of view "legalistic". The traditional moral philosophy is crammed with legal metaphor, and most of its vocabulary is that of the law. The two most typical of its modern exponents are Kant and Bishop Butler. Schopenhauer refers in biting terms to Kant's "judicial imagery"; in Butler—though one of the shrewdest and most enlightened of those who have ever discoursed upon "human nature"—it seems that most of the moral life is spent in a court of justice pleading a case before "the bar of conscience".

Now if the ideal of law is justice, the administration of law is none the less of necessity mainly utility. For in the last analysis moral justice is intimately personal. In the distribution of an estate, for example, a liquidation of the assets and a proportionate distribution of the cash-proceeds may be as remote from justice as Solomon's proposal to divide the child. The best to be said of it is that it treats all alike; but since all may be very different this is little. The ideally just distribution, especially where the property is various in kind, would be dictated by a careful regard for the personal tastes and the personal situations of the several parties. This, however, would be less a problem for a court, even for a court in equity, than perhaps for a friend of the family of long standing. But only the mutual understanding of the parties themselves could finally solve the problem. Yet if they are unable to reach an understanding, the rule of liquidation and proportionate distribution will be effective in closing the case.

Moral justice presupposes a personal acquaintance with the parties concerned. The justice of law is blindfolded; and in modern civilization justice is necessarily blindfolded by the fact that the parties to a suit can only in rare cases be known to the court. Hence such maxims of utility as that ignorance of the law is no defence. This rule would be outrageous in the administration of a family, not wholly justifiable in the administration of a school. If a child pleads that he didn't know, or even that he had forgotten, it would in most cases be simple cruelty not to inquire into the fact, even at cost of having to deal with the delicate and uncertain distinction between an excusable forgetting and no earnest desire to remember. But only the parent, who knows the child well, can form a satisfactory judgment. The judge, facing an entire stranger, would need more than the penetration of Solomon. His only way out is to accept no excuse whatever.

And this is the only *safe* course. Safety is indeed one of the most obvious motives both of law and of orthodox morality. Laws are made deliberately with this in mind, and nine just men are bound lest one unjust escape. Why should not mutual consent be sufficient for divorce? You will find many persons who see no reason in justice and decency why this should not be. But they will oppose making it a law; first perhaps, because it might open the door to legalized prostitution under the guise of marriage (which means that it would then be uncertain whom we could invite to meet whom at a dinner-party); but further because it would raise very complicated questions about the support of former wives, or of half-parented children, which our institutions are unprepared to handle. The motive of safety is no less apparent in legal decisions. Almost invariably indeed they betray a curious intermingling of two very different considerations: on the one hand justice as regards the parties in question, on the other the question of how far this justice might result in illegitimate applications on the part of others. Safety, again, is the motive of orthodox morality; one of whose maxims seems to be that, "This would be all right for you and me but it would never do for the masses". "Sound" and "dangerous" are its two most important terms. In that large and perplexing field of the morality of sex, fear of doubtful cases seems to be the ruling principle. Did George Eliot do wrong in living with Lewes as his wife? From her letters one's impression would be that few legitimate marriages have been so successful or so truly moral. Orthodox morality fears to render any judgment but "wrong", because in probably nine cases out of ten the result would have been an ignoble scandal.

This is not to say that I might not sympathize with a certain regard for safety. Personally I have little taste for adventure except in the fields of the spirit; although I cherish a secret admiration for those who do venture to translate thought into act and sympathy for those who fall. But I do not offer this as a criterion of "sound morality", but rather to suggest that this phrase embodies a contradiction in terms. What each may venture—which means, how much morality each may expect to get into his life—is a question for each to answer. All that I suggest here is that safety be not confused with morality.

All of these utilitarian considerations resolve themselves, it seems to me, into the simple pragmatic question of what to do. And I would point out that, in spite of the "law's delay", it is the first and most imperative duty of the court, not to dispense justice, but to render decisions—decisions that shall be as just as possible, but in any case decisions. And thus its function is to solve problems if it can but at all events to dispose of them. Decisions and methods of making decisions form again the most conspicuous element in the efficiency of the modern administrator or business man; who faces each day a heavy morning mail, and whose only safe rule is to dispose of it if possible all on the same day, because to-morrow will bring another. These inquiries are disposed of as far as possible in formletters, or standardized replies, the purpose of which is to enlighten the correspondent if possible, but in any case to silence him. The so-called moral standard is expected to perform the same function. When a man says that we *must* have a moral standard, all that he means is, I take it, that we must have some method of disposing day by day of the necessary business of life.

I will not despise the business side of life. It will be sufficient to point out that the business side stands for necessity rather than choice. It marks the region of activity that we cannot hope to make moral—or living. And therefore if you are looking for the special character of the moral life you must seek it in the *contrast* to business method. Business method aims at action and results, with the greatest economy of thought. The moral life is not so much action as thoughtful action, and the moral fruit of action is not "results" but experience of life. But the introduction of thought into action changes the whole character of the problem. Moral problems are continuing problems, inviting contemplation. The moral results of action are not so much conclusions as new developments of older questions. The moral problem, in short, is the problem of life.

Problems of business call for definite answers, to be given at once; the problem of life cannot be thus disposed of.

§ 13

The association of morality with authority, and of the moral attitude with the didactic, represents what is called "Positive" morality. "Positive morality" seems to mean that the moral world is a world of definite extent (and not hopelessly big), which is being gradually surveyed by successive generations of moralists, whose results, final as far as they go, are being steadily incorporated into certain ever more established principles. In other words, positive morality presupposes that ethics is a science; that the moral world is a world of fact; and that the moral life, however complex it appear to be, presents a specifically practical problem, capable in the end of a scientific solution. Traditional morality represents, then, the " accumulated experience of mankind", which, as the experience of a world of unchanging law, can be objectively stated and therefore taught with authority to the next generation.

Now things that can be definitely stated can indeed be taught. One may be taught the rules and forms of grammar, elementary geometry, the fundamental principles of physics and chemistry, and how to operate a typewriter, a printing-press or a motor-car. One may even be taught certain broadly recognized rules of literary or musical composition. And if morality could thus be taught, by those who know, we should have no alternative but to recognize their authority. In his "Liberty, Equality, Fraternity", Sir James Fitzjames Stephen (a fine representative of "positive morality") proposes a simple theory of government to the effect that those who know should tell the others what to do and make them do it. Those who know are certainly entitled to do so.

But those who "know" I suspect always of knowing nothing about morality. Upon them the significance of the Socratic "know thyself" is probably wasted. Morality I have defined as the self-conscious living of life. In this view morality is not positive but problematic. "Positive morality" is valuable mainly for childhood and youth. It would more fitly be presented under the title of "The Rules of Practical Wisdom". These rules—against the commission (*e.g.*) of lying, theft, adultery, and murder—may easily be taught, but so may the rules of grammar, and they bear the same relation to morality that the rules of grammar bear to the expression of meaning. Namely, the *meaning* to be expressed (for example, in the use of the subjunctive in Latin or German) emerges only when we contemplate the exceptions; and the more immediately language is alive with meaning, as for example in poetry, the more freely do the exceptions make light of the rules. For those not yet prepared to attack the problem of life on their own responsibility the rules of practical wisdom are safe rules. But the safer they are, the more non-committal and meaningless. The youth emerging into manhood discovers, perhaps with a shock, that none of these rules is intended, even by the orthodox, to be taken quite literally and absolutely. The rule against lying, if this be taken to stand for absolute openness and sincerity, is violated by good men every hour of the day; for no man, however honourable, fails to make some distinction between those who, by virtue of their relation to him, are entitled to have the truth from him and those who are not. And the attempt to systematize the rules leads only to endless casuistry.[1] Casuistry is only the legitimate refinement of orthodox ethics.

---

[1] Some persons find comfort in the distinction between concealing the truth and telling a falsehood—as if there were any object in concealing the truth except to mislead! Others find a curious satisfaction in preserving the form of honesty while parting with the substance. They think that somehow, while sinning in fact, they have preserved respect for the ideal. I wonder if they have done so. At any rate, I may recommend to them a study of the delightful Samuel Pepys, who somewhere in his "Diary" records that, having received a bribe from a captain in the navy in the form of a packet of sovereigns, he was careful, in emptying the packet into the drawer of his desk, to close his eyes, so that he could afterwards say, " I did not *see* any sovereigns in the packet."

When, now, the young man, come to himself, so to speak, questions the meaning of these rules, he discovers that the meaning of the same rules is different for different men, and also that different men prefer different rules. One man prefers honesty at the cost of brutality, another carries considerateness to the point of deceit. For each the significance of the rules, like that of the rules of grammar or of the words in the dictionary, lies in their use in expressing the meaning of life for himself. And for each the meaning of life is a problem, a personal problem, calling for an original solution.

This means that the moral life is an art rather than an applied science. It is a creation. And morality can then be "taught", or not, in just the sense in which art can be taught. One cannot be taught to create. One may, as I have pointed out, be taught certain rules of literary or musical composition, or certain laws of physics; but no one can be taught to be a new Shakespeare or Beethoven, to write novels equal to Thackeray's, or even to devise a really new machine. On the other hand no artist creates *in vacuo*. Beethoven's creations were based upon a study of the forms of composition used by those before him. The artist learns to create by studying the great masters: he becomes an artist when he ceases to imitate them. The great masters in morality—it would be difficult indeed to name them. They are not specifically the moralists. They are often for each of us those whom we have known most intimately. They include, in the end, all who, in history, art, literature, or philosophy, have had any important experience to reveal regarding the significance of human life and human nature.

But the masters of life are never "authorities". Their conceptions of life are not "standards". As a mode of expressing the attitude towards them of a morally responsible agent I find the sentence curiously fitting which Aristippus, not perhaps the most moral of the moralists, applied to the pleasures of life (having applied it in the first instance to his mistress, Lais): Ἔχω, οὐκ ἔχομαι.

"I possess, I am not possessed." I will enjoy the pleasures of life, I will not be dominated by them. And thus I may in the true and proper sense *enjoy* the moralities presented by the various experiences of mankind. I will understand them all, I will make them all my own : I will be in bondage to none.

CHAPTER V

THE MOTIVE OF AUTHORITY

§ 14. The categorical imperative. § 15. The basis of authority. § 16. The authoritarian tradition. § 17. Austere morality. § 18. Authority *vs.* morality. § 19. The sentiment of reverence.

§ 14

ORTHODOX morality has just been treated as standardized morality. In this chapter and the next I shall develop its implications as the morality of authority.

By the morality of authority I mean morality formulated in terms of *duty*. Among moral philosophers the most uncompromising exponent of this conception is Immanuel Kant; for whom it seems that the one necessary, sufficient, and all-inclusive criterion of morality is that morality commands.[1] Now for Kant this means that no merely utilitarian morality can ever be moral. The utilitarian says, Be good and you will be happy. But this, says Kant, is mere advice. It means only, Be good *if* you wish to be happy; and it is open to the reply, But I don't wish to be happy. The utilitarian imperative (Kant can speak only in terms of " imperatives ") is thus a hypothetical imperative, while the imperative of morality is always a categorical imperative. Morality offers no advice. Morality cares not to persuade you of the wisdom, or profit, or beauty

---

[1] This in spite of Kant's no less positive insistence that morality is also freedom. Of this Professor Dewey remarks (*The Influence of Darwin and Other Essays*, p. 65) that " The marriage of freedom and authority was then celebrated with the understanding that sentimental primacy went to the former and practical control to the latter ". I question " the understanding ", but this neatly describes the result.

of goodness. Morality is interested only in the authority of goodness. And therefore morality speaks exclusively in terms of "Thou shalt" and "Thou shalt not".

For Kant, then, the issue of morality takes the form of authority *v.* utility. And his vindication of morality is a laborious defence of this distinction. It is my purpose in the presentation of authoritarian morality to show that the distinction is false; and that not only is authority based upon utility, but that among the several elements involved in the assertion of authority utility is morally the most respectable.

§ 15

Although Kant wrote nearly a century and half ago, his scholastic formulation is valid to-day as an expression of the popular idea of morality. Even by those who propose to take their duty lightly, morality is commonly conceived as duty. But morality has not always been viewed as duty. In the ethical literature of the Greeks the conception is at least not prominent; and the modern reader of Greek ethics, at least the reader bred in the protestant religious tradition, has the sense that a certain undefined but familiar element is missing. Greek ethics is cast mainly in the form of a discussion of "the good". This suggests a very different picture from that to which we are accustomed. Instead of the child being admonished by his parents, or the soldier receiving orders from his superior officer, we have before us the picture of a youth to whom the various possibilities of life are being unfolded and who is now invited to choose for himself that which is most lovely and beautiful. His elders and friends may indeed take upon themselves the responsibility of enlightening his choice. But the assumption is that nothing but enlightenment is necessary. To judge that this or that is good is as a matter of course to choose it.

It is true that the conservative Greek morality was cast in the form of reverence for the gods and obedience to the law of the state. But the Greek gods were hardly adapted

THE MOTIVE OF AUTHORITY

to the role of moral authorities. Apart from the scandalous stories told about them, which Plato properly deplores, they seem to lack the necessary authoritative relation. They are authorities, it would seem, only in the sense in which to-day wealth and fashion are authorities in matters of taste and social convention. They may interfere in human affairs, if they care to do so, because they have the power, but it is not clear that their power rests upon any special basis of right.

The Kantian conception of morality reflects a totally different tradition, the tradition, namely, of protestant Christianity, which is mainly an Old Testament tradition, thus a Hebrew tradition. Kant, we remember, was bred in the atmosphere of German protestantism and German pietism. Now in the Old Testament God is Jahveh, or Jehovah, the tribal god of the Hebrews, and as the tribal god he is in some sense the father of the tribe. But the idea of fatherhood embodies two *motifs*. The father may be expected to forgive offences against himself, such as one in another relation will never forgive. On the other hand the father is especially authorised to punish. How deeply instinctive is this conception, both parents and teachers can testify. The parent who does not hesitate to punish severely is often fiercely jealous of punishment by another, and the child will take meekly from his parent what he would resent from the teacher. It may be said, then, that both the Old Testament and the New Testament teach the fatherhood of God. But while in the New Testament God is the tender parent, in the Old Testament he is the stern parent. The New Testament teaches God's mercy, the Old Testament asserts his authority.

But the tribal god was something more than a father to his tribe, in the customary human sense. The human father begets his children, but he does not create them; he is not infrequently surprised by what he has begotten. In the Hebrew cosmology God was both the father and creator of man, and likewise the creator of the world. This meant that the authority of God was absolute, and further that God was the sole and final source of any authority to be found in the universe. The logic of the conception is very simple : shall I not do what I will with my own ? And what is so truly and certainly my own as that which I have created ? That this is the true logic of property would be conceded, I believe, both by communists and by individualists; whose point of difference regarding property would then lie in the question of who has created it. But it seems that no human being does more than partially create. Even the novelist who creates characters is dismayed to find them taking courses of their own. God, however, is the absolute creator. And therefore he has absolute authority.

Such I take to be the final " basis of authority " underlying, however obscurely, every authoritarian theory of morality, not excepting those which are avowedly agnostic or atheistic ; underlying likewise every authoritarian theory of the state. In the mediaeval tradition, persisting well into modern times, morality was based squarely upon the will of God, all right was divine right, and all earthly authority was a question of to whom God had delegated authority. The doctrine of the divine right of kings, which came to a head in seventeenth-century England, was a reply to the divine right of popes. It fell before the divine right of the people—for the rights of the people had to be no less divinely authenticated than the rights of kings. The eighteenth century "rights of man" were still to come. It seemed out of the question to establish any human relations without erecting a "seat of authority", which was always God's authority. Thus we find divine right asserted quite as despotically in Puritan New England as in England herself under Charles the First.

§ 16

So long as the morality of authority implied the background of a theocratic universe, with God as the creator and father, it stood for an idea, and for a genuinely moral idea, even if, as I shall point out later, the idea failed to warrant authority. Under the growing influence of rationalism the theocratic conception lost its power and the authority of church and king declined. But the demand for authority survived—as it survives to this day. It was now, however, no longer an idea but a tradition.

In morals the seat of authority was now said to be, not external, but internal. The quality of authority was bestowed upon our perceptions of good and bad. The "moral sense" was defined and set apart, secure from criticism, from our sense of other things. And Bishop Butler set up the authority of "conscience." As Butler would have it,[1] the deliverances of conscience are in no sense my personal judgments, either reasoned or instinctive, of the goodness or badness of things. Conscience, like the "*daimon*" of Socrates, is "the voice of God", speaking within me and compelling me to do blindly what on my own judgment I should hardly choose to do. The tradition of authority survives to-day, somewhat attenuated and disguised, among the moralists who hold that the word "ought" expresses something unique and *per se* unanalysable, and among the political philosophers who find a similar unanalysable in the conception of "sovereignty". The implication is that these conceptions proceed from a power other and higher than ourselves. The authoritarian tradition survives under the seemingly most adverse theoretical conditions in the moral idea seductively described as "self-realization"; which, following T. H. Green, warns you that your only "real self" will be that which chooses a "common good", expressing in the end the will of God.

Modern science has parted with the will of God. It is the special claim of science that she brings us down out of the clouds of empty abstraction, romantic imagination, and

[1] As a matter of fact, Butler's analysis of " conscience " is really an analysis, so modern in some respects that he more than anticipates T. H. Green, of the process of reflection ; and it is interesting to note that, while Butler's sermons were written to oppose Shaftesbury, both moralists made the essence of morality to consist in reflective action—and both used the term " reflection ".

futile longing (which the Freudians have shown to be "infantile") to the ground of solid and tangible values. For the mysticism of the divine will science substitutes the realities of human welfare. And this gospel is often announced in tones that remind one of Lucretius, as a glad emancipation from religious superstition.

One might then expect that, here at least, the tone of authority would give way to gentle persuasiveness and sweet reasonableness. But not at all. The "orthodoxy" of to-day is as often scientific as religious. This scientific view of the world has merely appropriated the panoply of authority after destroying the person of the Author. The scientific sociologist proclaims the sacred authority of Society in tones that recall the ancient law of Sinai. The modern judge endeavours to awe the condemned criminal by explaining that he is sentenced for an offence against Society. The majesty of the law, which was formerly the majesty of God, is now (since the law cannot dispense with majesty) the majesty of the Social Order. And this conception of the sacredness of the group as against the individual is re-echoed down to the gangs of boys on the street-corner. A college Greek-letter fraternity[1] in expelling a recalcitrant member (who may have been too intelligent to take his fraternity seriously) conceives that it thereby places upon him a moral stigma.

The scientific biologist then fortifies the authority of society by explaining that in the struggle for existence the solidarity of the species is all-important. His special

[1] For the benefit of British readers it should be said that the Greek-letter fraternity, its name consisting of the two or three Greek letters forming (I understand) the initials of its Greek motto, is a secret society of students with intercollegiate affiliations. In each college the members of a given fraternity form a " chapter ", of perhaps twenty or thirty students, who eat together and for the most part live together in " fraternity-houses " which are often costly. Thus membership in a fraternity becomes an aristocratic distinction, varying with the fraternity, and those who are not fraternity-men, the non-Greeks (perhaps half or more of the college), are distinguished as " barbarians ". Membership in a fraternity is supposed to mark a mystical bond of union—with a corresponding exclusion. At any rate it is the man's fraternity that chiefly determines his social affiliations.

authority is therefore the authority of the Laws of Nature, and for the majesty of God he substitutes the majesty of the Species. His lead is followed by the scientific anthropologist, who discovers in the solidarity of the species the origin and ground of the belief in God, and now proposes to reconcile science and religion by demonstrating the solid usefulness of religion.

It was very interesting during the World War to observe all the more ardent militarists rallying quietly to the cause of religion. Omitting those whose thoughts were turned to serious things by the horror of the situation, perhaps by personal losses, I have in mind the many others, men of hard fact, not conspicuous at any time for the sentiment of reverence, and hardly to be charged with a longing for communion with God, who suddenly discovered that religion was a good thing. Directly or indirectly, they had learned from the anthropologists (what they might also have learned from Cicero) that religion is the necessary support of patriotism. Much of the religion preached today is of this pragmatic variety. It should be described, not as religious *belief*, but rather as a practical and utilitarian application of Voltaire's suggestion that if God did not exist we should have to invent him. For—and this is the major premise—if we are to have morality (that is, if we are to have social order) we *must* have authority.

§ 17

And so beneath "authority" we may read utility, or social convenience. But if social convenience were the only motive in question a moral law would be a simple business proposition, authority would stand only for sound judgment, and criticism of authority would be as little reprehensible as any other criticism. This would not wholly account for the attitude of authority. To explain this attitude I think we must add to the motive of social convenience (never quite divorced from the interests of class or party) a certain animal passion which manifests itself in the love of domination and the love of punishment. Authority which is neither masterful nor vindictive, authority which seeks only to persuade, seems to be—well, " lacking in authority".

Such at any rate is the reading to be derived from that more extreme form of orthodox morality which the radicals call "Puritanism", but which calls itself "austere". I have no doubt that "Puritanism" is often a jest at all seriousness. On the other hand, to identify the serious with the dogmatic attitude is begging the question. The Puritanical attitude is only the more resolute expression of the common orthodox morality of authority. It is because morality is identified with authority that it becomes the mark of "a moral person" to guide, instruct, admonish, and, if possible, to punish his fellows. It is authority that justifies "the good example" and "the brother's keeper"—functions hardly compatible with a respect for his personality. In the orthodox conception morality is inseparable from censorship. "Censoriousness" may indeed be formally deprecated, but it is only a saving censoriousness that separates positive morality from moral scepticism. To be tolerant of your neighbour's vices is to prove that you are yourself without serious convictions. Every moral person must then become a moralist, whose function is "to award praise and blame". In the older and "sterner" days moral earnestness had to be authenticated by a fierce denunciation of the evil-doer. But we still look for "moral indignation"—or "righteous indignation"—the assumption being that morality without indignation must be unreal, and that indignation is the only mood appropriate for a communication of moral values.

In a story by Nemirovitch-Dantschenko a mother—a peasant-woman, the mistress of a landed-proprietor, who by her own effort has become a person of some education—is giving some sad parting advice to her son, a lad of sixteen, who is to be sent to school, and from whom she is to be separated indefinitely at the instance of the father: "Do you, Sasha, not take it upon yourself to judge either your father or your mother. That is a sin. You do not

THE MOTIVE OF AUTHORITY

receive an education that you may learn to judge, but that you may learn to understand." To judge (*i.e.*, " to award praise and blame")—or to understand? This is the question. The question may not be free from perplexity. But I ask which of these two functions stands for a more characteristically spiritual achievement and which, on the other hand, is more nearly allied to animal passion and resentment. The morality of authority calls for judgment; that is to say, for punishment; in the end, for vengeance. "Who", cries Cotton Mather, in the book written to justify the burning of witches, "shall be the instrument of God's vengeance?"

Such was the "austere" morality of the Puritans—austere and forbidding. The illustration is doubtless extreme, yet it is the extreme that most clearly suggests the motive and raises the question. There are passages in Cotton Mather's diary which indicate that he rejoiced over the number of the damned—on the ground, rather evidently, that the chances of his own salvation seemed thereby improved. Viewed anthropologically, this representative of the Puritans appears to differ but little from any other primitive barbarian, red, brown, or black, who thinks to propitiate his tribal deity by the shedding of blood and at the same time enjoys in the practice of cruelty a liberation of atavistic impulse.

This atavistic explanation is suggested rather forcibly when we note how much moral indignation is expended, and with what mysterious ferocity of resentment, upon sins of sex—and quite apart from any question of betrayal or desertion. That the contemplation of cruelty or treachery should excite a desire to punish seems intelligible enough; but that this desire should be excited by the attraction of other persons for one another suggests something sub-human, something even more deeply and mysteriously animal than animal jealousy. One is reminded of the sudden nausea induced by the sight of blood or by contact with a corpse; or of that instinctive repulsion to suffering and mutilation which may even paralyse pity; or, again, of the disgust aroused by the tears of another when, logically and humanly speaking, he deserves our sympathy.

And yet I would not withhold my respect for the "austere" ideal in one who confines his austerity to himself. One must freely admire the man who, with a sensitive appreciation of the many sides of life, resolutely puts aside even most of its satisfactions on behalf of what his imagination presents to him as a great end. Some such resoluteness of choice must doubtless be a part of any moral life. We may question his valuation as we may question any other valuation of life. But if a man chooses to be austere with himself it is his right, and it may be his salvation. Yet this only means that it takes all kinds to make a moral world, and that the austere choice is one among others. And I fancy that he for whom it has been a choice, and not merely the result of insensitiveness, will be very slow to condemn those who have chosen differently. In any case, it seems that the austere-and-forbidding ideal conceals somewhere a contradiction. When it becomes possible to say (as I have often heard), "Well, he's not just what you would call a moral person, but "—but something rather more distinctively humane—the idea of the moral person must be out of joint.

Among the modern prophets of authoritative and austere morality the greatest perhaps is Thomas Carlyle. Carlyle's moral idea is the strong man, or "hero". His heroes, of whom Mohammed, Napoleon, Cromwell, and Frederick the Great are conspicuous examples, are seemingly men who do things without asking questions ; even the shrewd and benevolent Abbot Samson, pictured so persuasively in "Past and Present", was not much given to taking counsel. Like Sir James Fitzjames Stephen, Carlyle believes that those who know should tell the others what to do and make them do it ; and for him this is the gospel of duty. In a passage levelled anonymously, but obviously, at Carlyle, Herbert Spencer proposes an alternative explanation. The passage is too full of interesting implications not to be given in full :

THE MOTIVE OF AUTHORITY

"It is curious to see how the devil-worship of the savage, surviving in various disguises among the civilized, and leaving as one of its products that asceticism which in many forms and degrees still prevails widely, is to be found influencing in marked ways men who have apparently emancipated themselves, not only from primitive superstitions, but from more developed superstitions. Views of life and of conduct which originated with those who propitiated deified ancestors by self-tortures enter even still into the ethical theories of many persons who have years since cast away the theology of the past, and suppose themselves to be no longer influenced by it.

In the writings of one who rejects dogmatic Christianity, together with the Hebrew cult which preceded it, a career of conquest costing tens of thousands of lives is narrated with a sympathy comparable to that rejoicing which the Hebrew traditions show us over the destruction of enemies in the name of God. You may find, too, a delight in contemplating the exercise of despotic power, joined with insistence upon the salutariness of a state in which the wills of slaves and citizens are humbly subject to the wills of masters and rulers—a sentiment reminding us of that ancient Oriental life which the biblical narratives portray."[1]

I do not offer this as a final analysis of Carlyle. But to me his "delight in contemplating the exercise of despotic power" is unmistakable, along with his appreciation of its "salutariness". What shall we say then of the cult of the strong man? What of those who, to-day as ever, are thirsting for an exhibition of power; of those who would see "the masses" "taught to obey", "know their place," "stop this democratic nonsense", "go to work and keep their mouths shut"? Such recommendations are commonly presented, if not in the name of God, at least on behalf of an austere ideal of duty. For my own part, I prefer Spencer's interpretation: "devil-worship."

§ 18

Morality I have defined broadly as the self-conscious living of life. Under this conception morality is criticism of authority rather than deference to authority, and choice

[1] *Data of Ethics,* Chapter III, Sec. 15.

rather than duty. The moral situation is not the situation of the child under the direction of his parents, for whom the only moral question is whether to obey or to disobey; nor that of the soldier under orders, for whom there is no question; but rather the situation of one confronted with the various possibilities of life, who is to choose, to appropriate—rather, to create out of this situation what he conceives to be best—and best from his own point of view. Morality according to this view is not training. "Moral training" indeed is a contradiction in terms. Animals are trained; moral agents are at best educated and enlightened. " Train up a child in the way he should go, and when he is old he will not depart from it "—if he fails to develop morally. Otherwise it will be strange if his way shows no departure from his training.

The essence of morality, in brief, is responsibility; and responsibility implies freedom of choice. The docile child, who obeys his parents, is indeed a convenient member of the household, but not yet arrived at morality. His morality begins when, at the cost of disobedience, it occurs to him to do what he himself thinks best. The soldier who blindly obeys orders has renounced morality by giving a moral power of attorney to his superior officer. This is not to say that the child is moral because he disobeys. He is moral so far as he aims to do what he *thinks best*—according to ideas of his own. It is very inconvenient when children, or other persons under authority, develop "ideas". This I would not merely admit (even feelingly), but emphasize, in order to bring out clearly the difference between inconvenience and immorality. For to have ideas of one's own, however inconvenient to others, is a sure sign of morality.

Some time ago an essay appeared in which the writer condemned the moral laxity of our age, as evidenced especially in the frank appeal to sex which our young girls are said to make in their style of dress and manner of dancing. The question was asked, What are we to do about it? And the answer was, It is nonsense to appeal to self-respect; we must put the fear of God into them. I

THE MOTIVE OF AUTHORITY

have no doubt that the advice is good from the standpoint of social convenience, of their convenience at least whose sensibilities are offended. One need not question the utility of "the fear of God" as a preservative of social order, if only it can be sustained. My criticism would be that the result thus attained would be in no sense a moral result. It would be, not morality, but, in Spencer's phrase, "devil-worship". And it would reduce our young women, although then modest, well-behaved, and pleasing to contemplate, to the moral status of the dog on the street who gives me a comfortably wide berth as I pass him, not from innate courtesy, but from "the fear of God". The result would be moral only so far as the desired reform in dress or manners, from whatever source inspired, were the expression, on the part of the young women in question, of their own moral taste, their own sense of good and bad.

But when this proviso is included it is not so certain that a genuinely moral reform will take the direction anticipated by the reformers. Genuine morality cannot be predetermined. This I repeat here because it has been a favourite avocation of moralists, from Aristotle down, to work out demonstrations of the ultimate identity of virtue and happiness, duty and pleasure, law and freedom, authority and choice. My son, says the moralist, I impose upon you the duty of acting freely but I warn you that true freedom will only confirm the wisdom of the law. If freedom did thus justify authority the fact would be miraculous. If further experience of life revealed nothing more of the meaning of life morality would be an illusion. Sex-morality, for example. In the matter of sex-relations our ancestors of a few generations ago could quite confidently lay down the law. To-day nearly all that we can say is that, from the standpoint of morality, sex-relations are perilously significant, and critically balanced between all that is best and all that is worst in human life. The decay of decency I suspect to be illusory. One may not doubt that youthful extravagance is dangerous—as life is dangerous; or that "the experience of mankind" has important warnings to utter. Alas for those who ignore them! But it seems to me that here least of all may one venture to predict the law.

The supreme justification of authority is embodied, as I have noted above, in the idea of God the Creator. In this conception it is assumed that in the power that creates the universe, including man himself, we have at last surmounted the elsewhere impassable barrier which hinders might from passing over into right; and that creatorship, at least, imposes upon the creature an obligation that is absolute. Now I shall say nothing here about the existence of God. Granting the existence of God, it still remains to ask whether the relation of God to man is a relation of authority. And I leave in the background the question whether a moral agent can conceivably be created. Here I will suggest only that a moral agent can be under no bond of authority even to his creator.

The problem of creative authority is the subject of that profoundly suggestive drama contained in the third chapter of Genesis. Here we have a picture of the Creator dealing with his creatures. The creatures have eaten of the tree of knowledge. They have become moral agents. And thus they have profoundly disturbed the economy of God's creation—it is no wonder that the older theologians dated all the tragedy of life from the "Fall of Man". Hitherto the creatures have been obedient, but they have not been moral—not a bit more so than the other creatures in the Garden. Now indeed they are moral and they disobey. And to those who have learned to disobey, whether animals or men, the argument from authority has ceased to be relevant. From now on they must be controlled, if at all, by an appeal to their interests. The Creator may indeed make use of his power and bend them to his will by the hope of reward and the fear of punishment. Even so he will be dispensing not commands but inducements. And —though it be the infinite power of the Almighty—the creatures, having eaten of the tree of knowledge, may still conceivably reject the rewards and accept the punishments.

They too have become almighty in their power to choose, and to choose to suffer.

Such, it seems to me, is the inescapable logic of the situation—which, by the way, is more or less the situation of every parent or teacher. Picture yourself as a creator. So long as you create machines they will obey you implicitly, according to the measure of your creative power. But suppose you create (and suppose that you can) persons having the capacity of judgment and choice: *ipso facto* they are for ever emancipated from your control, and your relation to them, whatever it be, will not be a relation of authority.

§ 19

But the sentiment of reverence? For the possibility of reverence, it is popularly supposed, depends upon "reverence for authority". Well, I believe that I am voicing the sentiment of reverence. I take it to be a characteristic mark of insight in James Martineau that he puts the sentiment of reverence at the top of his elaborate and complicated scale of "springs of action"; and I also subscribe to that alternative statement of Kant's principle (fundamentally in opposition to his authoritarian prepossessions) in which he bids us treat other persons always as ends in themselves, never as means for alien ends; in other words, to respect the souls of our fellows—something which "authority" seems unable to grasp. But how to suggest in brief or in broader compass all that is involved in the sentiment of reverence, is somewhat beyond my power. Wonder, curiosity, yet also critical inquiry and a sense of the paradoxical and the humorous—if reverence be a *sentiment*, and not a blind propension, I should say that it involves at least all of these. Reverence is indeed the necessary implication of humane intelligence; that is, of imagination. Or going further back, the germ of reverence is contained in Aristotle's "all men desire by nature to know". For the desire to know is the desire for the enhancement of life; the outreaching of imagination towards the unknown distant;

the desire for the enlargement of my own life through the appropriation of the experience of life of other beings, and of all being. And thus in its more intensive form quite remote from "idle curiosity". Curiosity about your neighbour's household affairs is idle indeed, but especially characteristic of those who are lacking both in imagination and in reverence. But the imagination which makes you wonder deeply about your neighbour's soul, about how life feels and seems to him, is respectful and reverent.

Putting it more academically, I should say that reverence is the belief in significance and the search for significance. It is reverence to thirst to understand what goes on behind the countless faces that pass us day by day, and to believe that something does go on there; and it is lack of reverence —at least an assertion that reverence is unmeaning—to believe that nothing of any consequence goes on there. And it is the culmination of reverence—if only you can carry the assumption of reverence thus far—to believe that something significant goes on behind the face of nature and, with scientists, philosophers, and poets, to struggle to grasp that significance. This is reverence for the divine.

But not, as I conceive, reverence for authority. I have suggested above that the idea of the fatherhood of God implies a moral relation, and thus a moral obligation, while the idea of God the Creator implies, in itself, no obligation. But the fatherhood of God, while implying reverence, contains no implications of authority. In the human relation of parent and child I believe indeed in the exercise of authority, especially in dealing with younger children; not, however, on behalf of their moral character, but as a simple household necessity, which may on occasion be a life-and-death necessity. But here the parental authority is simply the filial fear. Reverence for the parent—the moral relation between parent and child—begins with the child's perception that the parent is his best friend and a person worthy of confidence and trust, a loyal help in difficulty, and a satisfying source of enlightenment in perplexity. But this sense of confidence involves no obligation to obey

Nay, the very fact of confidence means that the obligation has been thus far already loosened.

It is not different with reverence for God. We have to remember that, true or false, the idea of God is logically and necessarily the imaginative development of ideals of human character and of human relationships. Let us admit that Jahveh, the god of Israel, was the expression of a sublime reverence. It is still true that he represented the characteristic Israelitish vices of jealousy and vindictive hatred. So that a pathetically beautiful appeal beginning with, "O Lord, thou hast searched me and known me" may be followed a few verses later by, "Do I not hate them, O Lord, that hate thee?" The Greeks likewise attributed their own vices to their gods, making them crafty politicians and free livers. The Greeks were not much afraid of their gods; but it is no less true, I should say, that the Greek mythology, the fruit of an imagination graceful, curious, wistful, was the expression of reverence.

CHAPTER VI

THE ORDERED SOCIETY

§ 20. The order of reverence. § 21. The utility of the reverential order. § 22. The ordered society and the biological species. § 23. Ordered relations *vs.* social relations. § 24. The decay of reverence and the dawn of morality.

§ 20

I COME now to the motive of authority as embodied in the conception of social order. The characteristic phrase for this motive is "reverence for authority", or "respect for the constituted authorities"; to which the corresponding diagnosis for all social maladjustments is "the decay of reverence". The metaphysical development of the motive of reverence may be found in "The Philosophical Theory of the State", by the late Bernard Bosanquet.

It is, I suppose, an indisputable fact that every child is born with a determinate potential complexion—say, with red hair or black. For Bosanquet it seems to be a fact equally indisputable (and in the last analysis a necessity of the same organic kind) that every child bears at birth the mark of a determinate social class. And therefore it is axiomatic for Bosanquet that the only conceivable social relation is an arrangement of men in classes; which are to be distinguished (as every logic of social classification seems to demand) as higher and lower, and bound together in a system of reverence for authority. This view of the logical necessities seems to be also axiomatic for many other persons; among them (including, strangely, some of the more advanced exponents of democracy) those for whom the social problem is a problem of "leadership"—

THE ORDERED SOCIETY

as if the only conceivable social order were an order of leaders and followers. We have heard much about leadership since the War. But true reverence for authority is expressed in the recognition of "natural" or "right leaders", to be found only among "the intelligent classes", the distinction of classes being referred to the Laws of Nature.

And for a true sentiment of reverence a society thus ordered is the embodiment also of an aesthetic ideal. The ordered society is a thing of beauty; beautiful because in the last analysis its beauty is the beauty of nature. Perhaps it would be better to say that the ordered society is picturesque. Society is made picturesque by the presence of distinctions; and distinctions seem to require that men be graded. The ordered society is again conceived as a society distinctively and exclusively moral. Ideally it seems that there can be neither beauty nor virtue in the relations of men except in a relation of superior and inferior in which benevolence is exchanged for reverence.

The ideally "ordered" society is, accordingly, a society patriarchally or hierarchically ordered, in which men are graded, and ranked, according to a single principle of worth. The type of all such is the society pictured in Plato's "Republic" (presented as the social ideal both by Bosanquet and by T. H. Green), in which a broad distinction is made between a lower class of common-minded men, or artisans, and an upper class of high-minded men, or warriors, the whole being guided and directed by a select uppermost class of philosophers and (in the language of a later period) saints. A more familiar illustration, however, is the picture of English country life presented by the literature of the earlier Victorian period, in which society consists of an upper class of landed gentry, an intermediate class of tenant farmers, with whom are grouped some yeomen, or freeholders, and a lower class of farm labourers, all bound together by the feudal principle of mutual loyalty. The tenant was bound in loyalty to his landlord—woe to the tenant who should vote against his landlord ! But the landlord was bound to the tenant; and especially bound to respect his first right to a lease of the farm which had been held by him and by his fathers before him.

The moral principle governing these relations is the principle defended in F. H. Bradley's essay on "My Station and Its Duties".[1] According to this principle the whole duty of each man consists in faithfulness to that station in life to which it hath pleased God to call him. The duties flowing from this principle are substantially those tabulated in the church catechism under the several heads of "my duty to my superiors", "to my equals", and "to my inferiors". In this moral system it was at once the virtue and the pride of any man that he "knew his place". By this indeed he vindicated his claim to self-respect. For the matter of that, it would seem that the two motives of self-respect and respect for superiors were interwoven in a mutual understanding which becomes at times almost democratic. Squire and tenant-farmer might be warm friends and even good fellows; but the tenant never aspired to dine at the squire's table, and he condemned as vulgar those of his fellow-tenants who cherished such aspirations. On the other hand, it seems that for those who lay outside of the system, such as the village shopkeeper, a truly sound morality was out of the question. Honest Hodge, the farm-labourer, achieves dignity by removing his cap in the presence of the squire; Dawkins, the shopkeeper, achieves only servility. The commercial, or calculating, motive could offer doubtless only a hypocritical respect for authority. For this, in the end, was the principle underlying the system, not respect for the person but respect for his rank, and respect for the principle of distinctions involved in the ordered society. Respect for one's betters and condescension to inferiors were the two signs by which, according to circumstances, one indicated a belief in the moral order.

This tradition of reverence survives to trouble us, in

[1] F. H. Bradley, *Ethical Studies*.

a society supposedly emancipated, as an element in the servant question and the labour problem. As for the first, I will not be so rash as to suggest that the need of personal or household service, for many persons a truly vital need, can very easily be reduced to a "business proposition". It is none the less the question of status, the question of a "proper respect", that presents the greatest difficulty. Mrs. Brown, a lady of liberal tendencies, and a matter-of-fact person, will have you believe perhaps that all that interests her is so much work for so much money. But she addresses her cook as "Mary", and she would be stunned if the cook should address her as "Emily". She is also slow to abandon her traditional prerogative of supervising, on behalf of morality, the cook's goings-out and her comings-in, and especially her relations with young men. And when in consequence Mary the cook prefers a place in a shop or a factory, probably a more grinding task and on the whole less lucrative, Mrs. Brown will begin to wonder whether these persons know what is good for them.

It is true that Mrs. Brown and her friends, finding themselves in the position of Mary (which, however, cannot politely be suggested), would feel in honour bound to prefer the shop or even the factory to menial service, or possibly to starve on something lower than shop wages in an occupation conventionally more genteel; and those hardships which make it a foolish choice for Mary would for them make it heroic. But their case, they would explain, if brought to the point, is different. And if you ask, How different? the answer, I fancy, would boil down to this: that God in his wisdom has created different sorts of persons for different stations in life; to most of whom, appropriately, a servile occupation is not really objectionable. Mrs. Brown and her friends would probably claim to be Christian women. They would be dismayed to learn that they are following Aristotle, the heathen philosopher, who taught that some men are by nature slaves.

It may be supposed that the husbands of these ladies—

business men, captains of industry, and employers of labour—are untroubled by any of this nonsense about the proprieties. As men of hard fact, their imagination is supposed never to be deflected by sentiment from the line marked by the arithmetical balance of profit and loss. And Mr. Brown would tell you perhaps that as long as he receives a sufficient return for wages paid, moral considerations have no interest for him. But he has probably failed to grasp the full connotation of the term "moral". In England, I believe, the employers are still known as "masters", the distinction being that of "masters" and "men". In the United States we prefer the politer "employer" and "employee". But the tradition is the same; the tradition, namely, of respect for authority. The employee is supposed to remove his hat in the presence of the employer. The employer keeps his hat on, and his cigar in his mouth, and it is he who is supposed to fix the conditions of employment. Since the business belongs to him the relation is in no sense a partnership.

Until recently labour disputes referred mainly to wages. Now, however, it seems that the question of wages is overshadowed by the demand of labour for a share, amounting possibly to the lion's share, in the management of industry. At the same time, the editorial columns of the daily press have begun to issue solemn warnings to the labour world of its obligations to "the public". Formerly it was assumed that responsibility to the public, if any, was assumed by employers alone. Yet it seems that "the public" is as little disposed as the employers to favour the participation of labour in the direction of industry. Apparently it does not occur to these journalistic moralists that moral responsibility and moral obligation imply a power of direction. Obligation without choice, the precise negative of *moral* obligation, is indeed the principle of authoritarian morality generally.

Now if I were a stock-holder, say, in a railway enterprise, I am not sure that I should be eager for a partnership with labour; nor should I be in a hurry to advocate this from the standpoint of the public. But this attitude I should call utilitarian rather than moral. And what it means is substantially this : I know from experience that the employers can in some fashion run the railways, provide transportation, and earn dividends ; and I prefer to get things done, or to collect dividends, with as little discussion as possible. I may have before me the vision of a much more humane and intelligent situation, which eventually may also be more profitable from the utilitarian standpoint. But the process of realizing this situation will involve mental and moral effort, including much thought, perplexity, and doubt. In brief, it is an invitation to a higher degree of moral responsibility than, in this direction at least, I care now to assume.

On the other hand, as a representative of railway labour, I should certainly refuse to recognise any responsibility to the public until the public co-operated in securing for me the commensurate power of supervision. If asked to accept a reduction of wages on the ground that rates are too high for the public to bear, I should wish to be shown whether rates might not be lowered through greater economy of management. And the employers, Mr. Brown and his friends, if placed in the same position, would call this a plain business proposition. Nay, more—a moral proposition. For it is precisely their argument when they point to the Labour Board and the Interstate Commerce Commission as preventing them from fulfilling a moral obligation to the public.

From the terms in which the discussion of labour problems is commonly conducted moral considerations of any intelligent kind seem rather speculatively remote. Yet it is worth asking what the moral issue might be. The cruder form of the labour argument, which is suspicious of the value or productiveness of any work not done with the hands, prefers to ban the whole class of employers and capitalists as "parasites", at least to the extent of receiving much more than their services warrant. On the other hand the employer claims for himself the dignity and the authority of intelligence. He represents the traditional "intelligent classes". And in vindication of his intelligence he claims further that it is by virtue of his organizing ability that industry exists. One wonders, then, why so little attempt is made by either side to test this claim by experiment. Labour seems as little disposed to assume responsibility as capital is to grant it. My suspicion is that each fears the other may be right.

Meanwhile some light may be thrown upon the superior rights and dignities of the employer by considering the relation of employer and employee as a relation of exchange. The labourer gives work in exchange for money; the employer gives money in exchange for labour. In a fair exchange the values are presumably equal. Why, then, is the employer entitled to deference? Because he provides the intelligence or because he provides the money? There are curious superstitions connected with money. The neighbour who borrows my lawnmower without asking my permission is perhaps somewhat impudent but nothing worse. But what if he borrowed the price of the lawnmower out of my pocket-book? When I pay for the hat that I have just bought, the salesman says, "Thank you"; if I should thank him for letting me have the hat he would be very much amused. I have observed a substantial shopkeeper still obsequiously polite to his customer though a negro servant who was probably parting with nearly her last dollar—and she, in turn, was exercising upon him all of the dignity that goes with the disbursement of money. Though there is no reason underlying the dignity of money, there is a simple cause. Money is a liquid asset. If you have only goods to barter with, you are at the mercy of the relatively few who happen to need your special goods. But everybody wants your money. Thus money is power. Under present conditions it is the most conspicuous and characteristic form of power, and power is "the basis of authority". Among those who reverence authority one rarely observes any long-sustained reverence for persons who are powerless.

§ 21

Turning, then, to the moral quality of the ordered society I need only repeat here with a difference of application what was said in the last chapter: the ordered society is not so much a moral ideal as an ideal of convenience. The motive underlying it is not reverence, but utility, and yet, more exactly, not so much utility, in any more comprehensive sense, as business efficiency. For the two things are by no means the same. One may seriously doubt whether our modern business organization stands for a very high grade of utility, even from its own ostensible point of view of productiveness. Employers themselves see clearly enough that productiveness is not enhanced when most of the army of workers have little personal interest and no personal voice in the process of production; and while productiveness is being constantly increased by labour-saving machinery, it seems that the skilled artisan is becoming steadily and deliberately less productive. Meanwhile, however, the present form of business organization does "get things done". This is the true meaning of "efficiency"; a motive by no means contemptible indeed, but in no large sense moral or suggestive of reverence. Efficiency is short-time utility. Its aim is to get things done, not with a large and artistic completeness—so as to satisfy indefinitely—but first of all promptly, so that the business may be disposed of and the world may go on.

For purposes of efficiency the hierarchical order is perhaps ideal. In any emergency—and the housewife who knows that dinner must be provided whatever happens, will tell us that emergency confronts us day by day—in the case of a fire or a flood, however, what we need first of all is a leader whose instructions all will obey; and any leader, any organization, is better than none. Hence the hierarchical order is not merely "mediaeval". The finest and most logical embodiments of the ordered society are extremely modern and up-to-date; as illustrated in our large industrial organizations, but best of all in the organization of a great railway system with its elaborate hierarchy of president, several vice-presidents, superintendents, yard-masters, train-masters, and so on. But the ideal of course is the army, the purpose of which is to get things done though the heavens fall.

In the army, under conditions of ideal military obedience, all of the morality in the situation lies within the breast of the commander-in-chief—if, of course, we define morality as the self-conscious living of life. The private soldier is as far removed from the morality of the situation as the mechanism of the guns. But the order of reverence is better illustrated by the economy of life on the old-fashioned farm. There was first the farmer himself, the supreme authority; then his wife who (under the older theory at least) obeyed him in all things; the children, who obeyed their parents; the horses and the dogs trained to obey all the family; and finally the cattle, pigs, and chickens, taught to fear if not very definitely to obey. In this picture we have an extended reverential series—in which the reverence varies inversely as the morality. If we then carry the picture back to the days of the patriarchs we shall understand the poetic attraction of the order of reverence—and see that reverence for superiors implies the point of view of primitive man.

§ 22

This primitive conception of life has been fortified within two generations by the introduction of the conception of evolution, bringing with it a biological philosophy which carries human society back to the status of the animal species. It has been the custom of natural scientists to represent the progress of science as an emancipation from superstition; in which the fear of natural powers and forces is replaced by freedom of choice; in which also nature, formerly dictating and enforcing the ends of our lives, becomes the means for ends of our own. According to this view of the function of science, one might suppose that the laws of heredity (assuming them to be discoverable) would serve chiefly to afford each of us a wider range of enlightenment in the choice of a husband or a wife ; and it might be assumed also that the possibility of controlling reproduction would be welcomed as affording individual men and women a larger control over the determining conditions of their lives. The effect of the biological view has been rather to reinstate a superstitious reverence for "Nature". Programmes of eugenics betray at best little regard for human relations; just as little indeed, in their more resolutely scientific proposals, as the stock-breeder shows for the personal choices of his animals. Not our own ends, the biologist tells us, but the ends of Nature, that is, of "the species"; on whose behalf biologists and physicians are not infrequently to be found among the enemies of birth control ; or at least in the attitude of claiming authority to dictate on behalf of the species the ends for which birth is to be controlled.

One of the significant fruits of the biological point of view is the prominence now given to the sex-relation as a topic for literature and for polite conversation, in striking contrast to the reticence of Victorian days. For my own part, I believe that frankness in such matters is on the side of decency ; but I also cherish the conviction that the principle of sex-morality is reverence for what is perhaps the most deeply intimate of personal relations. To this view biology can hardly be said to contribute. Biology seeks rather to convince us that as animals our chief function in life is breeding ; and it then sets up as the moral ideal a conception of "good breeding" all its own. It is true that biology has helped to make breeding conscientious ; on the other hand it has helped to check the development of a humane attitude towards differences of race and towards personal peculiarities and deformities. Under the biological régime it has become a definitive condemnation of a man to call him "abnormal". The result is that sympathy and imagination are deprecated, while race repulsions and the animal repugnance to the abnormal are exalted as wise provisions of Nature for preserving the purity of the species.

In the early chapters of Genesis we are presented with a picture of the Garden of the Lord. It is not an unpleasing picture, in spite of the fact that it assigns to the man and the woman the moral status of only the most favoured among the favourite animals. The biological point of view has extended the Garden of the Lord to cover the earth and transformed it into the Lord God's stock-farm. Those who are disposed to question this *motif* should remember that Darwin got his clue to natural selection from the procedure of stock breeding—and they may also recall Plato's appeal, in the fifth book of "The Republic", to the principles employed in the breeding of sporting dogs and game birds. This conception of the divine stock-farm, in which we are bred for purposes not our own, is the finally scientific and up-to-date development of the ideal of the ordered society.

§ 23

As the alternative to the ordered society I will venture here only very briefly to suggest the motive implied in a moral society, having dealt with the subject at length in another volume.[1] If the motive of the ordered society is business efficiency, the motive of the moral society is "leisure"; or if you please, "humanity". The moral society, in other words, is not an *organization* of workers and business men, but a *society* of gentlemen. This, however, is not to suggest a class-distinction. We are all in some degree business men, and all of us—those of us at least who indulge in moral philosophy—are likewise gentlemen. "Leisure" is that part of a man's life which remains after he has made the sacrifice to efficiency. What is chiefly then to be noted is the change which comes over the motives, and over the whole view of life, of any man as he leaves his office or workshop and goes into his home or into "society". He has just been engaged in the

[1] *Individualism*, 1911.

practice of efficiency, doubtless with scant respect for the dignity of persons. In the world of leisure he is faced with the dignity of persons as the theoretically accepted principle. In his office he has been perhaps an authority; in any social gathering—at a dinner party, for example—let him be a person ever so important, he is just as much and just as little of an authority as any one else. Nor may it be said that the host and hostess are now the authorities; although they occupy commonly the two ends of the table it is not for the purpose of preserving order.

In brief, there is no "social system". "System", we may see now, is abhorrent to the motive of the *social*. And a "social organization" is a plain contradiction in terms. Bosanquet will have it that a man is not a man except as he is a member of "organized society"; what I would point out is that he is not a man except as he is more than a member of an organization. To see the contradiction, compare a group of four men who meet once a week, with no hard and fast engagement, to play a game of bridge, and a similar group of twenty-five or thirty. The latter can hardly be maintained without organization. But it will be noted that just so far as the element of organization enters the situation the social element departs. A "social glass", or a cup of tea, is properly named; to call the income-tax a "social institution" is misplaced sentiment.

Yet there is order, even within the group of four; and order sustained, not by any form of authority, but by mutual understanding. And there are, if you please, distinctions : just those intensively personal distinctions indeed, eluding all attempts to standardize them, which constitute the essence of a relation distinctively social. And I suppose that every one "has his place" (if that be important) in the regard and respect of his fellows. It is not, however, "that station in life to which it hath pleased God to call him", but inevitably the station that he is able to win by his talents and to demonstrate as his own by the force of his personality.

Nor may it be said that the world of leisure is an inactive or unproductive world. But in this world things have to be done with a careful regard for the rights and the tastes of those doing them; and the operating method is not the method of command and obey, but the method of co-operation by agreement. And the principle of agreement is the principle of mutual understanding with regard to taste and convenience—not mutual self-sacrifice, but that artistic completeness of convenience, rendering full justice to each, which though never absolutely attainable, becomes ever more nearly attainable as men come to a truly personal understanding with one another.

The practical moral problem—the problem both moral and practical—is then to import these humanly social relations into the conduct of men in business, so as to transform—without loss of efficiency, perhaps even with an eventual increase of efficiency—the world of business into a moral world. How far this can be done, how immediately in any given case, need not concern us here. What I would point out is that any such problem is faced with at least an immediate issue between the human considerations and the business considerations. To get things done is one consideration, to get them morally done is quite another. In this issue the ideal of the ordered society stands not for humanity but for utility.

§ 24

Morality, I have said, is the self-conscious living of life. From this point of view it is an advance in morality when men learn to choose what they will do, and to insist upon choosing, rather than when they "learn to obey the constituted authorities". And in illustration of this I will close this chapter with some remarks bearing upon "the decay of reverence"—which I will put somewhat in the form of a fable. It has often occurred to me to speculate upon the moral status of the lower animals, and to wonder why ethical theories are so seldom tested by reference to our attitude towards these, our animal kinsmen. I fear it may be because in the background we detect the presence of ominous questions.[1] Some time ago, however, I thought of asking, What if the horses and cattle were suddenly endowed with self-consciousness and the power of speech ? Suppose that the draft-horses became aware of what they contributed in the economic process, or that the food-cattle came to know that they were to be eaten and could tell us that they knew ? I fear that after a discussion of this subject with one of the then cultivated and instructed members of this species, we should find that a good beefsteak had lost some of its flavour. On the other hand, I imagine that the cattle would flatly refuse to be eaten. It would be useless to call Dr. Paley to explain to them out of the Bible that God intended them to be food for man ; and no less useless to dwell upon the superior importance of human life as compared with theirs. They very properly would never see it. If we threatened coercion, they could, as a last resort (what we should do in their place), threaten race suicide—or possibly immediate, individual suicide. Our only recourse would be to treat them as persons worthy of consideration, *i.e.*, as gentlemen, by offering suitable inducements, though what these inducements would be, I must leave the reader to imagine. But one point is clear : we should be facing a situation distinctively moral, confronted with moral agents whose rights, though newly created, we could upon no ground venture to ignore.

Well, the significance of the fable is that this is precisely the situation confronting the "intelligent classes" in the present crisis of social life. "The masses", so called,

---

[1] In his *Autobiography* Anthony Trollope offers an amusingly naïve justification of his favourite sport of fox-hunting, based gravely upon a computation of the pain suffered by the fox as compared with the pleasure of a hundred or two hunters. Trollope forgets that the importance attributed by him to the gratification of the hunting-instinct of the hunter places the hunter who chases the fox in the same order of nature with the fox who chases the hare—and then why bother about morality ? The fox does not.

"the workers", in present-day terms, have just lately (in the history of the race) acquired self-consciousness and the power of speech. Until yesterday these workers, representing numerically all but an insignificant fraction of the race, remained inarticulate in moral philosophy and nearly so in literature. As pointed out above, all Greek ethics, which continues to set the questions for academic ethics, is the ethics of a leisure class. Classical literature makes us almost forget that, then as now, life was supported by work. In ancient literature the worker, usually a slave, remains unrepresented except as Christianity voices his claim to respect in another world. In the Greek view of life he forms a part, not of the moral world, but of the natural world along with the horses and the cattle. All of our ideas of higher culture are derived from and still are impregnated with this conception of a social situation which involves the distinction of master and servant. So that, in spite of the change of ideas brought about by the industrial revolution, which makes it now possible to give the status of gentleman to a successful business man,[1] we do not yet clearly conceive what a really non-servile higher culture would be.

Meanwhile the industrial revolution, built upon the steam-engine, by segregating and massing the workers has made them class-conscious. In the utilitarian school of ethics we have, for the first time I should say in moral philosophy, the expression of an industrial view of life. One of the consequences of this view is now being presented to the world in emphatic and imperative if also somewhat insolent tones (in which, as betraying a sense of power, they are not peculiar) by the labour unions; whose leaders are proving themselves to be men of no mean intelligence, political and administrative. And of late the labour world, while not relaxing its demand for wages, has announced a

---

[1] What this means is shown in Mrs. Gaskell's "North and South", in which that clear-minded woman finds it evidently something of a task to show how the daughter of a very poor Anglican clergyman could be conceived to love, and honourably to marry, a well-to-do manufacturer, although a graduate of Oxford—this, of course, seventy years ago.

claim for participation in the direction of industry. The claim is doubtless shocking, but viewed calmly it seems that nothing could be more characteristically moral. What it means is : personal dignity (dignity in spite of a certain concomitant insolence) is asserting the rights of gentlemen.

Faced with this situation, it is useless to tell them authoritatively where they belong ; precisely from the moral standpoint, that remains to be seen. Nor will it avail to refer to the superior wisdom of the intelligent classes. Alas, I fear that, by the side of many of the labour men, the enonomic philosophy of the "intelligent classes" is only too often naïve ! And it is rather late in the day for "the fear of God". They have been warned ; and it is a peculiarity of the moral world that, although you may perhaps enlighten the unenlightened, you cannot so well dis-enlighten the enlightened.

How the rights and obligations of the situation are to be analysed, how they are to be adjusted, it is not my purpose to inquire. My interest here lies in the motive and conception of morality. Hence it will suffice to point out that this assertion of rights on the part of the workers, or the masses, so far from marking "the decay of reverence" deplored by worshippers of the ordered society, marks a significant extension—perhaps the most significant in the history of the race—of the territory of the moral world.

CHAPTER VII

THE UNITY OF THE SPIRIT

§ 25. Morality among the values. § 26. Utility and the system of means and ends.

§ 25

IN passing now from what has been mainly a criticism of the orthodox view to a more positive development of the conception of morality I will begin with a brief statement of the psychological thesis, or motive, which is to underlie all of the subsequent chapters, and which may be stated as "the unity of the spirit".

The contrast of morality and utility involves a distinction of "values" which suggests the more recent fashion of treating ethics as a branch of "value-theory". Among the several values we may distinguish *economic* value, relating to wealth, or more generally to utility; *aesthetic* value, relating to art and beauty; *ethical*, or moral value; and *logical* value, in which knowledge and truth are conceived as a species of value. The sum of these "values", assumed to be so many different kinds of value, is human life. Now among these values what is the place of morality? My answer will be, Everywhere.

To make the meaning of this clearer—it is for me one of the convincing merits of Benedetto Croce's philosophy of beauty that he makes the aesthetic a generic aspect of the human mind, or in his own juster and more graceful terms, of the human spirit. By this it is meant that creative art is not confined to "men of genius"; to exceptional and abnormal men, capable of a special sort of intoxication; or to exceptional and abnormal states of mind. "Since we all talk," he says, very significantly, "we are all artists." Any one who has ever attempted to talk (or to write) seriously, with a careful sense of responsibility for saying what he means, or who has observed a child struggling pathetically for the fitting word and dissatisfied with any other, who has compared this with that facile use of slang (in polite conversation or commercial correspondence) which is never at a loss and never means much, will see, I think, that serious talking is an experience both of art and of beauty. But then he will see that every experience, so far as it is *experience*—consciousness and not habit, is as such an aesthetic experience and has, in however slight a measure, the quality of genius—and thus, I maintain, the quality of morality.

It is therefore dismaying to find Croce, in a fashion characteristically Latin, dividing the realm of the spirit into the four seemingly separated "forms" of aesthetic, logic, economic, and ethic; such that, it seems, nothing that is any of these forms, or departments, of the spirit can at the same time be in any other. To be sure the four forms are somehow linked in "the unity of the spirit"; an evolutionary unity in which the spirit, beginning with the aesthetic, passes through the logical and the economic and reaches finally the ethical. But in this "unity" I find the aesthetic and the moral, to me the most intimately related, separated by nearly the whole field of the spirit, and the aesthetic (curiously, the field in which Croce's chief interests lie) degraded to the status of the most primitive form of consciousness. To me this is false aesthetic and false ethic; and I am led to suspect that Croce, who is a free spirit in the field of aesthetic, has in the field of ethics bowed to a pious convention—the convention, namely, that while art is self-expression morality expresses "the spirit of self-sacrifice"; that while art is individual morality must be "universal".

But my chief objection to these nicely differentiated "forms of the spirit" is that they perpetuate the tradition of the departmented soul; the soul conceived after the analogy of the house, or the factory, in which successive stages in the process of manufacture are distributed spatially among so many rooms, or buildings. The classical illustration is what James calls "the Kantian machine-shop", from which we derive the tripartite division of the soul into knowledge, feeling, and will; three rooms, in the first of which we find out what the world has given us (without yet suspecting what we want), in the second how we like it (without suspecting what we shall do about it), and in the third what we are going to do about it. Primitive conceptions of this kind will be found underlying most of the chapter-divisions in the textbooks of psychology. They doubtless enable us to talk about the mind, they hardly enable us to understand it.

Such at least is my prejudice: namely, that the departmented soul is no soul whatever. And therefore I must view somewhat sceptically the multiplicity of separate fields, each guarded by its own standard as by a tutelary deity, into which life, or "value", is divided by science and by common thought. A shopkeeper tells me that this is the right price. If I ask whether he means that the price is moral, I shall learn that prices are determined not by moral laws but by the laws of economics. A teacher of French tells me that "Sapho" and "Mademoiselle Maupin" are good literature, but hastens to explain that he means, not morally good, but aesthetically good. If I criticize Jones who has just lost his son for his choice of physician, I may be reminded that his fault was at most an error of judgment, and thus not moral but intellectual. Or (to introduce the traditionally most absolute division of moral philosophy) his fault was merely prudential—as if there could be a "merely prudential" in an issue of life and death! Other standards might be mentioned, such as the standards of manners (assumed to be independent of morals) and of correct dress.

In this common view morality appears to be only one of the many departments of life. And in the mind of the average man it seems to be somewhat apart from life's main business. The business man dismisses moral considerations on the ground that "business is business", calmly certain that morality belongs somewhere else. For the artist art is art. The statesman is convinced that morality should not obtrude upon diplomacy. He may even take pride in the reflection that he has allowed no moral scruples (all very well in their place) to qualify his pursuit of the national prestige. It seems indeed that among the departments of life morality is the least important. So that the common man may be forgiven for supposing that morality comes into play only on Sunday, that it is concerned mainly with domestic relations, and perhaps exclusively with the relations between men and women.

It is against this departmental view of life (common indeed but far from distinctively vulgar) that I hold that among the several "values" of life morality is everywhere. A Crocean released from the orthodox convention might prefer to say that beauty is everywhere. I could meet him more than half-way. My own starting point is morality; and I am interested in vindicating the moral quality of every movement of the mind, or the spirit. But I am no less interested in pointing out that beauty is everywhere and, possibly above all, that intelligence is everywhere. It is not my intention to elaborate a system of values, but the underlying thesis will be this: that morality and intelligence and beauty are only so many artificial and conventional separations, justified doubtless by convenience of communication, of what is inseparable in the concrete reality of mind, or spirit, or life. For ethics this means that the whole meaning of morality is nothing less than *life*, and that its subject-matter is as broad as "human nature"; and in the last chapters I shall go on to point out that human nature is still the issue involved in questions of knowledge and truth.

§ 26

So much for the place of morality among the values; now for the special character of utility. Morality, I have said, is everywhere. So far as the useful is the embodiment of human value, utility is also everywhere. Economic value, regarded as the expression of human need, is moral value.[1] And it is doubtless possible so to extend the application of "utility", by appealing vaguely to "the larger utilities", as to make it cover all of human life. But this is to give to the term a meaning and direction which is the reverse of the "strictly utilitarian". And it is my purpose thoughout this essay to suggest that, in this stricter and only distinctive sense, utility is on the contrary a motive at variance with the motive of morality and in like fashion at variance with the motive of beauty and of truth.

Morality, intelligence, beauty are expressions of life: utility represents the organization of life into a system of means and ends, the substitution of mechanism for choice and interest and of habit for critical intelligence. A world finally utilitarian would be a world from which choice and direction (hence, all morality) had vanished, a world to be referred in every detail to the operation of "economic law" —a situation far from being represented in any actual human world.

To describe an activity as utilitarian is to say that it is a means to an end; and this implies that it is done not for its own sake but for the sake of its results. The interest and value lie wholly in the end. The end is a subject for intelligence and choice. The intelligence to be applied to the means is strictly limited; and in a thoroughly organized system of means and ends, as illustrated in an up-to-date factory system, the function of intelligence will be reduced to a minimum. So far as a man's activity is merely

---

[1] I have dealt at length with the relation of the moral and the economic in a paper on " Moral Valuations and Economic Laws " in *The Journal of Philosophy*, Vol. XVI (1917), No. 1.

utilitarian it means that he has ceased to be a moral agent and has assumed the status of a machine.

Kant said, So act as to treat humanity, whether in thine own person or in that of any other, in every case as an end withal and never as a means only. This marks the moral as distinct from the utilitarian order of society. In the conception of an "ordered society", of higher and lower classes, the lower classes have relatively the status of means —to ends not their own. But the same implication resides in that more democratic conception of society which makes virtue for the individual to consist in being "a useful member" devoted to the common good. It may happen that in his social function, however humble, the individual finds food for his imagination and an enjoyment of life. But this consideration is irrelevant, and even confusing, to the idea of "a useful member". The ideally *useful* member is literally the machine; which alone exhibits a single-minded devotion to what it is designed to do.

The conception of utility is illustrated "in thine own person" so far as one part of life is treated as a means for another part as end. This is what we mean when we refer to the utilitarian motive most of the activities involved in making a living. What is implied is that no one makes shoes from any interest in shoes, but only for the money to be received for them. And perhaps the best picture of the utilitarian life is that of the business man who, as conventionally conceived, spends weary years in business in the hope of retiring on a fortune, or of the wage-earner who patiently accumulates savings in the hope of living to enjoy them. Such are the typically "useful lives", and the question I raise is whether they are the ideally moral lives. And the question may be extended to cover all of those conceptions in which life is viewed under the form of a "vocation" or a "career" subject to the issue of "failure" or "success"—even though success be defined in no sordid terms. Life may be good or bad, but I wonder in what sense, except as a means to alien ends, it may be said to involve the issue of success.

This is not of course a proposal to banish utility from life. The utilitarian organization of life into a system of means and ends is a necessity of getting things done; and there can be no doubt that things must be done. But this is not to say that the system of ends and means is an ideal conception of life.

CHAPTER VIII

THE PRAGMATIC ATTITUDE

§ 27. The forward-looking attitude. § 28. Anticipation *vs.* retrospection. § 29. Imagination and the specious present. § 30. Reflective intelligence and the flux of life.

AS a significant and interesting expression of the utilitarian motive (or at least as a means of further defining that motive) I shall consider now the pragmatic attitude as represented by Professor John Dewey, an attitude also defined as "experimental" or "empirical". The attitude is significant as expressing the spirit of the age embodied in the conception of "modern progress". And it is interesting as a basis of criticism because Professor Dewey is a thorough-going critic of orthodox morality, who conceives morality to be co-extensive with the meaning of "life", and conceives life as a process of reflective intelligence.

What remains, then, to give a utilitarian cast to the pragmatic attitude? I will put it as follows. For Professor Dewey it seems that the essence of immorality lies in the adoption of "fixed ends"; in taking any part of life to be of absolute and supreme importance, to which the rest of life is subordinate, or, as I should put it, in conceiving life as a matter of means and ends. He who adopts the orthodox programme of fixed principles and unchanging moral laws has forsworn moral choice and made of himself a mechanism for the illustration of "moral law". But he will be no less of a mechanism, no less of a non-moral being, if he has committed himself absolutely to the attainment of any specific end. The moral attitude will be at every moment an attitude of open-mindedness. "We are in a non-moral condition whenever we want anything intensely", *i.e.*, absolutely, so as to limit the possibilities of choice.

So far I follow him ; and I should take this to mean that a man's life is imperfectly moral so far as he sacrifices any part of himself past or present. But now it seems, as I understand Professor Dewey (and I will not claim to understand him finally), that for him morality does consist precisely in the constant sacrifice of the past—to the future or to the present. This is the essence of the pragmatic attitude. And what it means is that the morality of open-mindedness is committed to a progressive as against a conservative attitude. For Professor Dewey it seems that progressive and conservative are the equivalents of moral and immoral. In this progressive attitude I seem to see life defined and limited by the utilitarian—more concretely, by the modern business man's point of view.

§ 27

According to Professor Dewey, "anticipation is more primary than recollection ; projection than summoning of the past ; the prospective than the retrospective." This passage from the essay in "Creative Intelligence"[1] states the essence, the quintessence, of the pragmatic attitude. The pragmatic attitude is the forward-looking as against the backward-looking attitude. What it means is, Waste no time over unfulfilled hopes. Let the dead bury the dead, and don't cry over spilled milk. What you wanted in the past is of no consequence now. The past is dead and gone, hence non-existent and unreal ; the real lies all ahead—in the future, Professor Dewey seemed to me formerly to say, in the present as he seems more definitely to say now ; in any case in a present which for its aims looks forward only.

---

[1] *Creative Intelligence. Essays in the Pragmatic Attitude.* (By Dewey and others, 1917.) I am repeating here some of the things said in my review of this book in *The Nation* (New York) for July 26, 1917.

This forward-looking attitude is also for Professor Dewey the reflective attitude. One who looks forward intelligently must of course also look back; and thus it happens that in point of fact "reflection" constitutes the central topic of most of Professor Dewey's writings. By him, however, the function of reflection appears to be strictly limited. "Imaginative recovery of the bygone is indispensable to successful invasion of the future, but its status is that of an instrument."[1] This states the "instrumental" theory of reflection, of intelligence or of thought. According to this view, thought is a means for action as an end. The instrumental view is thus the opposite of any view (such as what I call the critical view) which looks for the realization of life in reflection itself and finds in unthinking action rather the vehicle, or means. The instrumental theory of intelligence is likewise a biological theory. It means, if I may state it crudely, that God has endowed us with reflective intelligence for the purpose of preserving our lives and of getting on in the world. For this practical purpose it is obviously necessary that we look back and recall which of the methods used in the past have been successful in attaining their ends. To do this is the function of thought just as reproduction is the function of sex; and therefore any preoccupation of thought in other directions—indulgence in retrospective enjoyment, sympathetic contemplation of dead hopes, revival of forgotten ambitions, any care whatever for what one formerly wanted, above all any present dissatisfaction because of past disappointments—all of this is an abnormality of the same order as the sexual abnormalities. From the instrumental point of view the past is only a means for the present, hence only something to be "used", so far as it may be useful, on behalf of the present.

Such is pragmatic "reflection"; a strange etymological fate, it may seem, for a word made out of *re* and *flectere!* To the ordinary man it will appear that reflection is better typified by those moments in which he, a "tired business man" returning from his office, or a tired professor

[1] *Creative Intelligence*, p. 14.

returning from a lecture, sinks into an easy chair, with his feet upon another, and having lighted a pipe, forgets about getting on in life and takes up again the threads of past desires, interrupted by business, and speculates longingly upon the possibility of satisfying them ; or decides perhaps to write to an old friend of years back, not because they have business to transact, or any plans to make, but because the memories are too precious to be lost out of life. Professor Dewey has his names for this species of reflective attitude. Formerly it stood for the "genteel tradition" of a leisure class [1] ; later it was "senile" [2]; but now, in his reference to "impotent wishes, compensatory dreams in consciousness",[3] I see him prepared with the Freudians to call it "infantile"—which means that a respect for the past is a form of sexual aberration.

§ 28

Anticipation, then, is prior to recollection—if this be more than the dogmatic assertion of a private prejudice, what is its ground ? For the life of me I can see but one ground, namely, the ground of practical efficiency, motived by the desire of getting things done, however done, and the necessity of getting them done now if they are to be done at all, since time and tide wait for no man. That this motive has its compelling logic will be clear enough. Upon it the business man has constructed a science. Knowing full well that the sole value of his present stock is what it will bring in the future he makes it a point when the season begins to decline to cut his prices ruthlessly with no retrospective regard to cost. Such a policy stands doubtless for reflective intelligence, yet for a process in which reflection is reduced to a minimum by the prior adoption of cash value as a fixed end, the only end that matters. And it is the exclusiveness of this end that makes the prospective attitude so exclusively logical.

---

[1] *Essays in Experimental Logic*, p. 72.
[2] Somewhere in *Creative Intelligence*.
[3] *Human Nature and Conduct*, p. 236.

Applied to matters more personal, the simply prospective attitude seems even less consistent with an attitude of reflection. When David shook off the sackcloth and ashes and became so quickly normal after hearing that the child of Bath-Sheba was dead, his friends naturally wondered. It was a trifle too practical and business-like. His explanation, that sackcloth and ashes are useless after the child is dead, is a really beautiful anticipation of the pragmatic attitude, but not suggestive of much depth of reflection. For the matter of that, however, the only practical attitude towards death is simply *not* to reflect upon it. You can make nothing of it. The thought of death paralyses action. And thus, as Freud has pointed out, death as a subject of conversation is universally taboo. Here at any rate the reflective attitude is not satisfied, but cut rudely short, by the practical attitude. To urge that grief is a luxury is to say, not Reflect ! but rather Forget ! For time is moving and hunger is pressing. Hence, on returning from the funeral the band plays "When Johnny Comes Marching Home Again" ; not, however, on behalf of a reflective attitude towards life.

Just after I had read "Creative Intelligence"—in 1917, when it seemed that college teachers would be without an occupation for the coming year—a colleague spoke to me of his intention of spending the next year writing a book for which he had long been gathering material, for the writing of which, however, under the then disturbed conditions, he had little appetite. "Then", I asked rather flippantly, yet interested to get his reply, "why bother about it?" "If I fail to write that book," he said, "I shall have wasted twenty years of work." Suppose now that he writes the book ? Shall we say with Dewey that the writing of the book is an end for which the twenty years of work will be (now) merely instrumental ? May we not as well say that the writing of the book will be merely instrumental in making good twenty years of work ? For my own part I cannot see that either point of view is more real or essentially more intelligent than the other. Any rejection of one on behalf of the other will be a matter of temperament. Some men—not usually accounted the least reflective of men—are disposed to emphasize loyalty to the past; for them nothing is life which fails to realize their earlier aspirations. Others are disposed to emphasize the possibilities of the future, and for them nothing is life except as it is pervaded by novelty and growth.

And since the latter is the temperament expressed in the pragmatic attitude, it will serve to point the issue if I confess to a considerable sympathy—temperamental rather than intellectual perhaps—with the former. To sit at a man's table and remember that the hospitality is the continued fulfilment of a friendship of many years gives me a peculiarly hearty satisfaction. I was delighted to discover some years ago after finishing a long task of writing that both the title and the motive were those of a crude undergraduate essay which I had written long before and forgotten. To many persons this might suggest only a persistent obsession; for me, I must confess, it was a confirmation of truth. Most of my life I have cherished an infantile ambition to build with my own hands in some pleasant place a small summer camp which I should all the more enjoy because I had built it myself. The time for that has probably passed. Yet while Freudians and pragmatists smile, I continue to meditate upon my plans. Suppose that it is done : why should I then apologize for an infantile obsession ? Why might I not rather point to the result as a rounded achievement of reflective intelligence ?

And then I wonder whether pragmatists themselves may not be the victims of "impotent wishes" and "compensatory dreams". The meliorists (among whom Professor Dewey enrolls himself), or the wide-awake men, would have us look upon the present era of history as a final emergence from a day-dream ; a dream of heaven as our compensation for the ills of earth. Modern enlightenment tells us that heaven is to be found, if anywhere, only upon earth itself, in social progress and reconstruction. This search for heaven upon earth is meliorism. But why should we expect to find it—or to find any approach to it? "Ah! *Vanitas Vanitatum!*" writes Thackeray at the end of "Vanity Fair", "which of us is happy in this world? Which of us has his desire? or, having it, is satisfied?" Do meliorists suppose that bath-tubs and trolley cars have intensified the *joie de vivre?* The whole trend of the "functional", or the meliorist's psychology is to show that things have a positive value only in the getting and only a defensive value when possession is assured. We cannot then indeed do without them; nor could we be easy at any time without them when once the idea has been suggested. Progress is indeed a necessity in the sense that it is an inescapable urge. But in what sense life is then made better meliorists do not pretend to make clear. Why, then, the eagerness of anticipation? May we not suspect that meliorism is but another compensatory dream—only now of a better time on earth to make up for the lost joys of heaven?

From the pragmatic point of view the typically unintelligent person is he whose views of life and plans of action, formed once for all, are never to be illumined either by reflection or by experience. That such persons are unintelligent may be readily admitted; and I will also admit, as an abstract proposition, that when pictures of the future produce a tendency to yawn it must be the mark of a defective imagination. Yet there is an opposite type of unintelligence of which pragmatists commonly take no account: namely, the superficial seeker after novelty whose imagination is so effervescently creative that he never holds a plan before him with sufficient steadiness to make it a subject for any reflection whatever. Which of these is the true type of intelligence and of the moral life, the stolid conservative or the brainless radical? The question may be condemned as itself unintelligent. It may suffice, however, to suggest that the moral life is as little to be defined by a preference for the future as by a preference for the past. Morality is not a simple question of conservative *versus* progressive.

§ 29

It may then help us to state the question if we remember that in the last analysis the pragmatic attitude is arguing for the enjoyment of the present. And so indeed am I. That which is not present enjoyment I take to be so much out of life. But "the present" —is this a conscious present or an unconscious present? The unconscious present is an abstract point of time which enjoys nothing. The conscious present—which James calls "the specious present"—is never a point of time. What the "content" of this present may be, depends upon the range of imagination. We may, as Royce has observed, speak with equal propriety of the present occasion or of the present century; or possibly of the eternal present of God, or the Absolute. Or with James of the present of "the tramp who lives from hour to hour; the Bohemian whose engagements are from day to day; the bachelor who builds but for a single life; the father who acts for another generation; the patriot who thinks of a whole community and many generations; and finally the philosopher and the saint whose cares are for humanity and eternity."

Now it will serve to characterize any attitude, as pragmatic or the reverse, if we can estimate the range of imagination implied in its present. And I will admit that I never quite know how much of reflective interpretation Professor Dewey may have tucked away in his "present". If we accept his announcement we must believe that "the antecedents of thought are our universe of life and love", including anything you please from the Monroe Doctrine to Botticelli.[1] And for aught I know his background in every present may be that of *ein gottbetrunkener Mensch*. But it will serve to define the pragmatic attitude (which is all that really matters) if I say that in reading the essays I get a very different impression; and that I seem to see him at every step clipping down the present until it represents the range of imagination of only the ordinary

---

[1] *Essays in Experimental Logic*, p. 75.

THE PRAGMATIC ATTITUDE

unreflective man ; at the same time characterizing what he has clipped away as "impotent wishes" or "romantic embellishments" of life. Thus he rejects the idea that actual life must be "a compromise with the best".[1] This idea implies an important conflict between facts and ideals, or between fact and imagination ; and "there is no wholesale discrepancy between existence and meaning ; there is simply a 'loosening' of the two when objects do not fulfil our plans and meet our desires".[2] In other words, there is nothing to justify what is called the problem of *life*, the meaning of *life*, or the *tragedy* of life. Problems, he tells us repeatedly, are always "specific" problems concerned with "specific" questions ; and anything like a philosophy of life should be left for the amusement of the poets.[3] Or, in other words, the end of action must lie in the action itself, and not outside.[4]

What, it may be asked, are the boundaries of "the action", of "the present", or (say) of life, so defined that you may point to something as lying outside ? If you are thinking of a movement of the body, of the present point in time, or of the span of three score years and ten, the meaning is clear enough ; and you can then point definitely to what lies "outside". But Professor Dewey does not mean this. Into "the action" or the "present" he will import some measure, however slight, of reflective intelligence, *i.e.*, of imagination. But when this is done the outer boundaries of the "present", of "the action", or of life, become wholly problematic. It is even a question what you mean. All depends upon the range of imagination ; and this may include God, freedom, and immortality, heaven and hell as well as the life on earth. In brief, there is now nothing but an arbitrary limitation of imagination by personal taste or by social convention—such as

---

[1] *Human Nature and Conduct*, p. 233.

[2] " The Intellectualist Criterion for Truth " in *The Influence of Darwin on Philosophy*, 1910, p. 135.

[3] " Intelligence and Morals " in the same volume, p. 71.

[4] *Human Nature and Conduct*, p. 223.

the convention established by the man on the street—which will mark off a pragmatic attitude from an attitude indefinitely "romantic".

In Professor Dewey's conception of the pragmatic attitude such a limitation appears to be assumed. Why is there no "wholesale discrepancy" between fact and ideal, hence no question regarding the meaning of "life"? Just because there is no "present", in no "action", a "wholesale" point of view. Human life is made to consist of a succession of temporary practical problems, each of them set and once for all given by the outcome of the last and each of them to be solved, or in some form to be disposed of right away. Arrived in Philadelphia, where do I go next? But where, I might also ask, am I to go after that? Even this question can hardly be considered, it will not be a real and present question, until I have arrived at the next place. Hence the moral question is always to be limited to the question of, What next? And not only to the question of, What next? (which may conceivably imply any range of imagination whatever), but to what bears upon that question *directly* and immediately. In other words, the imagination implied in the present tends to be confined within the limits, if not of the imagination of "the tramp who lives from hour to hour" or of "the Bohemian whose engagements are from day to day", yet of the business man who must give all of his attention to the task before him. Only as we conceive imagination to be thus restricted can we define a distinctively pragmatic attitude.

And in this connection it strikes me as a very interesting mark of the pragmatic attitude that (as I seem to note) when Professor Dewey will present you with an illustration of reflective intelligence he almost invariably introduces a business man, a manufacturer, or an inventor. Having got this impression before,[1] I was not surprised to find his chapter on "The Nature of Aims" in "Human Nature

---

[1] See, for example, pp. 24 and 35 of the important " Introduction " to *Essays in Experimental Logic*.

and Conduct" concerned mainly with bows and arrows and electric lights, and reflective intelligence represented by Edison. Metaphors and illustrations are often more illuminating than arguments. And it may serve again to mark the pragmatic attitude if I say that it would never occur to me to select Edison as a type of reflective in-intelligence as long as I could recall the names of Shakespeare or Goethe, Thackeray or Tourgenieff, Newton or Darwin, Washington or Lincoln, or our own William James. It is quite possible that I fail to appreciate the depth of reflection represented by the electric light; yet while the inventor of the pragmatic logic is bowing deferentially to the inventor of the electric light I find myself wondering whether the pragmatic logic, which has been for me a never-ending source of fruitful questions, should not, in terms of *reflective* intelligence, stand for more than all of the electric apparatus invented to date.

As a final suggestion of the meaning of the pragmatic attitude I will point to the contrast between the pragmatic attitude and the humanistic. The only term of the kind that I have cared to apply to what I call the "critical" view is the rather vague term "humanism". And "humanism" is the term applied by Dr. Schiller of Oxford to his own version of the pragmatic attitude. Professor Dewey seems to prefer almost any other, and I think he is right in feeling that between his pragmatic attitude and what is generally regarded as "humanistic" the difference is fundamental. As an expression of the humanistic attitude I can think of nothing finer than a passage from the close of Walter Pater's essay on "Pico della Mirandola":

" He had sought knowledge, and passed from system to system, and hazarded much; but less for the sake of positive knowledge than because he believed there was a spirit of order and beauty in knowledge, which would come down and unite what men's ignorance had divided, and renew what time had made dim. . . . For the essence of humanism is that belief of which he seems never to have doubted, that nothing which has ever interested living men and women can wholly lose its vitality—no language they have spoken, nor oracle beside which they have hushed their voices, no dream which has once been entertained by actual human minds, nothing about which they have ever been passionate, or expended time and zeal."

"Nothing which has ever interested living men and women can wholly lose its vitality." One can hardly state the limits of what this may be taken to mean. Such, however, is the attitude of humanism; and at the lowest terms it offers a complete contrast to the attitude of pragmatism. For whatever else the pragmatic attitude may mean, it means this—and such is Professor Dewey's constant iteration: that nothing which has ever interested living men and women can have more than a passing vitality.[1]

§ 30

So much for the pragmatic attitude. The pragmatic attitude, speaking in the name of reflective intelligence, makes the past life an instrument for the present. As against this I am urging that an intelligence genuinely reflective will refuse to treat any part of life as a mere means to another. Reflection I will identify with "imagination"; and a reflective living of life means that we live each moment in the light of the largest possible range of imagination.

But what this would mean in terms of a temporal progression, or of a pattern of life, is a question hardly to be answered. Rather it is to be answered in countless ways, but by poets (speaking in the larger sense) rather than by scientifically prosaic philosophers. It seems that life as thus conceived must be ever continuous yet ever creative; ever a present enjoyment which embraces both a fulfilment of the past and a fulfilment of the future. But how? For imagination works variously. It has, for example, a strangely transforming effect upon the common relation

[1] See the very interesting essay on "The Significance of the Problem of Knowledge", reprinted in *The Influence of Darwin on Philosophy*, 1910.

of means and ends. To go through a hard and dreary grind for an end to be enjoyed only, if at all, in the distant future, is not morality but brutality. Yet so far as the vision of the future is clear some of its enjoyment is realized in the present. Thus we find grown persons more content to wait, happier in the waiting, than children; at least trained to patient resignation. But patient resignation is by no means a moral ideal. If this is the best one can do with the present way of life, it is better to try another. Yet it may also be that imagination directed upon the present means may make them interesting for themselves. Because a man enjoys eating bacon for breakfast he may be willing to cook it—thus far the eating is profit, the cooking is loss. But presently he may discover that to cook bacon properly is a nice problem from the standpoint both of reflective intelligence and of artistic skill; and then he may find himself eating bacon mainly for the pleasure of cooking it. I make the illustration purposely crude to suggest that the distinction of end and means is a function of imagination and that indefinite possibilities of present realization may lie in the *reflective* treatment of the means. The business man whose professed purpose is to make money may be really interested in "business". Thus far his attitude has ceased to be merely utilitarian.

In a fashion likewise uncertain and difficult to describe, imagination deals with the past. It does of course make the past available for present uses, as instrumentalism claims. But it also makes the past real and present—just as real and just as present, *when you are not disturbed by the need of getting on,* as the present moment itself. And thus imagination works to destroy that past-and-gone feature of the temporal past which most of all marks the so-called reality of time: nothing would be irrevocable if your imagination were all-sufficient. Again, however, it makes the past desires living. Yet at the same time it may show us that in ways not contemplated at their inception they have been satisfied and fulfilled.

If I should offer an imaginative picture beginning with, "Life is like—," the reader would be reminded of the host of parables and metaphors in which men have sought, each according to the quality of his imagination, to concentrate into one picture the whole meaning of life. How shall we picture the life of reflective intelligence—reflective and also (as pragmatism teaches) creative? Resorting thus to metaphor I might say that for me the life of reflective intelligence is not a business enterprise, in which each past term is only a means to a prospective end; nor, again, a logical exposition, in which the premises are interesting only as leading to a conclusion; but more of the nature of a work of art, such as a symphony, in which there is temporal progression yet no distinction among movements of means and ends, each present passage having its own serene worth, quite as retrospective as prospective, and there is no thought of getting anything over and done with. But to make this an experience of living you must put yourself within the movement of the progression. And then, as I conceive, each new present will be indeed, as pragmatists teach, a newly created unity, a new plan of life, the fruit of ripened experience; yet a unity which will gather together the unfulfilled aspirations of the past quite as much as it looks towards the future.

CHAPTER IX

THE WISDOM OF THE SERPENT

§ 31. Intelligence and the serpent. § 32. The moral fault and the intellectual. § 33. The clever rogue and the simple honest man. § 34. The critical life and the question of intelligence. § 35. Intelligence *vs.* intellect, mathematical and logical. § 36. Intelligence personal and critical.

§ 31

"NOW the serpent was more subtle than any beast of the field which the Lord God had made." This announcement marks the opening of that brief but portentous drama, representing the conflict between authority and intelligence, which comprises the third chapter of Genesis. And the selection of the serpent to play the part of intelligence expresses an ancient and deeply-rooted human prejudice; a prejudice further illustrated by the choice of Mephistopheles or Iago for the villain of the play. Authoritarian moralists, it goes without saying, are committed to a discouragement of intelligence; since it can never be predicted that an exercise of intelligence will confirm authority. And probably many a parent with a son at college is consoled when the lad learns little by the thought that he might learn too much. Related to these is that considerable class of slow-minded but sentimentally " sensitive" persons whose intercourse with others, ever uneasy, seems to be dominated by the fear of exposing their private thinking to the test of criticism. They have indeed the practical justification that the test may serve only to worst them in an argument without proving anything; and one need not be a sentimentalist to realize that a finally satisfying conviction, if there is to be one, will not be a matter of argument.

Yet aside from all this, it seems to be a part of the natural man to be irritated by the presence of critical and imaginative persons who, though they refrain from comment and inquiry, may not be trusted to take what we tell them at its face value, but may rather be counted upon to form their own opinions and to entertain further questions. As a protection against such persons we erect an inner sanctum in which our motives may be stored safe from outer criticism—and also from our own. And in this attitude we have the support of all "sane and practical" men, whose point of view is well expressed by Shakespeare's Caesar when he says:

> Let me have men about me that are fat,
> Sleek-headed men, and such as sleep a-nights,
> Yon Cassius has a lean and hungry look,
> He thinks too much: such men are dangerous.

Remembering Caesar's ambitions we may sympathize with his desire to have men about him who sleep at night while he remains awake. But this may lead us to look more tolerantly upon the lean and hungry Cassius. And we may then acquire a certain respect for the serpent if, divesting ourselves of the tradition in which most of us have been bred, we read the story as an episode in mythology. As such it will take its place beside the many heathen myths in which the all-powerful gods are unaccountably baffled by the activities of their own creatures. And read in this light it will appear, I think, that of the four characters in the play, the Lord God, the man, the woman, and the serpent, the serpent is the clearest representative of critical intelligence; for he is able seemingly to perplex the Lord God himself.

Nor is his intelligence a mere vulgar cunning. For, strangely, his most insidious suggestion embodies what may be regarded as the deepest truth of moral philosophy: "For God doth know that in the day ye eat thereof, then your eyes shall be opened, and ye shall be as gods, knowing good and evil". It will be interesting to compare this with the words of Jesus in the Fourth Gospel: "And ye shall know the truth and the truth shall make you free."

The moral aspect of the situation seems likewise altered when we transfer the conflict of motives to a more modern setting. Reading the story in the spirit of the ancient conceptions of property, regarding the man and the woman as the Lord God's creatures—and remembering perhaps that knowledge hardly adds to contentment—the serpent appears to be only a mischievous intruder upon the peace and harmony of the garden. But if we substitute for the Lord God a Russian landed-proprietor before the Emancipation, or a southern planter before the Civil War, or a capitalistic employer of to-day claiming by virtue of his position the right of master; and for the serpent one of those who would awaken the subjects to a consciousness of their power and a sense of their manhood; it may then be difficult to see how the part of the serpent differs from the part played by those whom to-day we honour as deliverers from ignorance and superstition, or how a communication of the wisdom of the serpent is other than a communication of moral responsibility. And it will strengthen the suggestion if we remember that in conservative eyes the critic of social institutions wears invariably the aspect of a serpent, whose wisdom is merely specious and "subtle".

§ 32

The opposition of morality and intelligence belongs to that departmental conception of the soul to which I have referred above, and according to which all of the knowing, or the intelligence, is done in one room of the soul, all of the willing, or the morality, in another, while a third is occupied exclusively by feeling, or taste. On this theory it becomes possible for the abstract "moral self" to charge some of his errors to the account of the abstract "knowing self", who may then be treated as morally suspicious and "dangerous".

When, however, we examine concrete cases of error, on the part of ourselves or of others, it seems that we are hardly able to effect a complete separation between the moral fault and the intellectual. Jones has wrecked his motor-car in an "unavoidable" accident. Knowing that some persons are more liable than others to unavoidable accidents our first inquiry may be directed upon the personality of Jones. From our human standpoint there are doubtless accidents truly unavoidable, due to contingencies which, as we say, only a divine wisdom could have anticipated. But even this is not to say that they could have been anticipated by no wisdom whatever. And the dividing line between human and divine wisdom, between what could be expected of Jones and what could be expected only of a higher order of being, remains always uncertain. Meanwhile we do know that one's vision of danger, even if limited ultimately, may be broadened indefinitely by a more intensive sense of responsibility. And if Jones is a morally sensitive person, and the accident has resulted in death, especially the death of one near to him, it is doubtful whether, though he has used ordinary foresight, he will ever rest comfortably in the conviction that the contingencies bringing about the accident were beyond the limits of any possible foresight. In the light of later reflection he is likely to go through life tormented by the thought, "I might have known, and therefore I ought to have known."

In this he will be stating the most essential proposition of moral responsibility and free will. This doctrine rests, I should say, upon a fact; at least upon an experience: upon the experience, namely, that retrospectively it is never possible to see why—whatever range of imagination might be implied—you or I could not know what it was possible for some other intelligence to know. It is the old story of Columbus and the egg, illustrated in the solution of any problem you please. In the light of the solution you and I can never see why we had to miss it, and the fact that we did miss it is now more or less humiliating. Physical powers, it seems, have their well-defined limits, but mental powers appear to have essentially none. Hence that A can lift a heavier weight than I can lift, I am content to accept as a fact; but to say that another intelligence has seen what I did not see is always in some degree to say that I also ought to have seen.

Suppose, again, that Brown has been betrayed by an agent whom he has trusted. It is worth noting that errors of this kind are peculiarly humiliating. And if Brown were a morally sensitive person his reflections might easily take form as follows: What it all means is that I did not quite know an honest man from a rogue; and this in turn can mean only that I am not a sensitively honest man. And his reflections would be supported in the gross by the consideration that those who are seduced into buying worthless stocks by the promise of extraordinary dividends are not likely to be of the purest type of character—at least, they are betrayed by an overreaching cupidity; and if he will recall the simple tricks by which in the older days "the honest farmer" was fleeced by the clever stranger, he may note that usually the sharper's art consisted in making the farmer believe that he, the farmer, was getting the best of an innocent stranger. *Integer vitae scelerisque purus*— honesty implies certain powers of perception, and there is some truth in the idea that in a world of rogues the honest man—the truly honest man—is peculiarly safe.

§ 33

"Behold, I send you forth as sheep in the midst of wolves: be ye therefore wise as serpents, and harmless as doves." Any separation of the moral from the intellectual seems bound to issue in a division of men into two classes: in one class the wolves and the serpents, in the other the sheep and the doves; in one class the "clever rogue", or the "astute diplomat", shrewd but unscrupulous, in the other the "simple honest man", or "simple rustic", naïvely scrupulous. The popular mind finds it difficult to believe that a "brainy" man can be altogether honest or that an honest man can fail to be somewhat deficient in "brains"; and the more reflective mind may still be confronted with an ever curious question. This clever rogue—is he so very clever? This trustworthy honest man—is he trustworthy only because he is a fool? My own conviction is that any attempt thus to classify the men we meet only reveals the futility of the distinction, and I am inclined to put the clever rogue and the simple honest man into the class of convenient fictions. But in moral philosophy there are no authoritative opinions, and the point is to see what the question means.

Take first the "clever rogue". From the superior standpoint of "the intelligent classes" we are likely to find him writ large in the patent medicine-man and the cheap politician. Yet if we note the temerity with which these persons reproduce pictures of themselves in the newspapers and on the advertising boards, displaying countenances in which it often seems that the word "rogue" is written in every line, we must surely doubt whether they are so very clever. Do they, let us ask ourselves, know what impression they are conveying to every more critical mind, and do they then deliberately defy that judgment for the sake of deceiving the stupid? I think this is greatly to be doubted, and I suspect that even the shrewdest of them display their pictures because, like you or me, they conceive their countenances to be impressive.

It is a fair supposition, I should say, that there is nowhere any striking difference of level, either moral or intellectual, between a political or other representative and the average of his constituents—he is not the wolf among the sheep or the serpent among the doves. Some years ago Miss Jane Addams printed an impressive study,[1] based upon intimate experience, of the typical corrupt alderman

[1] " Ethical Survivals in Municipal Corruption " in *The International Journal of Ethics*, VIII (April, 1898), No. 3.

and his typical constituency of foreign-born citizens. As against the current view of political reformers that these voters were without moral ideals, it was shown that on the contrary they were guided by what was from their point of view a very reasonable conception of "a good man": the man who stood by them in difficulty, who provided coal and warm clothing in winter, who found jobs for their sons and helped on occasion to adjust their difficulties with the police, and who above all (a very large consideration in the minds of the foreign poor) saw that no constituent lacked the dignity of a reputable funeral. That the funds for these benefits came from bribes for street-railway franchises, they knew well enough, but this they could excuse as only a mode of restitution. What shall we say, however, of the alderman himself? I think we can have no ground for supposing that he did not take himself just as his constituents took him, as a good-hearted and generous man. In other words, he was no more intelligent than he was scrupulous.

This is doubtless to put the question at only a vulgar level, and (it may be objected) in terms of an intelligence hardly to be compared with the refined astuteness of the Macchiavellian diplomat who really sets our problem. But it is my purpose to raise the question whether the situation as just presented will not be true for any level. No one can of course pretend to have measured the heights of intelligence. All that any of us can do is to ask himself whether a closer acquaintance with those who within his personal environment are famed for Macchiavellian astuteness increases his respect for their intelligence. And in this matter it would prove nothing to offer personal observations unless they could be made concrete. What shall we say, however, about Macchiavelli himself? Defenders of Macchiavelli are accustomed to endow him with a marvellous insight into human nature—chiefly, it seems, because of his lack of moral scruple. Yet in the end they convict him of having underestimated the force of moral considerations—as if these considerations were somehow accidental to human nature. Now it would prove nothing to say that Macchiavelli's personal career was a failure. Nor should we forget that "The Prince" was a serious political philosophy, presenting perhaps the earliest vision of the modern nation-state, conceived as a united Italy. Yet in reading Macchiavelli to-day (after four centuries, to be sure) it seems to me that what is chiefly remarkable is not so much his cool advocacy of treachery and assassination as a policy of state—which was probably only to stand for "realistic" statesmanship under the conditions of his day—as his simplicity in supposing that the end that he had in mind, the unification of Italy, could be established and indefinitely maintained by mere ingenuity of statecraft, and with so little regard for the needs and the aspirations, and the economic conditions, of the peoples to be unified. Such, it would seem, must be the reflection of any modern historian. But a crowning simplicity seems to lie in the idea of the essay itself. If the instructions to the prince were to be of any value whatever it must be in the form of a private document, yet the essay is a contribution to literature.

This is to state the point of the whole question. What of the Macchiavellian diplomat who has acquired a Macchiavellian reputation? Let it be remembered that these are the only Macchiavellians we can be called upon to consider. The secret Macchiavellians are fated to remain indistinguishable among the mass of moderately decent citizens. What shall we say of the intelligence of a man who, however competent otherwise, prides himself upon his *finesse*—that is, upon his ability to play a game with his neighbour—and who thereby establishes a reputation for *finesse*? At this point it seems that his grasp of human nature is defective; he has failed to see the consequences of establishing a reputation. It seems not too much to say that any man who prides himself upon his knowledge of human nature thereby proclaims himself a fool: all that he proves is a naïve conception of human nature.

And on the other hand what if a man does understand

human nature? Can his understanding be then dissociated from moral scruple? We do not find men whose business it is to inflict pain—surgeons and judges, for example— expecting to fortify themselves by understanding the pain they inflict. And if it should happen that further acquaintance with one of the reputedly "shrewd but unscrupulous" only increases my respect for his intelligence, it seems to me that one consequence is inevitable: I must then deeply question my own previously formed moral ideals. For if his insight is generally so superior to mine how can he be altogether mistaken about what is really good?

Turning now to the "simple honest man", I shall assume that the "simple", or stupid, man is not to be confused with the merely uneducated. To find uneducated men who are sensitively honest does not mean that you have found this honesty in the stupid. The question that I raise here relates to the convention of "simple honesty" —the conjunction of these two terms—and I wonder how any person who has faced the problem of honesty can suppose that honesty is "simple", and therefore a virtue peculiarly appropriate to the unintelligent. In the business world honesty is simplified by convention. Holding a piece of real estate which I expect (perhaps as the result of private information) to diminish in value, I decide to put it upon the market; and to escape inconvenient questions I put it into the hands of an agent. I let the buyer take care of himself; I tell him no lies; and thus I remain conventionally honest. But suppose I learn that a person of my acquaintance is about to buy the property as an investment, putting into it perhaps the whole of a rather small capital. Ought I to warn him? The question of honesty is at least not so simple now as before. Yet, in any of the relations between men, the questions of honesty presented by matters of business are among the relatively simple. What shall we say when honesty becomes a question of honour and loyalty, between friend and friend, between man and wife, or father and son? It seems that "simple honesty" must now be the equivalent of a fine and discriminating intelligence.

And therefore I will put the case of the simple honest man as follows : Do you find men who respond to you with a finely discriminating sense of what is fair and honourable, from whom, however, you can obtain no intelligent response, with whom you can hold no intelligent conversation, upon any other subject ? Or do you find men with a highly intelligent appreciation of other aspects of life who in any question of what is just and honourable are simply obtuse ? I know that the existence of such persons —geniuses without conscience and dull-minded saints—is accepted as a common matter of fact. The question will be whether the conventional statement of fact will satisfy your personal experience; which will naturally include more dull-minded persons than geniuses. For my own part I do not seem to find among the dull-minded what we mean—what we all mean—by "an honest man". What I rather expect to find is a low cunning. An honest man is no lifeless pattern of rectitude, but a communicable soul; towards whom you can safely expand, with whom you can be confidential, and whom you can trust precisely because you can communicate with him. And he who is thus communicable I can hardly rank among the dull.

It is not to be denied that the clever rogue is very frequently successful. But to make success a test of intelligence would be to affirm what I am most concerned to deny, namely, the identity of intelligence with practical wisdom. Hence I will not only admit, I will even insist, that one may be easily too intelligent for success in business or in politics or in social life. The practical man's objection to the Cassiuses who "think too much" is from his own point of view perfectly sound. To work easily with other men it is an advantage to be able to take them at their own estimate. To sell goods with the best success you must believe in the goods you are selling. A piano-salesman whom I met on the train, who after many years with one company had entered the service of its chief rival, told me with some humour that he had found it rather embarrassing at first to "talk up" to his old customers the piano he had always condemned; and he had only overcome his embarrassment by dismissing the moral question. Had he ventured upon further researches into moral philosophy I fear his salesmanship would have been ruined. Would he then, however, have been less intelligent?

But this is to suggest that the question of fact is at bottom also a question of the meaning of intelligence; which is the form of the question to which I am coming.

§ 34

Morality I have defined above as the self-conscious living of life; more bluntly as knowing what you are doing. And therefore for me morality is intelligence. As a believer in intelligence I believe in analysis without end. I believe in looking a gift horse in the mouth, in letting your right hand know what your left hand is doing, and in letting no false respect for persons forbid an intimate analysis of motives, of your friend, your wife, your child, or your grandmother. But I believe that morality is above all an analysis of your own motives.

As a believer in intelligence I repeat Aristotle's statement that all men desire by nature to know; only adding, more explicitly, that in the desire to know we have the central and fundamental fact of human nature. To William James's statement that knowing is always for the sake of doing I reply that the only valuable fruit of the doing is the knowing. What is the value of "doing things" if we don't know what we are doing? Or how is one to be credited with *doing* something if it be not a knowing-doing? To do in any significant sense is to do self-consciously. And therefore as a believer in intelligence I place the satisfactions of knowing—spiritual expansion and the enlargement of vision—against all the utilitarian advantages of knowing; which themselves must be measured ultimately in terms of the knowing itself. 'Tis better to have loved and lost than never to have loved at all; and, if there be any better in the universe, better to have lived and lost. It is better to have played the hand and lost it (I am thinking of the game of bridge) if the hand presented any worthy problem. You have lost your money, or your points, as the case may be, but you have gained in insight. And for the believer in intelligence this is the real score of the game.

To profess the belief that morality is intelligence is at once to suggest the Greek view of life. Among the Greeks, as I pointed out above, morality was conceived in terms of the "good" rather than of "the right"; and thus in terms of choice rather than of authority. And all of the Greek moral philosophy is marked by a belief, in some sense, in the doctrine of Socrates that virtue is knowledge. Yet the doctrine of knowledge, and the Greek view of life, presented a problem, even for the Greeks. Plato, for whom virtue is nothing if not knowledge, sees that knowledge may be mistaken for a calculating prudence and is at pains to distinguish true knowledge from the specious wisdom of the sophists. Aristotle suggests that virtue calls for something more than knowledge, yet he concedes that perhaps the whole question is a question of what is true knowledge, or intelligence.

And thus, having stated the creed, we face the question —to which I have thus far been leading—what is to be understood by intelligence? For I fancy that no one who finds inspiration in the thought that morality is intelligence will say that for him life is a matter of accounting or of engineering. The question involves, then, the distinction between two competing conceptions of intelligence, which I may describe as, respectively, mechanical or mathematical intelligence and personal or critical intelligence; or again as scientific intelligence and humane intelligence. What this means I will venture to suggest through a very humble illustration.

Several years ago one of my children returning from a summer holiday brought with him a black kitten about four months old to which I was appointed, partly by force of circumstances, and partly by the choice of the kitten, the guardian and next friend. The kitten discovered quickly not only that my study was a quiet and comfortable place but that I was for him an indulgent person. He learned also that the study, having one door opening into the hall and another leading to a side porch, was a convenient passage in and out of the house; the more so since he could always rely upon me at his call to let him in at one door and out of the other. But what he never discovered, and what I could never teach him, was, in going out to stand back so that the opening door should not strike him in the face. To the end of my guardianship he never got out without having his nose thumped; at which he never ceased to be surprised and resentful.

Was the kitten intelligent? Although unable to comprehend doors, he seemed very well able (and in more ways than I have stated) to comprehend me. He was lacking in scientific intelligence, but he seemed to have humane intelligence. Was he, however, really intelligent?

An animal psychologist would have set him down as hopelessly unintelligent. The animal psychologist is accustomed by tradition to test the intelligence of an animal by putting him into a box with some sort of latch to it and then noting how long it takes the animal to master the latch—as if Bergson had never reminded us that man alone is interested in such things. Or he puts the animal into a maze and again notes how long it takes him to find his way out. But not only the animal psychologist. The same sort of test is to-day applied to human intelligence. The so-called intelligence-tests are full of puzzles and tricks which, if not, like locks, embodied in metal or wood, are built upon the same mechanical principle. And among the populace the mechanical criterion of intelligence is now well-nigh universal, the wisdom of the serpent (which strikes me as after all a more humane sort of wisdom) having been replaced by the wisdom of the machine. The proud parent points triumphantly to the signs of intelligence in his son, the signs being that the boy has quickly and thoroughly mastered the secrets of the motor-car or of the radio-set. Whether the lad will ever understand a line of poetry, or sit comfortably through a good concert, enjoy a good novel, look with interest upon a good picture, or grasp the meaning and motive of courtesy—these questions the parent omits to ask.

And so, before rejecting (or accepting) the doctrine that morality is intelligence, it is needful that we consider the alternative conceptions of intelligence.

§ 35

The scientific and mechanical conception of intelligence identifies intelligence with "intellect". And those who adopt this conception are called—by their critics, however, oftener than by themselves—"intellectualists".[1] For this view the type and ideal of intelligence is found in the "cold-blooded reasoning" which is characteristic of arithmetical calculation, of geometrical demonstration, and of the syllogisms of formal logic. And such is the fascination of numbers, forms, and syllogisms that some philosophers, among them Mr. Bertrand Russell,[2] following Pythagoras and Plato, find in them a revelation of the divine nature, while many mathematicians are now telling us that for the essence of logic we must go to mathematics. Mathematics, they mean, is not merely an illustration of logic ; mathematics *is* logic, and the only logic.

Now I would not for a moment question the *utility* either of mathematics or of formal logic. The apparatus of the syllogism supplies useful weapons for defence.

---

[1] In an article on " Intellectualism " in *The Nation* of some years ago, expressing the same views as those given here, I took the name of " intellectualist " for myself. The only difference here is that I reject the name. " Intelligencist " would convey my meaning ; but the term is hardly permissible.

[2] In *The Problems of Philosophy*, at least. From an article by Mr. Russell, printed since the above was written, I judge that the view is now repudiated.

To point out that your opponent is reasoning in a circle or has converted an A-proposition simply is usually to silence him—even though you suspect that a true A-proposition ought to be capable of simple conversion and that reasoning ought in circular fashion to make ends meet. And it is worth noting that for Aristotle, the inventor of formal logic, the question constantly uppermost is, If your opponent says this or that, how will you reply to him? Logic, it seems, is concerned with the game of debate; and "formal logic" is a statement of the rules of the game. One recalls the question credited to Jowett, Is logic a science or an art? and his answer, It is neither, it is a dodge.

It is not, however, upon merely sporting grounds that I would concede the utility of logic. Nor merely concede. Rather is it an important part of my argument to insist that there is a solid basis for logic in a utility soberly practical and business-like. Formal logic, I should say, is the casuistry of thought just as formal ethics, or right-conduct ethics, is the casuistry of motive; and just as formal ethics substitutes utility for morality so in formal logic is utility substituted for intelligence, or thought. Now logicians themselves are not as a rule prepared to say that the forms of logic are a simple portraiture of thought. Logic, they are likely to tell us, is a method not of thought but of demonstration; not of discovery but of proof. Logic, again, is a method of settling disputes. In dealing with the plain man, whom I meet in the person of the undergraduate student, I am constantly confronted with such questions as, Well, how are you going to settle the question? Who is to be the judge? Or perhaps, Who is to be the umpire? In such questions the plain man supposes naïvely that he is expressing a demand for truth; and if you reply that you are not primarily eager to settle the question he will set you down as a lost soul. It is not perceived that to *settle* a question means only to dismiss the question and get it out of the way while the *answer* to the question lies perhaps indefinitely far beyond. Yet questions that cannot be answered must none the less be settled.

I believe we may state the whole case by saying that logic—likewise all of scientific method, but in particular logic—is thought sacrificed, trimmed and pared down, to certain vitally important needs of *communication* : to the very vital need, in short, of communicating something to another person in such a way that you can be absolutely certain that he has received your communication just as you intended it. One need not be reminded how vital is this certainty of communication to the conduct not only of business but of all practical life. In this age when practical activities are tending universally to become socially organized activities it is the necessity underlying all other necessities. Yet it is no less clear that the more absolute you make the terms of communication the less you can communicate, and the less you can convey of your personal meaning. The only absolute language, we are told truly enough, is the language of mathematical notation. Formal logic states, then, not merely the rules of a game but the conditions of a contract. It is the embodiment of a *modus vivendi*. A contract is supposed to express a meeting of minds ; but every one knows how little of the meeting of minds can be embodied in the terms of a contract and how much must at best be left to personal understanding. Even a contract is not to be relied upon in dealing with a rogue.

An essential mark of the cold-bloodedness of cold-blooded reasoning, be it noted, is the absolute lack of uncertainty, of hesitation, of any process of deliberation, with which, in a process ideally intellectual, the thought, or argument, passes from each point to the next. Given A ; therefore B ; therefore C ; therefore D. He who in this derivation pauses to deliberate—thus implying, for example, that some other term, M, might conceivably be contemplated by the side of C as a possible consequence of B—is thus far defectively intellectual. And he who would venture to inport into the logical process an element of personal choice or taste is a traitor to the intellectual ideal. By a strange paradox it seems that the ideally intellectual process is marked by a complete absence of that activity of weighing and judging—that activity of imagination, we might say—which from any other point of view seems to be just the most characteristic mark of any process of thought or reflection. The presence of imagination, suggesting that thought faces possible alternatives, means that the thought is not perfectly logical. And thus imagination becomes the mark of a mind defectively logical; for the intellectualist defectively intelligent.

A writer of popular detective stories of a few years ago desiring to present his detective (always the same person) as the ideal of cold-blooded thinking called him "The Thinking-Machine". This, I should say, unwittingly states the case. Why this so-called logical process should be venerated as the truest revelation of the world of the spirit is more than I can see. For conceived in his perfection what we find before us in the person of the "logical thinker" is—not indeed any metaphorical "thinking-machine" but literally the machine itself. The logician Jevons betrayed this implication when he invented the logical machine. Had he lived later he would have found his logical machine, in one form at least, ready to hand in the adding-machine which we see at the bank. This alone of all beings in heaven and earth exhibits the perfection of "logical" thinking. In it the intellectual process is never corrupted by personal choice—just because it does not think.

This is not to say, however (God forbid!), that mathematicians do not think, but only that they are not thinking when they are "thinking mathematically". I will not pretend to a too close acquaintance with the mental operations of mathematicians, nor will I venture to say what significance attaches in the last analysis to the beauty and elegance of their forms and relations. Modern mathematics one is constrained to accept as a mystery, like transubstantiation, known only to the initiated, who on the other hand seem unable to explain it. Yet I will venture to suggest that the relation of logic to thinking may be illustrated generally, with application to mathematicians among others, by contrasting any schoolboy's presentation of his "original" proof of a geometrical proposition—given A is B, to prove that M is N—with his process of arriving at the proof. Heaven only knows how many foolish ideas, how many genial suggestions—involving perhaps "illicit" operations, such as drawing lines for the purpose of getting a hint of the terms of the proof—may have entered into the process The completed demonstration, supposing it to be presented in good logical form, would have you believe that the lad's mind could never have contemplated going from "A is B" to "M is N" by any but the most direct route and that on the way his imagination has never once been deflected from the path directly ahead. This, however, as even the logicians will tell us, exhibits not the process of thinking but the results of thinking—the practical results, I should add, marking also the point at which thinking stops.

Thus also the perfected machine marks the end of the inventor's thinking; something very useful indeed, but from the standpoint of thinking no longer worth thinking about. One is tempted to say that the logical demonstration is the corpse of thinking presentably laid out for burial. But perhaps the better figure would be the gentleman in evening dress who would give you the impression that this is a simply logical derivation from his personality. Any real activity of intelligence, in brief, is a genial operation, a process of trial and error, full of foolishness as well as of seriousness, of comedy and often of tragedy. The logical presentation of thought is that aspect of the process which we venture to make public.

§ 36

For myself, then, I seem compelled to say that there is only one kind of intelligence, namely, personal intelligence. And if this be true, then it will follow that the attitude towards the world in which the "intellectual" ideal is supposed to be embodied—the impersonal, scientific, matter-of-fact attitude—is either unintelligent or not so impersonal as it seems. The latter is what I suspect. But to make the intent of the distinction clear, let us assume once more that there are two kinds of intelligence ; and let us say now that the two kinds are manifested respectively in the knowing of things and in the knowing of persons. Scientific intelligence is manifested in the knowing of things ; personal, or humane, intelligence in the knowing of persons.

On this score I claim a certain respectable intelligence for my kitten. And if I were attempting to estimate the intelligence, say, of a fifteen-year old boy, I doubt if I should be greatly interested in his manipulation of gasoline motors or radios. I might not indeed care to look too closely into his taste for literature or his ability as a literary critic, since these things are more or less a matter of circumstance and education. But I should think it relevant to ask how certainly he grasps the meaning of anything said to him, whether in jest or in earnest ; and in particular I should ask how well, when he is entrusted with a commission, he understands the meaning of his instructions as distinct from the letter. How safely can you rely upon him to do the wise thing in an unexpected contingency ? How far does he really understand *you* ?

This will suggest my reply to those who object that for intelligence in the proper sense I am substituting "taste", or "culture", or perhaps "mere feeling", which is then by a *tour de force* labelled "intelligence". I do indeed select the manifestations of taste and culture, so far as they are genuine, perhaps also of feeling, as the best expressions of intelligence ; and these as against "intellect"and "science". But such manifestations I take to be not exclusive or peculiar but only finer developments of that intelligent insight, that intelligent common sense (not crude common sense), which has been illustrated above in our intelligent lad. And this means that taste and culture (and likewise feeling) are in the true and proper sense to be regarded as operations of intelligence and of knowledge—in the true and proper sense of marking an awareness of realities not myself.

For it is naïve to suppose, as it seems many persons do, that the exercise of taste is something which, as distinguished from any operation of science, is concerned only with the state of one's soul ; that it marks only an ecstasy of appreciation ; or a state of the soul directed, if directed at all, upon such abstractions as beauty, harmony, sublimity To appreciate Wordsworth is not merely to be tickled by Wordsworth; not merely to be stimulated by Wordsworth to thoughts of the sublime ; it is in any case *to know Wordsworth*, to grasp objectively the workings of Wordsworth's mind. To appreciate Plato's "Republic", nay to read the "Republic" in any sense worth mentioning, is not merely to apprehend certain facts about the history of political theory or what not ; nor yet to indulge in a private exercise of critical powers upon a book—it is merely puerile to suppose that when you read Plato you are reading a book ; but to read the "Republic" is to form an acquaintance with Plato. And it is no less true that to enjoy or to appreciate a Beethoven symphony is to enter into the mind of the man Beethoven. Of all of these so-called "appreciations" I insist that either they are knowledge or they are nonsense. They stand for real knowledge and real intelligence if persons are real. And if persons are real at all—if, in other words, there be a moral world—they stand for an intelligence inseparable from morality.

But personal intelligence is critical intelligence. And it is the critical quality that makes intelligence an operation distinctively "moral". For I suppose it will be admitted that any moral world is a world of relations among persons, and many are content to define morality simply as the adjustment of personal relations. But the adjustment of personal relations—above all, of the very personal relations of married life—what is this but a process of criticism without end ? For a person is never a finality ; never, therefore, a fact which may be defined once for all and then counted upon to remain what it is. It is an elementary fact of the personal life, at any stage and of any person, that life is a process of reflection, a constant transition from "what one is" to a *consciousness* of what one is ; and then one is somewhat other than before. Of the more interesting persons of our world, perhaps of any persons to whom we can come sufficiently close, this is obvious ; and it is their charm. However deeply we see into their souls there remains ever something new just beyond in the form of a fascinating problem. The same is true of the world of literary, historical, and artistic criticism. Of the knowable facts about Plato's life there may conceivably be a final statement, but Plato himself will be a problem for criticism to the end of time.

Now it is precisely this critical aspect of intelligence which, as I suggested above, leads us to think of all intelligence as the wisdom of the serpent. The natural man is suspicious of criticism. And before I listen to another man's criticism of my motives I may very reasonably wish to have some assurance of his competence as a critic. He might demonstrate his competence by understanding my motives, and this demonstration would disarm suspicion. But in the end the really important criticism is my own criticism. Alas! it is the serpent within that disturbs repose. Of the identity of morality and intelligence this is the most distinctively moral consequence. For the self-satisfied, for those who conceive that they have taken the final measure both of their fellows and of themselves, there is no salvation. They are dead souls. The moral process is a process of endless inner inquiry, of never-ending self-criticism. This is what we mean by the development of character. And this is clearly what was meant by Socrates when to the statement that virtue is knowledge he added the deeply ironical "Know thyself". To know yourself is to be committed to a task that will have no end.

And this will then give the answer to those many persons who think that to conceive morality as imtelligence is to convert morality into a mean and calculating prudence. By prudence they mean a calculation of the external conditions of life which assumes that the motives of life are once for all simple. Such indeed is precisely the intelligence assumed by the utilitarian school of ethics. By this school morality is conceived as a process of developing the means of life's satisfactions while the motives to be satisfied remain for ever fixed; and fixed, therefore, at the point of simple sense-gratification.

A grim insistence upon the unchangeable baseness of human nature is the distinctive characteristic of the moral philosophy of Hobbes. On one occasion Hobbes created a difficulty for himself by giving sixpence to a beggar. "Would you have done this if it had not been Christ's command?" he was asked. " 'Yea,' said he. 'Why?' quoth the other. 'Because,' said he, 'I was in pain to consider the condition of the old man; and now my alms, giving him relief, doth also ease me.' " I suspect that Hobbes was here risking his immortal soul on behalf of philosophical consistency. But such at any rate is the theory of prudence. What it means is that whatever light Hobbes might get upon the outer world nothing could possibly throw further light upon himself or reveal a more generous motive than "ease". A curiously arbitrary limitation of intelligence, if you stop to think of it, and hardly to be identified with an "enlightened" self-interest; yet undeniably convenient. It is not true, alas! that the comforts and advantages of prudence are for the intelligent; they are reserved for the self-satisfied stupid.

To those who are accustomed to formulate morality as "doing good to others", "loving your neighbour", or "trusting your fellow-man", this view of the moral as the critical attitude will, I dare say, seem repellent. Yet what is meant by a love and confidence which dispenses with critical insight—what the spiritual realities are here conceived to be —is more than I can comprehend. I should like to be able to offer a more intimate illustration. But I recall, as it happens, a schoolmaster, the proprietor of a small school, who once said to me, "I must admit that I am not impartially just to my boys. I am often compelled to grant the requests of influential parents, releasing their sons from obligations to which the other boys are held. But I try to be just as I can." Does such a confession repel or attract? I must confess that this piece of confidence has left me with a deep respect for this gentleman and with a warm sense of personal understanding. He was, by the way, a true gentleman, a conscientious and effective teacher, much respected by his boys, and the profits of his school were probably little more than a living. And I compare my feeling with regard to him with my distrust of the more usual schoolmaster, who never admits injustice, and is probably never aware of it, because his sense of justice is not too highly developed.

It is often said, when other justification seems lacking, that we love our friends for their weaknesses. "Weaknesses" I suspect to be a mark of deference to authoritarian morality. I should prefer to say that we love our friends for what they are. And we love them—we are close to them—just because we know so well what they are, because we know that they know, and that they know that we know —because, in one word, there is *intelligence* between us.

CHAPTER X

THE BEAUTY OF VIRTUE

§ 37. Aesthetic taste and moral law. § 38. The experience of beauty and virtue. § 39. The beauty of utility. § 40. The moral ground of aesthetic criticism.

MORALITY, truth, beauty; or conscience, intelligence, taste: in saying that among the values morality is everywhere, my thesis is that any of these conceptions when critically interpreted—with a view to the meaning underlying the conventional form—will be found also to mean each of the others. And thus to say that morality, or conscience, is everywhere in life is also to say that intelligence and taste are everywhere.

In this chapter the centre of attention will be beauty, or taste. It is not my intention to demonstrate a theory of beauty; for which indeed I have too little experience in fields specifically aesthetic. I shall be content, in this direction, with what may be suggested in the course of dealing with some of the customary arguments for regarding morality as one thing and beauty as another.

§ 37

Prominent among the arguments for demonstrating this irrelevance of beauty and virtue is the argument which links the two conventions, namely, that there is no disputing about tastes—*de gustibus nil disputandum*—and that "what is right for one is right for all", into the doctrine that judgments of beauty are subjective, and therefore not to be questioned, while judgments of morality are objective and are therefore to be enforced by law.

That there is no disputing about tastes I take to be plainly false, together with the implication that there ought to be no disputing about tastes; for if we must dispute about anything I wonder what other material for dispute is so well worth while. As a matter of fact people are constantly disputing about tastes, and with hardly less animus than in their disputes about morals. It may be doubted whether the sternest Puritan hates the evil-doer quite so sincerely as the professional aesthete loathes those who prefer the banal and the vulgar. The aesthete closes the discussion with the cool and verbally modest retort, "Well, our tastes differ", while the Puritan consigns his opponent to the world below; but their meaning is the same.

And if it be urged that the aesthetic point of view tolerates different *genres*, or types of beauty, Mozart and Wagner, Watteau and Leonardo da Vinci, finding each in its own way beautiful, then we must ask, repeating the question of earlier chapters, whether the moral point of view does otherwise. It is supposed somehow to mark the disinterestedness and liberality peculiar to the aesthetic point of view to say, for example, that the lover of Mozart need not quarrel with the lover of Wagner. Not, I should reply, until it becomes a practical question of arranging the programme of a concert. But it is only upon some practical question, concerning the possession of land, or money, or the like, that the Anglo-Saxon finds any real need of quarrelling with a Russian, the Gentile with the Jew, or the capitalist with the labourer. Art as conventionally conceived is likely to be artificially restricted to such expressions as pictures, music, and the like. We forget that art may cover the whole of life. In the conventionally restricted application, different aesthetic tastes can live more comfortably in the world together than different moral ideals, because they can more easily keep out of one another's way. Logically and essentially, however, the aesthetic point of view is not more a matter of privacy than the moral.

Persons of taste very commonly distinguish good and

bad taste—and quite as properly, it seems, as when these adjectives are applied to differences of moral character. For even in the field of taste it is not enough for a man to take his stand upon the simple assertion, This is my taste. If he cares to have his assertion respected—and if not why should he utter it?—he must justify his taste; not indeed by reference to a standard of taste, but certainly by showing that when the meaning of his taste is developed (suppose it to be a cubist or futurist taste) there is revealed a consistency and significance of motive of which any interest in the world of taste must at least take account. This is to give to his assertion an objective significance, objective in just the sense in which moral assertions are objective (see § 44). But it is also to incur an obligation. You cannot take a stand or make a claim without incurring an obligation, and moral obligations rest upon nothing more.

Persons of taste have also a way of condemning as "bad taste" conduct which moralistic persons, if they pass any judgment on such conduct, would call "wrong"; such as wilful disregard of the sensibilities of other persons present in the choice of a subject of conversation. What they mean by bad taste is, however, really a disregard of *moral* considerations. And if you or I prefer the term "taste" in this connection, it is not for the purpose of ignoring the moral aspect of the issue, and of calling it purely aesthetic, but simply to claim for the expression of taste a finer and deeper insight into the *moral* values.

Nor, on the other hand, shall we find many persons to assent to "What is right for one is right for all" if this principle is to be taken literally to the extent of an absolute disregard of the individual conscience. Even Kant, who embodied the principle in his "categorical imperative", had to assume that the individual conscience would of its own accord ratify the principle. During the World War, when absolutism was in the saddle, the principle was applied to military service; yet by virtually universal consent exemption was accorded to conscientious objectors who could demonstrate that their objection was conscientious. It is true that the demonstration was reduced more or less to a convention, such as membership in the Society of Friends or other religious body committed to pacifistic teaching. Yet the convention itself was significant. Morality is not "objective" in the sense of disregarding personal taste, conviction, and point of view. And yet in a truer sense morality is indeed objective. Any modification of demands to fit a particular person may require him to show that he is really what he claims to be, a pacifist by independent conviction and not a pacifist for the present emergency, created by the demand for military service. If you are to be a pacifist in time of war you must also be a pacifist in time of peace; and your life must show that you are essentially a man of peace. To meet this test the Quakers could point to a consistent policy of pacifism, embodied in a religious conviction, covering two centuries. The fact that the claim was allowed at a time when all exemptions were disputed, shows that, even when emergency seems to strengthen the principle, we are not quite ready to assert that what is right for one is right for all.

In brief, then, it is not true that morality is "purely objective" or that beauty is "purely subjective". It is not true that morality is absolute obligation, beauty mere choice. In the moral world or in the world of beauty, every choice involves an obligation, every obligation rests upon a choice.

§38

That beauty and virtue are irrelevant is said, however, to be a matter of common fact and experience. Since we may no longer speak with Aristotle of the "virtue" (*e.g.*) of a watch or a motor-car, the comparison must be mainly in terms of human beauty; and since in our day we prefer not to apply the term "beauty" to men (a very significant illustration, by the way, of the conventional limitations of the term), we find the question concentrated upon the relation of beauty and virtue in women. Now, passing in review most of the beautiful women of whom we have read, beginning with Helen of Troy, it seems at first glance that the observation must be true : beauty and virtue need not, at any rate, go together.

But moral philosophy is not limited to the first glance, nor again to what are called the plain facts of experience. Of the aesthetic quality of these plain facts I shall have something to say in the next chapter. Here I will say that appreciations of beauty, at any rate, are not such plain facts. They are not something stamped upon us instantaneously once for all as by a rubber stamp, but highly complicated and subtle continuing processes. Any appreciation worthy to be called a judgment of beauty is developed through a series of experiences. I hear Richard Strauss' "Also Sprach Zarathustra" for the first time (harking back twenty years), and I loathe it ; the second time, and I wonder about it ; the third time, and I am deeply impressed by it. On the other hand the seasonal popular song may upon first hearing have all the sparkling charm of a freshly opened bottle of champagne ; to be flatter after a week than stale champagne. It might be a good rule of thumb to say that the test of beauty is its staying power. But this would be only a crude way of saying that the test of true beauty is reflective experience : reflective analysis and reflective taste.

And this means that the question of beauty and virtue is not a question of whether they are found apart as a matter of unreflective fact—while beauty and vice, virtue and ugliness, rest comfortably together—but a question whether they can remain apart in the course of reflective experience and reflective taste. My thesis is that they cannot remain apart. You may easily say upon first acquaintance that this woman is wonderfully beautiful, while yet you know her to be treacherous and false. There is nothing that we may not *say* while the vocal organs remain unimpaired. "Beautiful" and "treacherous and false" are thus far for you only a word and a phrase. The question is whether beauty will be an *experience* after "treacherous and false" has also become an experience.

And for the answer we need not quite passively wait for the bitter experience. We may try what Royce called a "thought-experiment," or an experiment in imagination —where, I suspect, the decisive experiments are usually performed. As one form of experiment I will propose that you take the following sentences:

A lovely and beautiful woman.
A beautiful woman, but what a liar!
A beautiful woman, but stupid as a beast!

Then ask yourself whether these three women are equally beautiful and equally likely to remain beautiful upon further acquaintance.

To carry out the experiment I will ask my male reader to suppose that by some mischance he had married the second or the third of these beautiful women. Is it a bad guess that after a year or two we should find him contemplating with ironical amusement the fact that other men thought her beautiful? On the other hand suppose a man to have married a beautiful woman with a rather disreputable "past" and then to have found in her a loyal wife, an intelligent and sympathetic companion: must we not suppose that any jealous bitterness with regard to her past will be modified, at least, by the thought that it was a tribute to her loveliness? And must he not also then conclude that chastity in women is a virtue rather overrated? It should be remembered that no youth under the spell of an infatuation doubts that his siren is *good*. She is not the conventionally "good woman", but then why should she be? In any case it seems that when beauty is associated with vice and virtue with ugliness there is a mistake somewhere. Suppose, once more, that in the midst of the description of a person in a novel you read that "his countenance which expressed nobility and intelligence was ugly and repulsive"—surely, before accepting this, you would read the sentence twice.

How, then, do we come to believe that beauty is one thing and virtue another? Because, I will suggest, the question as commonly treated is referred not to our experience of beauty and virtue but to conventions of beauty and virtue. The moral world of daily intercourse is peopled largely by dramatic conventions—such as "the clever rogue" and "the simple honest man". In the world of conventions the moral man is the "Puritan". The intelligent man is represented by Mephistopheles or Iago—or by Edison. And the aesthetic man is the disciple of Oscar Wilde wearing long hair and a red carnation. But in the special question of morality and beauty I suspect that, even by more discerning persons, the issue is conceived vaguely as lying between the Ten Commandments and the Parthenon; or between Christianity and paganism. Morality is conceived as the special and peculiar property of the ancient Hebrew people, beauty as the exclusive property of the Greeks. This is a strange assumption if you pause to think of it; stranger than the assumption of one race of people born blind, another born deaf—since these functions can easily be separated. It is upon such an assumption, however, that the Greek profile comes to be the standard of human beauty, the Puritan (whose views of life are mainly from the Old Testament) the standard of goodness—as if God had by a *fiat* fixed the standard type of beauty once for all and had thus ordained that beauty of countenance should be for ever unattainable by a negro, an American Indian, or even by an Anglo-Saxon!

If this be the issue of beauty *versus* virtue, it is clear enough that the two need not go together. Yet I suppose that all of us have known persons whose faces bore all the conventional marks of ugliness, whom nevertheless we have found to be altogether attractive and delightful, noble and high-minded. And after learning to know them we have not merely tolerated their ugliness, or put it out of our minds. Rather we have come to find it fascinating and significant, their faces "distinguished", if not now vaguely beautiful. And thus perhaps we have come to see what is meant by saying that beauty is a matter of mere association, or convention. It is precisely "a mere convention" so far as beauty is a matter of standard, habit, or fashion. And then we see too that if all the snub-nosed men had the genial wisdom of Socrates, while all the Greek profiles marked the "Hoi Polloi", it would presently become difficult to see in a snub-nose an aesthetic defect or in a Greek profile a mark of beauty. Suppose that all of the lovely and delightful women weighed more than two hundred and twenty-five—or suppose that they were all spare and (as we should say now) emaciated: what is now referred to in a pitying whisper as a species of deformity would soon be hailed as a mark of transcendent beauty. The cynical critic may object that "nature" would still fasten the sexual attraction to the Venus of Milo or, better, to the lovely "Sleeping Venus" of Giorgione. But if he is right (and the many divagations of sexual passion suggest that he is wrong), it would mean only that sexual attraction had lost its last shred of sentiment or of moral significance.

Yet the question is after all not quite exclusively concerned with the beauty of persons. The souls of persons are expressed also in objects either of art or of use made by human hands. And here it is a question, not quite of beauty and utility, as we shall presently see, but of beauty and significance, involving the question of sincerity. We face here the perplexing question of decoration, or adornment. Such indeed is the power of habit and association that things continue to give the impression of beauty after they have ceased to be significant. A coat-sleeve without buttons still looks ugly, though the buttons have long since ceased to function. A generation ago, after side-pockets had disappeared from cut-away coats, it seemed that beauty still demanded the pocket-flaps.

Yet mere "impression" is never final in the life of a conscious being. The pocket-flaps have now disappeared. Within little more than five years the bobbed-hair girl has begun to be beautiful; and I wonder if we may not soon begin to think of a rich and luxuriant mass of hair, so impressive to Victorian taste, as a stupid and uncomfortable survival of the aesthetics of primitive man. At any rate when the conviction of absurdity is become finally clear the impression of beauty is dissipated. There are modern office-buildings which present a fine appearance of massiveness, gigantic columns at the entrance seeming fittingly to support the many stories of wall above them. But no architectural genius avails to preserve this impression of massive beauty in the mind of one who *knows*—*i.e.*, that the columns support nothing and that the walls are like so much wall-paper, set into and supported by the steel frame of the building.

Once more, this is not to say that beauty is merely subconscious utility. Beauty, we shall see presently, is if anything deliberately chosen utility—which is quite another matter. I have read that Henry Ward Beecher used to carry with him a small bag of gems for the sheer delight of handling them and feasting his eyes upon their colours. For myself I can sympathize with the man who is willing to pay the price, and forgo something else, for the pleasure of having his clothes made of those fine, soft, fluffy woollens so caressing to the hand that rests upon the knee—provided that he will not then basely turn about and explain that such cloths wear longer. And so if the lover of the massive appearance should claim that this gives delight and comfort to the eye I shall conceive his taste to be justified if he can explain himself. Unfortunately for his explanation, it seems that the appeal is here not to the eye but to the mind. The beauty of the massive columns lies in what they suggest, and what they suggest is false.[1]

---

[1] In *A Theory of Knowledge* (1923), p. 89, C. A. Strong says, referring to the kind of considerations just mentioned, that this " is to forget that our enjoyment of it [i.e. architecture] is, after all, primarily a pleasure of seeing". Does he mean seeing without imagination—is this aesthetic enjoyment ? How, then, does aesthetic enjoyment differ from the purely sensual ? But if imagination is involved I wonder how he manages to halt the mental process at the point of merely seeing .

THE BEAUTY OF VIRTUE

§ 39

The question of the beauty of virtue brings with it the question of the beauty of utility. In what has just been said reference was made to the view that beauty is only a kind of refined utility, utility in the larger view. And among those holding this view, it seems we must reckon Croce, who says that an object is beautiful "if perfectly adapted to its practical purpose". Now it is quite possible, I should say, to hold that beauty is only a larger view of utility if we utter the word "only" with a certain accent of caution and of irony—if, that is to say, we have taken into account the possibly revolutionary character of the transformation effected by the larger view. For my own part I prefer the so-called beauty of utility, I dislike all adornment, and I am suspicious of "objects of art". Beauty, I will say with Croce, is perfect adaptation to the practical purpose. And this seems to me a comfortably simple and definite view—until I endeavour to state for myself the meaning of the practical purpose.

When the practical man explains that a writing-table, for example, is for him purely a matter of utility, it is pertinent to ask how sensitively he has questioned his need for the writing-table. He thinks possibly that a packing-box turned on its side would really serve the purpose and that anything more is a concession to reputability. If so we may point out to him that a packing-box would probably be unsteady—to build a solid and durable piece of furniture is, by the way, a matter of engineering art and skill. The rough surface would offer impediments to writing and to the easy disposition of papers, and it would be unpleasant to touch. It would also gather dirt. We might go further and suggest that, if the table is to be used for any length of time, it should be of a colour and form comfortable to the eye. Here the practical man will doubtless object that we are introducing considerations that go beyond utility. Perhaps he is one of those who can see the utility of a warm overcoat, but despises the silk lining which makes the coat so much easier to put on and off (thus mitigating the nuisance of an overcoat) and so much more comfortable on the body. Then we may ask why the appeal to certain sensibilities is to be described as purely utilitarian, to certain others as purely aesthetic. Why is the convenience of the writing-table to be credited to its utility, and unpleasing colour and form to be charged against its beauty? Or why is the noise of my typewriter to be accounted a merely aesthetic defect? If our practical man boasts that he is untouched by these so-called aesthetic defects, alas! that means, I fear, that he wishes to be classed among the cruder forms of animal life. If, on the other hand, he undertakes to question his need for the writing-table deeply and then to satisfy this need completely, he will discover at the end, I think, that he has achieved a work of art and created a thing of beauty, if he has not also expended a considerable sum of money.

From utility to beauty is then, I should say, a passage from the crude mechanism of life to life itself; from the relatively unconsidered gratification of desire to its deliberately conscious gratification; in other words, from the uncritical to the critical life. Utility, as I have pointed out above, marks the presence of ends taken for granted. When the practical man says, This serves my practical purpose (and there is no more to be said), what he means is that the purpose itself is not to be questioned. But this means, not that it really satisfies any purpose intimately personal, but that it removes a present difficulty and enables life in some fashion to go on. The "strictly utilitarian" consideration is limited to what will just pass. If he will refer the question seriously to his own purpose, asking, say, What must this writing-table be if it is to be comprehensively satisfying, and satisfying to *me?* he will discover that his purpose implies much more than any conventional utility has provided for. It is only by an artificial limitation—imposed perhaps by business considerations of time or money—that he can exclude from the purpose of this or that object of use any of the purpose of his life. Then he will discover that nothing manufactured will really serve his purpose, nothing indeed but a work of art created by himself, embodying and expressing his personal life as that life is already embodied in his face and his hands. And when from this point of view he recalls the original "practical purpose" it seems now that the practical purpose represented only a schematic outline of life, workable indeed, yet from the standpoint of life itself a kind of caricature, and related to life much as a saw-horse is related to a real horse or as the painter's manikin is related to what he will express with his brush.

This means, again, that from utility to beauty is a passage from the dumb, relatively speaking, to the consciously articulate. Art, as Croce says, is expression. This element of expression will be clearer if from the practical man's writing-table we turn our attention to his coat. When a man says, A coat is for me a matter of pure utility, and therefore I consider nothing but price, durability, and warmth, it means either that he forgets or that he will deny that the clothes express the man. The fact that a man is indeed known by his clothes, he can hardly deny. He may condemn the fact as standing for an artificial association; but then he may have to explain why the use of c-a-t to indicate a certain soft furry animal with claws is not the product of an association even more artificial. When the consciousness of expression is borne home to him it seems that, simply as an honest man, he is faced with a problem; which is now indistinguishably an aesthetic and a moral problem. He may seek to evade the problem by wearing only the most neutral of coats. But hardly with success. It does not indeed follow that a severely plain choice in matters of dress and household equipage marks an insensibility to beauty; it may mark only a mute rejection, despairing or contemptuous, of the satisfactions available. But any attitude whatever implies a certain judgment, which is both moral and aesthetic, upon the values represented in the current conceptions of life.

§ 40

Finally it will be said on behalf of the separateness of beauty and virtue, but mainly now for the protection of art and beauty, that it is not the function of art to teach moral lessons. But neither, if I am right, is this the function of moral philosophy. And here I think we have the root of the whole matter : the separation of beauty and virtue is inspired mainly by a fear of that authoritarian conception of morality which defines virtue as right conduct and makes it the function of ethics to "teach".

Yet, though it is not the artist's function to *teach*, it is surely his function to *express ;* and if not moral lessons, then impressions, conceptions, appreciations of life ; and thus to express what is in the most significant sense moral. If moral philosophy is a study of life, I think we must find in art and literature, and most clearly in poetry and fiction, its most important experimental laboratory ; and to me a study of the aims and motives of literary criticism reveals far more adequately than most of the treatises on ethics the distinctive logic and *motif* of the "moral" world. There is indeed a superficial literary criticism which is concerned with style—and a more superficial study of literature which, seeking to be accounted scientific, calls itself philology. But the style is after all the man. And the fundamental peculiarity of any distinctively "literary" treatment of a subject—that which makes it seem so trivial and unworthy to any properly scientific mind—is just that it tends to regard the form and even the subject-matter of any writing as somewhat less interesting than the mind and personality of the writer himself. And thus the really critical question for literary criticism becomes the question of the man himself and his outlook upon life.

I have referred above to the Carlylean "strong man". When we "study Carlyle" the chief point of interest is— just Carlyle. In his "Heroes", in "Frederick the Great", in the Abbot Samson of "Past and Present" he has given us Carlyle's own ideal of man ; and what is more, a comprehensive view of what he conceives to be worth while in human life. His style is a subject for dispute. But this is only to say that Carlyle is a conspicuous illustration of the fact that the style is the man. So long as you find a suggestion of worth and greatness in his presentation of life you will find him eloquent and impressive; and while he remains eloquent he remains significant. If this impression is dissipated his eloquence becomes tirade.

Likewise of Dickens. What makes "David Copperfield" to most persons the most impressive of his novels is the fact that there clearly you have Dickens himself. In his characters and in their difficulties the writer of fiction reveals his personal conception of the problem of life. If you are a lover of Dickens and rank him as in some manner a true artist it means that in the sober middle-class ideals that stand forth in his pages and in his sympathetic handling of lower-class life you find some of the value and essence of genuine humanity; and if you dismiss him as a sentimentalist, it means that you question the significance of middle and lower-class virtue. I suppose, again, that Arthur Pendennis is largely Thackeray himself—Thackeray taking himself humorously yet none the less offering an *apologia*. Pendennis, I fancy, is just the sort of decent, wholesome, yet withal clever and intelligent young Englishman most congenial to Thackeray's taste. He is not quite a man of genius, and he is no hero; but this only means that Thackeray has no very high appreciation of heroes—a moral estimate, be it noted, in which there will be others to agree with him.

Granting that seemingly great artists are sometimes seemingly the most immoral of men—seemingly, I mean, for the first look—it will be no less true that the final estimate of the art will coincide closely with the final estimate of the man. One cannot remain for long an admirer of Villon and also a Puritan moralist. Nor, again, will Tolstoi's four volumes of "War and Peace" remain an artistic monstrosity for one who has come to share Tolstoi's belief in a mystical humanity, the life of which is revealed not in the passing acts of individuals but in the slower movements of nations and races; by one, in other words, whose moral ideal for the individual is self-effacement and absorption of self into humanity. For my own part, though I find Balzac's novels fascinating and compelling when once I am past the beginning, I cannot rate him as the great artist that his admirers usually find in him; and mainly because to my taste his slavish admiration of the manners of high life casts a blemish of vulgarity upon nearly every scene. And I have little appreciation of the much-praised "art" of de Maupassant because it seems to me that his "effects", so far from indicating either breadth or depth of experience of life, are just the customary shallow tricks of the journalist who creates dramatic situations (*i.e.*, "news") by the simple distortion of fact. On the other hand, I am disposed to rate Tourgenieff as a very great artist because I seem to find in him (possibly indeed because I know him to have been a serious student of philosophy) a background of gravity and brooding contemplation, a sense of the tragic complexity of all human motive, which gives suggestiveness to the simplest of his sketches of Russian country life and to his revolutionists, such as Basarof and Roudine, a significance almost Shakespearian.

Any of these judgments of mine may be disputed. But it will be found, I think, that the ground of the dispute will include the moral ground. It will be claimed that I have wrongly estimated not merely the artist but the man.

CHAPTER XI

THE BEAUTY OF KNOWLEDGE

§ 41. Aesthetic impressions and scientific facts. § 42. History as a branch of art.

ONE of the more obvious objections to any conception of the unity of the spirit is that which takes the form of saying that there is no element either of the moral or of the aesthetic, no element of choice or of taste, in our knowledge of facts. Facts, it is said, are in no sense formed or created, they are simply given. The question is too large for comprehensive treatment, and the present brief chapter is merely to suggest what can be said for the thesis that knowledge of fact involves creative imagination. This suggestion I will convey through a more or less free rendering of Croce's theory of "impressions" and of his seemingly paradoxical theory that history is a branch of art.

§ 41

According to Croce art is expression; the *ex*pression of an *im*pression, as he also says—that and nothing more. This means that in a certain perhaps proper sense of the word art is absolutely democratic. A peasant or a duke, a mill-worker or a poet, a hotel-waiter or a gentleman-and-scholar—one subject has as much of the possibility of beauty in him as the other. There is no intrinsically ugly. And thus Croce takes issue with an authoritarian aesthetics which, like authoritarian ethics, believes that God in his wisdom has put a finer kind of human nature into some frames than into others and has marked each with an appropriate sign.[1]

But he also faces a scepticism more coldly factual. Art the communication of impressions! one may exclaim. What nonsense! When the cook tells me that she finds in the refrigerator only one pound of butter and four eggs she communicates an impression, but the communication is not art. It seems (so runs the objection) that Croce has missed the difference between two kinds of impressions. On the one hand we have the painter's impression of a landscape, or of a person, which he tries to express on canvas. Of this kind are the properly aesthetic impressions, and these we welcome as art. On the other hand are those ordinary impressions of matter of fact which the psychologist calls sensations, or sense-perceptions. The communication of these impressions is not art but plain information, or perhaps science.

Now to the reader of Croce it will be clear that he has not for a moment forgotten this difference. It is rather the chief purpose of his argument to show that this difference, the difference between the aesthetic and the matter-of-fact impression, is not in the last analysis a real difference. At best it is a difference of degree and circumstance. And if we remember that in the Greek the term "aesthetic" covers both the artistic impression and the matter-of-fact perception we shall find ourselves asking whether after all every experience of matter of fact is not in its own measure an artistic experience. If so it will mean that all of our experience is in its own measure—so far indeed as it is any conscious *experience*—aesthetic experience; in other words, that all experience is, just as experience, a "sense of life".

This I believe to be profoundly true, but how to make it demonstratively true is another matter. For in most of

---

[1] Here let me repeat a *caveat*. Croce also offends authoritarian ethics by teaching "art for art's sake"—along with, as it happens, " duty for duty's sake". This blind service of two irresponsible masters implies that art is irrelevant to morality, and this it is my chief purpose to disprove.

our experience we *seem* to take the world just as it is given, most of all the world of common fact. Here we talk about "data" and "presentations". And here at least it seems that the mind is truly a *tabula rasa*, taking what comes just as it comes, without exercise of taste, with no regard for taste; nay, forewarned—by the scientist and the logician, by the psychiatrist, and most effectively by the brutal common sense of the plain man—against any exercise of taste. And thus the word "impression" comes to mean an inertly passive experience, to be described not as an activity of mind but as a "mental state".

Yet to any one initiated into the practice of self-consciousness, to one become curious about his "mental states", it will be clear, I think, that the passive character of the perceptive "states" is chiefly a convention. Even those who insist most upon the "given" character of sense-experience recognize the seeming activity of "apperception", or selective attention. But what this means we may best realize in the fatigue that follows a multitude of impressions —for example, after a day spent in a comfortable Pullman car. Then it seems that, so far from receiving passive impressions, it has required a day-long strain of attention to keep our world straight through a welter of shifting scenes. Here at least, it seems that the world is not given to us in a rational, intelligible, and harmonious picture. We have to form the picture. And to form an intelligible picture out of the daily run of modern experience is often a terrible effort. A pupil of mine just recovering from nervous prostration told me that in Chicago, where he lived, he could not venture down into the business district, since the sign-boards alone were too much for him. One need not succumb to nervous prostration to understand this.

Perception of fact is not, then, as it seems, a case of having an impression stamped upon us; it is always a process of forming and creating. We do not simply get an impression of the world before us, we *form* an impression. If the activity of forming is not always in evidence it is because in our transactions with the routine of daily fact the process is more or less mechanical and stereotyped. It is in the experience of, so to speak, coming back to fact that we best catch ourselves in the act of forming. Waking from sleep in the morning, especially from a sound sleep —if you attend to this, I think you will see that it is never instantaneous and never a mere change of state, a substitution of one picture for another, but a complex and very interesting logical and artistic process of re-forming out of chaotic matter a world that you have for the time lost. Sitting before the fire, let your mind wander; in other words, loosen for a moment your "grip on reality"; at once your world, now indeed rather passively perceived, assumes shapes most illogical and fantastic; suggestions present themselves which at other times never even show their faces; and ideas and images (so called) assume new and strange and often forbidden fellowships. It is thus, I will suggest, that dreams occur; by a relative cessation of the forming process; and thus also the ravings of delirium and the obsessions of the insane. For the matter of that, if you are looking for a world of passively received impression, a world characterized by the innocence of the mind, I suspect that in the experience of the insane you will find it at its passive best.

When you have once caught the forming in the act— in the process of coming back to fact—you may then, I believe, find it, vestigially at least, in half of the perceptions of daily life; especially if you happen to be an absent-minded philosopher and college professor whose punctual engagements, demanding alertness when they occur, are few as compared with those of the business man, and who may thus let his mind wander from fact a good part of the time. The clock strikes; the telephone rings; I need the scissors which lie just before me on the desk. Even the scissors I seem not to perceive without a complex, though exceedingly rapid, formative activity, logical and aesthetic. And if you say, Yes, but it is the fact of the scissors that determines the outcome, well, that is just the question, the very big question, that I wish to suggest as lying in the background. It is true that practical perception is confronted by a seemingly resistant "matter", but so also in some degree is artistic creation. And it may be that the resistance is a question only of my insistent demand for the scissors. For my own part, at any rate, I can see no essential difference between coming back to fact after a night of sleep and coming back to any other interrupted activity of the spirit; coming back to a pleasant day-dream after an unwelcome ring of the telephone, or to the composition of a novel, a poem, or a song, a philosophical or a scientific theory. And for a typically aesthetic activity give me the process of constructing a scientific theory; for the sake of which observations are emphasized here, others minimized there, still others (no less factually observations) rejected as positive errors, all on behalf of the author's intuition. Nothing is more suggestive of the sculptor's process of modelling in clay. But in all of these cases alike, it seems that coming back means only that the course of imagination is resumed.

It is a persistent illusion—and no less an illusion because so necessary to the business of life—that we all live in the same world. The illusion is so persistent that even for the instructed it requires an effort of imagination to realize that an infant six months old in the same room with grown-ups cannot see what they see; or that what they see could not be seen by an Australian blackfellow suddenly set down among them. The ordinary modern living-room contains chairs in which we *imagine* persons to sit—and this defines and forms what we *see*. Again rugs which we may imagine to be removed from the floor—as merely seen they might as well be built in. Glass bulbs which we imagine to become incandescent; a huge box, called a piano, which (strangely) we can imagine to give forth sweet sounds; and book-shelves displaying rows of rectangular patches in various colours which we imagine to be removable, and then to be capable of developments and transformations which our blackfellow would surely attribute to magic. It would be very interesting to get his impression as his eye falls upon the book-shelves. But no, I fear it would be very uninteresting; for what I suspect is that the book-shelves convey to him no impression whatever, just as they appear to convey little or no impression to the infant.

But what, then, of our own impression? The answer seems to be that our own impression of this apparently given and self-existent room is the last expression of an infinitely subtle and complex activity of imagination, co-ordinately logical and aesthetic, the motives and grounds of which we shall never finally bring to light. It is as distinctly an artistic product—expressing, if we go into the finer points of the character and quality of what we see and of what we refuse to see, the nature of our souls —as the work of any painter. And as for what is "given" as a basis for the activity of imagination—seen and not imagined—it seems that nothing is absolutely given. The given, the datum, resolves itself in the last analysis into a kind of formless something which is saved from being nothing only by a seemingly inert stubbornness. The room, the object of our formed impression, seems to be even less given than the angel which Michelangelo saw in the block of marble.

Croce puts this point neatly, if somewhat too summarily, when he disposes of the common idea that the difference between the artist and the plain man is a difference of skill or technique. This common idea Croce takes to be that, while all men see alike, only the artist knows how to express what he sees. Against this Croce points out that the superiority of the artist lies in what he *sees*, it is a difference not of technique but of vision. This difference we can all readily appreciate when it comes to the painting of a portrait, especially of one who is near to us. The painter's impression is awaited as a kind of possibly fateful revelation. But the point applies no less to the cook's humbler impression of the pound of butter and the four eggs in the refrigerator. The painter of still life might well see more than the cook; and yet the cook's impression is also an activity of the human spirit. She too is no merely passive photographic plate but, in Croce's words, a creator of life.

And since (as Croce himself insists) we are all artists, the advantages of superior vision will not lie exclusively with those who make art their profession. It is a too common vice of aesthetic philosophy to consult only the professional artist. The cook may conceivably see something in the butter and eggs which is hidden from the painter of still life; and the physician may see that in a man's face which the painter happily misses. The criminologist or the life-insurance agent may each see something else. And in the end what I would emphasize (as expressing my own idea, at least) is that every impression of the world is an individual impression. It is no doubt practically convenient to assume that we all live in the same world of fact, but it marks a lack of imagination if we believe it to be true. The machinist and the carpenter, the sailor and the miner, the railway-conductor and the salesman, the lawyer, the physician, and the clergyman, the zoologist, geologist, mathematician, or literary critic—no two of these live in the same world of fact. Each of these worlds stands for a certain type of imagination; a certain point of view, unconsciously embodied in metaphor and trick of speech, for the determination of reality and of fact; and for the literary artist each contains, no less than the sailor's point of view, the potentiality of romance. But the profession is not yet the individual; and what is true of the class is truer still, and perhaps only then true, of the individual himself, and only so far as he is a conscious and genuine individual. Every thinking man's impression of the world is an artistic intuition. As a thinking man he is not a mere recipient of impressions, but the artist and architect of a universe; or, once more, a creator of life.

And yet his impression of the world is knowledge of the world. How this may be, our imagination may not easily grasp. But we may appreciate the cognitive quality of our impressions, and at the same time the aesthetic quality of our cognitions, if from the world of "things", seemingly given once for all, we return to the more sociable and negotiable world of persons; where indeed the unity of the spirit, the identity of the moral, the aesthetic, and the logical, is most clearly in evidence. Suppose that some one asks me about Smith—say that he is considering Smith as a candidate for an important appointment. Since Smith's family and mine have always been neighbours I know all about Smith. But it will not answer his question to give him, however completely and accurately, a coldly impersonal record of the facts. Though the facts be important, such a restricted account may even arouse suspicion. And he is likely to interrupt me with something like, Yes, but what is your *impression* of Smith?

What he wants is not scientific fact but aesthetic appreciation—a task of another dimension. The facts are easy to convey; but my impression? If I have any intimate insight into the character of Smith my impression is bound to be complex and perhaps problematic. It will not suffice to use the customary slang and say, "Oh! first-class" or "no good". And if I succeed in really conveying my impression it will mean that I have the art of a poet. But it will be no less a matter of art even to give that impression form to myself; that is, to form the impression. Yet my questioner in seeking my impression is not merely curious about the quality of my taste; he is paying a compliment to my intelligence, to my capacity for knowledge. The facts about Smith he will take from any reasonably careful person, but for impressions he wishes to be assured of a discriminating insight. And that cognitive insight he expects to find in the expression of my taste.

THE BEAUTY OF KNOWLEDGE

§ 42

So much for the matter of impressions. And now we may perhaps see why for Croce history is a branch of art. For history in any worthy sense is not a chronicle of events but an insight into the life of persons. Even if we adopt the (to me repugnant) theory that history deals with movements and tendencies we have still to answer the question—if history is to bear any relation to human life—what was the movement or the tendency for those who lived within it? What was the twelfth century for those who lived in the twelfth century? What was Locke's essay for those living in the year 1690, or in 1700? Surely not a "dear old book", as it was for William James. But this insight is just the limit, in the mathematical sense, of all historical inquiry; even the limit defined, as by Royce, as the point just beyond any possible concrete attainment—as the number 2 lies ever beyond the sum of $1, \frac{1}{2}, \frac{1}{4}$, etc. And scientific historical inquiry, however important as an accessory, will never quite yield it. A man may spend a lifetime reading the twelfth century, and the result may be only a card catalogue. Insight into the twelfth century—a grasp of that impression of the twelfth century of which the literature and events of the twelfth century are the corresponding expression—is reserved for imagination and for art. Historical criticism, literary criticism, art criticism and moral criticism, are in the last analysis identical activities.

A very important illustration of the Crocean logic of history is suggested by Albert Schweitzer's genial and fascinating "*Geschichte der Leben-Jesu-Forschung*", or history of the investigation of the life of Jesus. It would be not too much to say that for the part of the world called Christendom the life of Jesus is history's greatest problem. No field of historical inquiry has been overridden by a greater number of theories or by a stranger variety; and none has raised questions more poignantly personal. The world has never seen, says Schweitzer, such a bitter, intense, and self-denying struggle for truth as we find in this field during the century or more past.

What is the problem? The records of the life of Jesus are full of yawning gaps. How are they to be filled? At the worst, says Schweitzer,[1] by phrases; at the best by historical imagination (*historische Phantasie*). The sources give us, so to speak, the phenomena; but we do not understand them historically—they are not *history*—until we comprehend them as consistent and intelligible and grasp them as expressions of the life of a specific individual person. And this can be done, according to Schweitzer, only by an historical experiment; by which he means an experiment in imagination of the same kind as that which I have proposed in the last chapter as Royce's "thought-experiment". In other words, if we are to comprehend the facts of the life of Jesus in their true sequence and inner consistency, and if we are to distinguish fact from fiction, it will be through imaginative insight into the mind of Jesus. We must grasp the life of Jesus from the standpoint of his own self-consciousness, feeling that life as he felt it, seeing the world as he saw it. Now to the orthodox Christian this is almost suggestive of blasphemy; to the student of history I fear it may be equally suggestive of irony. Yet in all soberness it seems to me to state the historian's problem, a problem which is possibly never finally to be solved, yet to be solved more or less as other problems of life are solved. Could we once see Jesus as he saw himself, then all of the critical questions, the vexing questions of chronology, of sources, of genuine documents and spurious, of original accounts and interpolations—for all of these questions we should soon find the answer; and the key to the answer would be the happy insight.

And thus the life of Jesus is an artistic and aesthetic problem—a problem of the same order as the problem of painting a portrait of Jesus. The portrait could never by any scientific method be constructed from the "data", yet

---

[1] See his introductory chapter, entitled " Das Problem ", zweite Auflage, Tübingen, 1913.

THE BEAUTY OF KNOWLEDGE 151

the successful portrait would account finally for all of the data.

So much, then, for the beauty of knowledge. I will close the chapter by suggesting a question. It will not be doubted that history is knowledge. Yet history is at once an exercise of intelligence, of taste, and of moral judgment —in a word, of imagination. But it seems that what is thus true of knowledge directed upon a world of persons is true also in some degree when knowledge is dealing with impersonal facts about "things". There too we have imagination. And what is more, it seems that even in this impersonal region, whenever knowledge becomes eager and passionate, the assertion of an experience rather than of the fulfilment of a criterion, of realities rather than of "phenomena", it tends to personify its things. My belief is that Kant's "things in themselves", which scientific method could never know, were metaphorical persons. This suggests the deeply interesting question whether, if knowledge is to be an experience, and not the formal fulfilment of a logical requirement, we human beings can possibly have the experience of knowing anything but persons ; or, putting it otherwise, whether a world of impersonal fact, or of inanimate things—an "unthinking substratum", as Berkeley calls it—must not always be a world which is thus far not known. A successful development of this suggestion would be the consummation of "the unity of the spirit".

CHAPTER XII

JUSTIFICATION BY KNOWLEDGE

§ 43. Judgment *vs.* criticism. § 44. Objectivity and rationality. § 45. The illusion of deliberate wickedness. § 46. "*Tout comprendre*" and "*tout pardonner*". § 47. The moral question and the practical.

"YOU do not receive an education that you may learn to judge, but that you may learn to understand". These words of the peasant mother to her son (quoted above) might stand as the text for the present chapter. The motive of an enlightened morality is not "to award praise or blame" but to understand. Moral intelligence is not judgment but criticism.

Yet to understand is certainly in some fashion to discriminate, and thus to distinguish the real from the merely apparent, the true from the false. If morality is just anything you please—anything you choose to call "life"—the word is without meaning and we understand nothing. Morality cannot be "purely subjective". There must be an objectively real quality in any genuine morality even though we refuse to abide by any objective "criterion". Now in the first chapter my thesis was stated simply, by saying that morality is knowing what you are doing; it is not then a question of what you do. The present chapter is to show how the reality of the knowing constitutes the objective moral quality; how action or expression is justified by knowledge.

§ 43

Morality, I say, is criticism. Let us look, then, at the logic of literary criticism. Suppose that you have a book to review. The authoritative method of criticism is to compare the thesis of the book with what is recognized by the best authorities and to measure its style by the recognized standards of style. But this method, while useful for disposing of the common run of inconsiderable literature, is not criticism. It is no true judgment of the book. For a true judgment it matters not at all whether the message of the book is warranted by the authorities. As for such "authorities", the history of any subject is a succession of conflicting authorities. The important question is, Is the author familiar with the authorities? This we mean when we ask, Does he know his subject? Or perhaps not even this. He may be one of those rare cases of the untaught genius who knows his subject without knowing any of the authorities; who by native insight has anticipated the authorities. And so the question is resolved into this: is he prepared to meet the authorities? Does the development of his position indicate that he is alive to the questions to which such a position is open and that he is prepared to meet them? Or is he writing blindly and naïvely, repeating possibly what many have said before him, unconscious of pitfalls that await him? If he does know, he is writing intelligently; and his book, whatever its thesis, is worthy of respect. By virtue of his knowing his treatment of his subject is objective.

And as for his style—I recall the words of an architect who once said to me, "You may break all the rules of architecture if you have mastered them". Likewise may you break all the rules of manners if you have mastered them. But here again it is not a question of mastering the "rules" but of being a master of style—there are seemingly untaught masters of style. And this question is best answered by asking how finely and justly, and with what deliberateness of expression, the style communicates the meaning. Does he know how to make words respond to and express his thought? If so he is a master of style no matter how strange his style.

Such I take to be the logic of literary criticism. Such is likewise the logic of art criticism as understood by Croce.

According to Croce art is expression. It matters not what you choose to express. There are no laws determining for the artist what is beautiful or ugly. Yet not everything is art that calls itself art. Croce speaks of "absolute art"; that is, of art as having an objective quality. Art is the *ex*pression of an *im*pression. Of any work of art we may therefore ask how perfectly the impression is expressed or conveyed. But this is only to ask how far the words, the statue, the song, or what not, contain a meaning. Is there "speculation in those eyes which thou dost glare with"? So far as there is meaning there is beauty and art—absolute and objective art whatever the meaning.

And such precisely, as I conceive it, is the logic of moral criticism. To select a possibly crucial example from the standpoint of the orthodox view, suppose that a man and woman are planning to live together without the form of marriage, or to form some sort of conventionally illicit union. Where the parties are free to marry there might seem to be no important question, and the increasing ease of divorce would seem to dispose of most of the other cases. Yet one may conceive of cases where divorce might be undesirable and of others where parties free to marry might nevertheless wish to escape the complications imposed by legal and social convention. In any case we are here facing the question whether one's life is one's own or the property of the social order, whether marriage (so to speak) is a personal relation or a public institution.

Authoritarian judgment would of course condemn any illicit union as simply forbidden by the ordinances of society. Such judgment, as I have pointed out in Chapters V and VI, would be the judgment not of morality but of utility. Such criticism would not be moral criticism. On the other hand it would be as little in accord with the logic of moral criticism for the parties in question to toss their heads and say that they will do what they please; and that what they please is nobody's business. This animal gesture suggests the morality of the slums. Other persons may at least raise the issue of whose business it is by asking

JUSTIFICATION BY KNOWLEDGE 155

questions. The questions may well be impertinent questions, but they are not demonstrated to be such by a refusal to answer them. The only moral way of meeting a question is either to give it an intelligible answer or to show that it is the question of a fool. And though—on grounds mainly utilitarian—you may reasonably refuse to answer anybody's and everybody's question, the important consideration remains—and this is the moral consideration—could you give an answer to the question if you wished to do so?

The moral question will then be something like this: the parties in question propose, quite properly, to do as they please, but do they know clearly what they please to do? Have they considered the matter "prayerfully", in all of its bearings? Have they, to begin with, faced the external consequences; the economic consequences, if they are not pecuniarily independent; then the social ostracism and relative isolation, with the possible limitation of their acquaintance to the relatively undesirable; the probable rupture of old ties—have they considered for each case what answer they will have to give? Again the scorn of the self-righteous and the abuse of the vulgar? Have they not merely faced these things as facts, but realised them in imagination as experience? And are they then prepared to meet the consequences cheerfully and uprightly without whimpering about wounded feelings? Have they also faced the more intimately personal consequences? What these may be, cannot of course be predicted; or just as little as we may predict the outcome of an authorized marriage. But the unrecognized union is on its personal side beset with peculiar difficulties—forcibly set forth by Tolstoi in his "Anna Karenina"—and here even oftener than in marriage what has begun with ideal devotion has ended in personal aversion and mortification. They are undertaking something difficult and perilous—have they faced the nature of their undertaking?

So far as for such questions they have found satisfactory answers I say that they have answered the moral question.

The questions are not essentially different from those involved in any regular marriage. Only here it seems that we are ready to take the will for the deed, the form for the reality. In either case, however, the essentially moral question is the question of the thoughtfulness (if you please, the conscientiousness) embodied in the act.

Meanwhile the act is transformed by consciousness of the act (if indeed you may call anything an act apart from consciousness of the act). Here as everywhere in life *consciousness makes a difference.* Or self-consciousness, if you prefer— to me they are the same. Now when I say that morality is not a question of what you do, but wholly a question of knowing what you do, I expect to be greeted by the unimaginative with a scornful scepticism, by the pragmatic with the statement that the knowing must at least make a difference in what you do. And by both I may be asked to explain—possibly "to figure out"—just how knowing what you do will transform what you do. Such a test I must reject as irrelevant. It presupposes all the logic of authoritarian morality: namely, that moral action is determinate and predictable, and that the principles of action, if not also the particulars demanded by the principles, are laid down once for all without reference to individual motive and significance. It presupposes also that to become conscious of one's action is a fact of the same order as that of attaching, say, a governor to a steam-engine, the effect of which upon the behaviour of the engine can of course be calculated. Knowing, I say, is of the nature of art. That knowing will make a difference in the doing stands as a matter of course. What you will say next will ever depend upon your realization of the meaning of what you are saying now. But what in fact you will say, though possibly to be anticipated more or less in sympathic imagination, is beyond the possibility of logical or scientific prediction. All that we can predict is that those who understand will see the moral significance.

Compare, however, the man and woman of our illustration, assumed now to have formed the illicit union, with any man and woman—of the slums or of the so-called fast set of fashionable society—who have been drawn together simply by the present excitement of a good time. The difference comprehends most of the difference between the man and the beast. We may expect a difference in behaviour; in the one case an observation of the decencies and delicacies appropriate to relations intimately personal which we may not find in the other. And a probable difference in the outcome: those who know what they are doing are thus far fortified against disloyalty. But these are outlying considerations. The morally important difference is the immediate difference of quality, expressed in the distinction of spiritual and animal. Those who in mutual intelligence know what they do have precisely thereby formed a "spiritual" union; a bond never to be created, except magically, by the ceremony of marriage, of which this ceremony can never be more than an outward and visible sign.

And in this fact of intelligence they have become *responsible*, in the strictly etymological and at the same time the most significantly ethical use of that term. To be responsible is to be capable of giving an intelligent answer to an intelligent question; it does not presuppose, rather it distinctly repudiates the presupposition of an expected answer. "What do you mean by doing this"? The child who struggles to reply to your impatient question, protesting that he had perfectly good intentions which you would appreciate if only you could understand, has in him the element of moral responsibility however strange his intentions may seem to you. He is socially and morally accessible; his attitude is reasonable. The child who meets you with sullen defiance, with stolid indifference, or with dumb submission, protesting nothing because he has no protest to make, is thus far morally impossible. His attitude is characteristic of those persons, neither normally intelligent nor quite imbecile, whom the psychologists call "morons".

Such, then, is the logic common to criticism, literary,

aesthetic, ethical. It may help to confirm and possibly further to clarify the conception if I add that such also is the logic of historical criticism. And history, as I have said above, is criticism—and moral criticism. But the moral attitude of historians is commonly very unsatisfactory to orthodox moralists. For while interested at every point in the *moral quality* of policies and persons, historians are curiously little interested in correcting the course of history or in classifying its important persons as good and bad. The historian takes any of the interesting personages —such as Napoleon, Frederick the Great, Plato, Martin Luther, Macchiavelli, Bismarck, Edmund Burke, or Benjamin Franklin—more or less as he finds them; and then he asks what measure of genius, of greatness of thought or conception, may be found to be expressed in their careers.

The effect of the question itself will be doubtless to transform them—to create, at the same time to bring out, a new region of fact with regard to the careers. The question will still be the question of moral justification. Was there a greatness of political wisdom embodied in the policy of Napoleon, or was he only a vulgar bandit and politician favoured by extraordinary circumstances? Was Mohammed, as Carlyle would have him, a case of where "the inspiration of the Almighty giveth him understanding" or, as suggested by Eduard Meyer, a prophet of the same order and on the same level with the Mormon prophet, Joseph Smith? Otherwise expressed, was the gospel of Mohammed the expression of a spiritual experience or was it simply words? Such a question, it would seem, is asking about an objective reality, however difficult the answer. Such is the question of historical criticism and such also is the question of moral criticism.

And such, then, is the meaning of justification by knowledge. So far as any form of expression, *i.e.* of action or behaviour, is intensively conscious—so far as it is thoughtful, reflective, self-conscious, so far indeed as it is in any proper sense experience—it is thus far morally significant and morally justified whatever its factual character. One might even say, with Pater, so far as it is a "passion", if we add his significant warning, "Only be sure that it is a passion—that it does yield you the fruit of a quickened and multiplied consciousness". On the other hand the nature and course of the action will then be transformed by the consciousness of the action. Take any action you please. Then put consciousness into the action. You cannot say how the action will be transformed; and no law can prescribe how it ought to be transformed. But this you can say: those who understand will mark the presence of moral quality and for them it will have moral dignity.

§ 44

I will now point out briefly that this conception of morality is not so very foreign to the categories of common sense, however it may be opposed to orthodox doctrine. And first the category of *objectivity*. An experience, I have just said, is objective—and it is objectively an experience—so far as it is critical; and this means that it is cognizant—objectively cognizant—of other experiences. Now when the term "objective" is used by philosophers and men of science it is likely to suggest a set of rules formulated on behalf of logic or of scientific method. But these rules are nothing but more or less ineffectual attempts to define the *experience* of objectivity; an experience suggested more directly when the literary critic speaks of objective criticism. And this experience of objectivity is only the experience that we have when we think our thoughts in the light of (not in conformity with) the thoughts of other persons. It does not mean that we follow a rule or that we substitute the thoughts or plans of other persons for our own. Objective thinking is, so to speak, fresh-air thinking or broad-daylight thinking, while subjective thinking is chamber-thinking, fearing to expose itself even to itself. Objective decisions are decisions reached after criticism. And as thus objective and responsible I may also point out that morality is in the true sense "social"—as against the customary sense of sacrifice for the common good.

Next the category of *rationality*. Thoughtful action is *per se* rational action. Yet not to be measured by any "rule of reason". Here again the rule is but an ineffectual attempt to transcribe an experience. This is shown in a very interesting way when we inquire into the motive of that most resolute of all attempts to reduce morality to a rule of reason which is embodied in Immanuel Kant's "categorical imperative"; which commands us to "act as if the maxim from which you act were to become through your will a universal law of nature". What did Kant have in mind here as the aspect most characteristic of the action of a moral or rational being—*uniformity* of action or *consciousness* of uniformity? The answer he has already given by saying: "Everything in nature acts in conformity with law. Only a rational being has the faculty of acting in conformity with the *idea* of law".[1] Note carefully the implications of this, and you will see that the one certain mark of a rational being is that he knows what he is doing; and whether such a being will then feel bound to emulate the uniformity of nature is another question.

In the end it seems that what Kant had before him was the simple eighteenth-century distinction to the effect that men have reason, while brutes (and *a fortiori* inanimate nature) have it not. This man-brute distinction marks the experience of rationality; it is *par excellence* the experiential meaning of morality. All of moral philosophy is an attempt to say how man differs from the brute. Kant's categorical imperative was an attempt to reduce the distinction to a kind of mathematical definition. For myself I prefer simply to point to the experience which Kant tried to define, the experience, namely, of knowing what you are doing. But this, I should say, is just what any man whose mind is undebauched by logic means by acting rationally. When we say of a man emerging from delirium

[1] From Section II of *The Metaphysic of Morality*. The translation is from Watson's *Selections from Kant*, p. 235.

that "he talked rationally" we do not mean that he talked in syllogisms. We mean simply that he knew where he was. The darkness of delirium had been succeeded by "the light of reason". And the concrete designation for an irrational impulse is invariably that it is "blind"

There remains, however, an implication which I would probably best not pretend to reconcile with the usual categories either of common sense or of orthodox ethics. And the implication is vital. Moral action, I say, is thoughtful action, and this is sufficient. Moral action, in other words, is deliberate action. Now in the common view moral action must indeed be deliberate. But this common view is likely then to insist upon the reality of deliberately immoral action. And this of course I deny. I do not say, be it noted, that deliberate action is certain to end in being right—thus implying a miraculously pre-established harmony between deliberate choice and an orthodox standard. I say rather that it is "right" in being deliberate. The distinction of deliberate wrong-doing is then a distinction introduced by the authoritarian standard.

The reader will perceive that we have again before us one of the *dramatis personae* of an earlier chapter in the person of "the clever rogue". One of the most interesting of his kind is the great American humbug; who, however, is not exclusively American. There are two beautiful studies of the humbug by Alphonse Daudet, one in a lighter tone in the trilogy of "Tartarin", the other in a graver, almost vindictive, tone in "Numa Roumestan". We find him everywhere in life—and never quite certainly not in ourselves; in the college professor who, having lost his zeal for study, will now authenticate his profession by oracular observation and edifying sentiment; in the politician who, his pockets lined with tainted money, lays his hand upon his heart and talks about his service to his country. The divergence between profession and fact seems so obvious that we assume the deception to be deliberate. Carlyle betrays this assumption when he seeks to vindicate the character of Mohammed by denying that he was "a poor *conscious* ambitious schemer". Yet we reveal our perplexity by putting the assumption in the form of a question; how is such deliberate mendacity and hypocrisy possible? How can the fellow expect any one to believe him?

Why should we, however, assume deliberate mendacity? Why not adopt the more probable assumption (nicely worked out by Daudet in "Numa Roumestan") that the fellow deceives himself? Not that he may not suffer from occasional terrible moments of self-revelation. But when he gets out before the audience, and hears the intoxicating sound of his own voice and the plaudits of the crowd, why should he not believe that after all he must be very much what he pretends to be? Does this mean, however, that he is to be reckoned among the rather innocent citizens of a moral world? By no means, I reply; the citizens of the moral world are not among the "innocent". The fact that he deceives himself is just the most decisive ground for banishing him. The habit of deceiving other persons is sufficiently doubtful as a mark of intelligence, but he who deceives himself must be set down as hopeless. Alas, these conscious hypocrites, these clever rogues, these shrewd diplomats, they have so little in them! Were they deliberate hypocrites, it would mean that they had sounded depths of wisdom by you or me unsuspected. And then for us they would be adding to the significance of human life.

And thus I continue to reject the distinction of the good man and the bad, as a distinction morally irrelevant; and the discrimination that I have in mind is between the presence of moral significance and the absence of it; which seems to me to mark the critical attitude. For my own part, I seem to find ever less use for such terms as "wicked", "sinful", "nefarious", and the like. They seem to me to correspond to nothing real. And I tend rather to think of those who are morally inadmissible as "coarse", "brutal", or "insensitive". Nor can I very easily digest the simple distinction suggested by "the criminal classes". I doubt very much whether the criminal classes

JUSTIFICATION BY KNOWLEDGE

have that character for themselves; and I suspect that many of them are only persons born belatedly, out of due time, persons who might have won a title of nobility in the free-booting ages of Elizabeth or of Anne, for whom however the present age is too civilized and sophisticated. And as for Milton's Satan with his "Evil, be thou my good", he is only the *reductio ad absurdum* of orthodox morality. I believe I am not the first to note that Milton has here invested Satan with a sublime moral dignity.

§ 46

The motive of morality, I have said, is not to judge but to understand. Now I dare say that the attentive reader has been already reminded by this of *"tout comprendre est tout pardonner"*; often translated to mean that to understand is to forgive. And this French saying is commonly accounted to be the last word in sentimentalism. For what it seems to mean is that morally there is in the end no real difference between men. We are all well-meaning men, and the only problem of the moral life is to understand one another. Am I to confess, then, that sentimentalism is the final meaning of the morality of intelligence?

Now I am not certain that *"tout comprendre est tout pardonner"* may not be a fair expression of my meaning—although personally I do not care to consider the moral problem under the aspect of forgiveness. For aught I know there may be behind the action of any man and of every man a depth of reflection beyond my grasp. And I should say that a truly critical imagination will not easily be satisfied to abandon the search for meaning and the hope of discovering a meaning. Meanwhile, however, this is not to say that every man has for me an achieved moral quality; and I am not so much of a sentimentalist as to assume the moral quality without some verifying experience. That which is already comprehended has its moral significance assured. But of any form of behaviour raising the issue of criticism, it still remains to ask whether it is comprehensible; and behaviour is not made comprehensible by showing that it is merely to be expected.

The point is so interesting—and so full of dramatic significance when it comes into the more intimate personal life—that I must regret my inability to offer more than a seemingly trivial and prosaic illustration. Many years ago I went into a Chicago department-store for a pair of shoes. The salesman, a man between twenty-five and thirty, whom I marked at once as a blundering, "feckless" sort of fellow, and rather shabby for so pretentious an establishment (he was probably an extra man), showed me four pairs, all, he explained, of the same price. I selected one pair as being clearly better than the others, besides being of the shape I wanted. The salesman picked up another pair and began volubly to assure me that of the shoes he had shown me these were in every respect the best. I told him that I would none the less stand by my choice. Then in great confusion he explained that he had made a mistake; those that I preferred were considerably higher in price. And he added, rather sullenly, that if I insisted, he must sell them to me at the price named—and himself make up the difference. When I explained that I did not wish to save money at his expense, he seemed pathetically relieved—and the transaction was closed.

But the point of my tale is this. As I was leaving the place the salesman said to me in a confidential tone, half in bravado, half beseechingly, "You see why I didn't talk 'em up to you, don't you?"

Did I see? That question, very amusing at the time, has stuck in my imagination for twenty-five years, and has come to embody for me one of the deepest questions of moral philosophy. Of course I saw that he had lied to me. But I also seemed to see more. I seemed to see in him one of those pathetic, well-meaning incompetents who will never be good for much and will never know why. And I guessed that after the fashion of his improvident

JUSTIFICATION BY KNOWLEDGE 165

kind he had probably taken to him a wife and begotten a child or two for whom it was a desperate task to provide. The discovery that by his blunder he had made a hole in his week's wages was more than he could bear. And so, naturally and inevitably, he lied.

Was this a case of *"tout comprendre est tout pardonner"*? Hardly, I should say. I could not resent the lie. But absence of resentment is not, except for authoritarian morality, moral justification. To note that an action takes place "naturally and inevitably", as I have just put it, is by no means to comprehend the action. To comprehend an action is nothing less than to appreciate the meaning of the action from the agent's point of view. This is to assume that there is such a point of view; in other words, that the action has moral quality.

Suppose, then, that reading my thoughts, he had replied with something like this: "I know what you are thinking; and what you suppose is mostly true. I am indeed one of the incompetents. But don't suppose that I lied to you unwittingly; because I couldn't help it; because I had no sense of the offensiveness of a lie. I did know, and it was in spite of knowing—or, if you please, in the light of knowing—that I lied deliberately. I resent as an imposition a rule that compels an employee to make good out of his own pocket, for the supposed honour of the establishment, a blunder that might easily and harmlessly be rectified; and I feel that I am justified in protecting myself against the customer who will use this for his own advantage. In your case I seem to have made a mistake; but as a matter of general policy I say that the lie was justifiable."

To put this speech into the mouth of the person I have described may seem far from realistic. But if so it will only bring out the point of the illustration, namely, the realistic character of the moral distinction and the difference between a true moral judgment and a mere outburst of sentiment. The moral question is the very nice question of interpretation: how much consciousness of meaning may

I believe to lie in or behind this act? How far is it self-conscious, how far merely automatic—how much "speculation in those eyes"? And had I encountered such a rationalized justification as I have endeavoured to suggest, then, even while loathing a liar on general principles, I must certainly have abandoned with shame the superior attitude I was tempted to assume, and I must then have recognized in the man before me a person of moral dignity. I need not have assented to the necessity of lying. I might have thought, vainly perhaps, that I myself could have found a better way out. But this will only help us to see how remote are the casuistic questions—such as, Is a lie ever justifiable?—from the vital issues of morality.

In justification of my general thesis I will venture to offer one more illustration. Some time ago I chanced upon an autobiographical work by a Jewish writer, an American of foreign birth. The book was a very personal document, in which an interesting experience and an interesting point of view were presented with genius and literary skill. At one point the writer was at pains to explain to his reader that he could find none of the supposedly Jewish traits in himself. Evidently it was his purpose to prove that there is no difference between a Jew and a Gentile. Personally I do not understand why a Jew, representing a people which has contributed so much to the culture of the race, should wish to deny that there is any distinctive quality in a Jew. It happens, however, that other Gentile readers have agreed with me in thinking that the book in question exhibited rather markedly some of the more unpleasant traits commonly attributed by Gentiles to Jews.

And in particular the following. The writer referred more than once to his wife and to his married life in terms that should win respect, yet with a certain defensive, not to say truculent, eloquence which made one wonder at the necessity. At the same time he commented in terms most contemptuous upon the "commonplace" and "uninteresting" wives of men with whom he had been associated; men who, it seemed, had not only done him no ill but had been generally friendly to him, and whose chief fault seemed to be that they preferred the society of their wives to his own society. Now this lack, I will not say of chivalry, but of objective decency and fairness—this childish and ill-mannered disposition to write one's own sensibilities large and the sensibilities of others small—is unfortunately just what the common Gentile world—whether truly or falsely, matters not for our purpose—is most inclined to regard as the peculiar mark of the Jew. And whether truly or falsely, how could he fail to be alive to the nature of the prejudice and to provide for it? Either, it seems, he must then have deleted these offensive passages or he must have justified them by explaining his point of view. And I think he must then have gone on to make as persuasive as possible the beauty of the Jewish character.

The difficulty with this writer, I guess, was precisely that he was unaware of these so-called Jewish traits. He did not know what his attitude would mean to his reader, nor just what it meant to himself. This was the root of the moral difficulty, and this constituted his offence and his offensiveness. After all, one can permit a man to say anything he pleases to one—or, apart from its practical aspect, to do anything he pleases—provided he makes clear the significance of what he is saying or doing. And in spite of all race prejudices, any racial trait tends to justify itself and to compel recognition when it expresses itself consciously and responsibly. The unconscious race-tendency is a trait merely brutal; the self-conscious expression of tendency is a contribution to life.

§ 47

So much for the justification by knowledge. Now I fear very much that some obstinately practical reader will be certain at this point to ask me what we are going to do about it when the carefully meditated purposes of different persons issue in conflicting lines of action—when, for example, one of a married pair is thoughtfully resolved upon divorce, the other no less thoughtfully resolved against it. To him I can only repeat what has been said before, namely, that it is not the purpose of moral philosophy to draft a schedule of what to do. Such a task is reserved for those—the law, or possibly the police—whose function it is to frame utilitarian schemes of social order; in which I am here not interested.

Meanwhile I may remind him once more of the difference between settling a question and answering it, between the disposal of a problem and its solution. The only conceivable *moral* resolution of a conflict is that which issues in mutual understanding after conference and discussion. The moral world knows nothing of judges, umpires, courts, and laws. If the parties should appeal to me I could give them only the rather easy advice to state their case, each to the other, with the utmost possible frankness. Putting it very vulgarly I might say, Begin by laying your cards on the table—if only you know what cards you are really holding. Any card-player will be reminded by this figure that consciousness makes an important difference; after seeing your careless opponent's hand at bridge it is very difficult to play as if you had not seen it—you do not know what your own hand alone would have suggested. In like fashion your own case is likely to look very different after you have grasped the point of view of the other party; and the difference makes the two more negotiable, more capable of a resolution satisfying to both.

But it may be that with the best will to negotiate there will remain elements of flat opposition of interest. This will mean only that, humanly speaking, the problem is morally insoluble. But if the problem is not morally soluble, in the sense of yielding complete mutual satisfaction, there may still be found a compromise, involving reciprocal sacrifice, which it will pay both parties to accept.

Let us not, however, mistake this mutual sacrifice for a moral solution. And if no practicable compromise is discoverable—well, if I were one of the parties I should then make the typical utilitarian calculation of profit and loss and ask myself how far it would pay me to yield the points now left in dispute, how far to fight for them. But when it comes to this we have left the moral world well in the distance.

CHAPTER XIII

THE ENJOYMENT OF LIFE

§ 48. The Epicurean attitude. § 49. An Epicurean confession. § 50. Epicurus and Pater. § 51. Enjoyment and imagination. § 52. The enjoyment of friendship and the enjoyment of religion. § 53. Serious enjoyment.

IN connection with the pragmatic attitude it was said that the significance of any temporal moment of life, or the meaning of any present desire, might be anything you please; "the present" is a question of the present scope of imagination. The same indefinite possibility confronts us when we think to define the boundaries of human nature. Could we think of the human being simply as an organism with a definite habitat and a restricted span of life, we might then formulate a definite "science of ethics", based upon human nature as a natural fact, undisturbed by suggestions metaphysical. But such a science of ethics would hardly merit the name of moral philosophy. The "moral nature" of man implies that he is not a mere organism but an organism which is self-conscious and critical, an organism with imagination. To human nature as thus conceived it seems difficult to assign any "natural" boundaries.

In the previous chapters I have found it convenient to take human nature, generally speaking, as it "is". But now it seems that to leave the story at this point is to omit all the deeper issues of moral philosophy; and to impose upon the critical life a termination artificially abrupt— even though we foresee that further inquiry will be inquiry without end. Accordingly I shall go on, in these remaining chapters, to pursue as certainly as I can the more

THE ENJOYMENT OF LIFE

reflective implications of the critical life. I shall begin in the present chapter by asking what is meant by the enjoyment of life.

§ 48

The question relates to the possibility of maintaining in the form of a critical life what in general terms may be described as an Epicurean attitude. Now it happens that the Epicurean (using the term in its broadest sense) is the person who is supposed to make the critical life his special profession; by which I mean that he lays a special claim to sophistication, regarding himself perhaps as the finally sceptical and disillusioned. It is he who has laid bare the vanity of most of the satisfactions that men seek, the vanity of social or political or literary distinction, the vanity of wealth and no less the vanity of the satisfaction afforded by the crude gratification of sensual appetite. But above all it is he who has demonstrated the vanity of religious hopes or fears, the vanity of all considerations relating to the fact of death. Reading Epicurus or Lucretius, one feels that in their view the one thing necessary for human salvation is indifference to death. The gods exist—perhaps; but whether they exist or not, we may be sure that the matter is no concern of ours. Human life must stand upon its own basis. Therefore let us cultivate our garden and not look beyond.

What, then, has life to offer? Well, for the Epicurean not a great deal, but something worth while if we moderate our expectations. The enjoyment of friendship, for example, if we are careful not to expect too much of our friends; and this calls for an attitude of amiability and cheerfulness, of urbanity and graciousness, and a kindly tolerance of human weaknesses. The art of life is to take men and things as we find them and to cultivate a taste for what they actually have to give us. To Epicurus and his friends it seemed that the chief fruits of the garden were the persons of one's inner circle. The Epicurean of the modern sort attaches more importance to the enjoyment of beauty and he may even add to this the enjoyment of religion. Any aspect of life may conceivably appeal to his taste for enjoyment simply as an aspect of life; that is, as a variety of sensation or of feeling. But in all such he conceives that he is dealing only with immediate and tangible realities. The sensation or the feeling is a realized fact; the cognitive significance of a sensation or a feeling is a vain speculation. And whatever may be true or false in the realm of speculation, it cannot change the nature of what is perceived, or felt, as a matter of fact.

§ 49

Whether I am by nature and temperament an Epicurean, I hardly know—certainly I find the Epicurean urbanity a difficult achievement. But as a moral philosopher I should be willing to call myself an Epicurean if only I might be permitted to remain a critical Epicurean; and in any case it has been my purpose in the foregoing chapters to justify the Epicurean demand for the enjoyment of life as an element essential to morality. I will therefore venture to illustrate my Epicurean sympathies somewhat as follows. When I see a group of children playing happily together, or at least with fair success managing their own affairs, my instinctive feeling is, Leave them alone. It seems to me something of an impertinence to show them how they ought to manage their affairs and especially to show them how they ought to play their game. And if it be said that the game if properly supervised could be made an instrument of self-culture and of moral discipline, my reply would be that they are getting the best sort of discipline as it is if only they are alive and playing the game. It may be only too necessary presently to interrupt them for the purpose of "training" them, along lines not spontaneously suggested by their interests, to meet the demands of a sternly practical world. But I do not feel called upon to add to the sternness of the world. I suspect indeed that sternness closes the mind instead of opening it.[1] And I should really like to believe that education could be left to the play of native interests. I am compelled rather to believe that native interests might fail to assert themselves apart from the discipline of life. Even so I can see no reason why I should artificially intensify the discipline of life.

As an Epicurean I should like to extend to men in general the kind of indulgence—deference, I prefer to call it—that I have in mind for the children. I wish to respect men's enjoyments, to let them live, and grow through living. I have no desire to "organize" them; and I refuse to be organized myself beyond what is plainly necessary for practical purposes. I might almost say, with Mr. Santayana, that I wish them only "simple happiness". At any rate I will quote his words as saying so much better than any of my own very nearly what I mean:

"I find that I am sometimes blamed for not labouring more earnestly to bring down the ideal good of which I prate into the lives of other men. My critics suppose, apparently, that I mean by the ideal good some particular way of life or some type of character which is alone virtuous, and which ought to be propagated. Alas, their propagandas! How they have filled this world with hatred, darkness, and blood! How they are still the eternal obstacle, in every home and every heart, to a simple happiness! I have no wish to propagate any particular character, least of all my own; my conceit does not take that form. I wish individuals, and races, and nations to be themselves, and to multiply the forms of perfection and happiness, as nature prompts them. The only thing which I think might be propagated without injustice to the types thereby suppressed is harmony; enough harmony to prevent the interference of one type with another, and to allow the perfect development of each type."[2]

---

[1] Bosanquet, the high-priest of absolutism, quotes from Mark Pattison "the force of individual character generated by the rule of Calvin at Geneva"; which means, I suspect, that dogmatism on the part of the master generates an equally dogmatic opposition on the part of the pupil. Calvinism is a system by which each exacts retribution from his children for the discipline inflicted by his parents.

[2] From his essay, "On My Friendly Critics", in *Soliloquies in England*, London, 1922.

And yet a "simple happiness"? Alas! I suspect that there is no simple happiness. The search for happiness inevitably develops complications and problems. And above all that supreme happiness which we hope to find in the intimacies of personal love and understanding. Happiness seems to be nowhere uncomplicated with "discipline". Yet even so I will let my neighbour find his discipline for himself. If he must go out of his way to find it and follow William James's moralizing advice (so incongruous, by the way, with William James) to do something disagreeable every day just for the sake of discipline—well, his demands upon life must be rather simple.

But why men—but more especially women—should delight in the imposition of discipline passes my comprehension. When I see a young working-girl exulting in outrageously gaudy finery, her young man presenting the glass to fashion in the most grotesque of ready-made clothes, I feel in myself no disposition to rebuke their taste however little it be mine. What I mainly ask is that she should genuinely enjoy her fine feathers and that she should not be wearing them in imitation of fashionable ladies or in blinder obedience to department-store advertisements. And if her fine feathers bring her to shame—well, alas! When I read in "Adam Bede" of poor Hetty Sorrel driven by a terror of shame to causing the death of her illegitimate child I am apt to forget all that has been said about her vanity and selfishness, and I am impressed chiefly by the brutal cruelty of a social order which inflicts such terrible penalties upon the irregular satisfaction of impulses so essentially innocent—so remote, at any rate, from anything malign or treacherous.

And it is just this desire to punish others for their sins of sex, or any desire to regulate the sex-relations of others beyond the minimum of utility, that as an Epicurean I find most unintelligible. If Brown has married a woman with a past I feel no impulse to push Brown off the sidewalk. If Brown and Mrs. Brown are happy together what more is there to be said? And who knows whether a shady experience may not turn out to be after the fact a superior opportunity for moral insight ? All that I ask of them is a decent reticence. Or if I should hear that Smith and Mrs. Jones are suspected of being too intimate —well, as a gentleman it is not for me to inquire further except perhaps as I may be in a relation of personal responsibility to Jones or Mrs. Smith. As for the other two they have set themselves a task sufficiently hazardous— why should I wish them disaster ? Sufficiently hazardous indeed is the task undertaken by any young man and woman who are seeking in marriage their happiness in one another. Surely the problem contains its own discipline, and failure is sufficiently humiliating ; why should we care to add to the discipline imposed by the problem itself ? And all of this is not because I would treat the sex-relation lightly ; rather because to my own feeling even as an Epicurean the sex-relation is so deeply committing, although I will not say that it must be such for all persons under all circumstances. But in a relation so essentially private who but the principals can say where the real loyalties lie ? And if there has been a betrayal what but the free conviction of the traitor himself can ever make good ?

And therefore as an Epicurean, but also if you like as a very serious moralist, I believe in "birth-control"; because it would add freedom to the sex-relation, and moral freedom in the sense of separating the personal motive from the utilitarian. Authoritarian moralists are generally united in the endeavour to suppress knowledge of methods of contraception and to hinder the attainment of any clearer knowledge. They claim that it would encourage "immorality". But I wonder how, except from a motive meanly curious, this could concern themselves. And I also wonder about the immorality. I wonder if this is not a case of Macaulay's Puritan who forbade bear-baiting, not because it gave pain to the bear, but because it gave pleasure to the spectator. Moreover, I suspect that it is not immorality that they most fear : what they dread, for their children perhaps, is the significance of the issue which will be presented when sexual intercourse is definitely freed from the fear of consequences; and they fear to face a question purely moral. As for those who condemn birth-control as an interference with nature, their point of view I am obliged to put upon the level of that of the Mohammedan of the desert.

I have dwelt upon the sex-problem because it seems to me to embody in acute form all of the problems of personal relations. And in my view all moral problems are in the end problems of personal relations. Accordingly, I do not deny that from the standpoint of social convenience and utility the rules of sex-morality may have an important justification, and therefore for the individual from the standpoint of worldly wisdom, and I would not be too disdainful of worldly wisdom. I even suspect that those may be right who tell us that happiness, in the sense of contentment, would be increased if marriages could be arranged in the good old-fashioned way by the consultation of parents. But, precisely as an Epicurean, I cannot identify contentment with the enjoyment of life, or social respectability with personal chastity.

Since all moral problems are problems of personal relations, I am disposed, here again as an Epicurean, to refer all morality to the principle of good manners. In sex-morality I feel that good manners would supply the determining principle. And above all in matters of religion. A man's wife, a man's religion—these two most momentous choices of his life good manners forbid me to challenge or rudely to question. And on the other hand, since I am not called upon to worship his wife, why must he insist that I worship at the shrine of his religion? As an Epicurean it seems to me that religious differences ought of all things to present the least practical difficulty. That, I shall be told, is because I have no anxiety for other men's souls, because religion is for me a matter of no significance. No, it is because I would respect their souls, and therefore their privacy, and because, precisely from this standpoint, I take their religion to be the matter of most significance.

And I might go further to suggest the validity of good manners as a principle for broader fields, even for the field of international relations. If the moral ideas governing these relations could be made to approximate those governing the relations of decent individuals; if national honour meant what honour means to-day to a man of intelligence and a gentleman, namely, a scrupulous sincerity and a scrupulous regard for obligations instead of a swaggering challenge to the issue of force ; if peoples could refrain from expressing contempt for one another's stock and for one another's religion and if such contempt could cease to be regarded as an evidence of patriotism ; if jealousy and revenge could be thought as vain and unworthy in a nation as in an individual—my impression is that the necessary economic adjustments would come rather easily and that we should presently have peace on earth and good will to men.

Here, therefore, I differ from those who would distinguish manners from morals, and the difference is one of principle. I am not thinking of course of merely formal manners, though I appreciate their great convenience. Nor do I feel it to be an important sign of good manners that a man knows the proper tone to use towards a servant. The motive of good manners, as I understand it, is the motive of respect for the personality of your fellow. Good manners properly conceived thus constitute the perfection of moral refinement. Those who would distinguish manners from morals will reply to me, Not good manners, but brotherly love. To me, however, brotherly love divorced from the motive of good manners is morally offensive. What doth it profit a man to heap him with benefits if you respect not his soul ? And I think that it calls for a peculiarly Epicurean sort of imagination to sense the nature and varieties of soul.

§ 50

So much for the Epicurean confession. A few words now about Epicurean philosophers. As an Epicurean who is also a student of philosophy I refuse to interpret even the ancient and classical Epicureanism as meaning, Eat, drink and be merry, for to-morrow we die. This is perhaps what logically Epicurus ought to have meant, since it seems that for him and his school the chief fact of life was that life is short. But it seems also that the Epicureans, with a painful inconsistency perhaps, arrived at a very different conclusion. We are but beasts that perish, therefore—shall we, therefore, enjoy the life of the beast? By no means. Therefore, rather, let us rescue from life what possibilities of sweetness and humanity it may have while yet there is time.[1] Epicurean morality, in other words, though confronted with the fact man is a perishing animal, is based, like every other morality, upon the idea that man is an intelligent animal. Its question then is, What is the best life for an intelligent being? The Stoics replied to this question by an attempt to invest life with dignity and greatness. The Epicurean doubted the possibility. But he still hoped to make life genial and humane. And this was his conception of the enjoyment of life.

I would not, however, pin Epicureanism to the philosophy of Epicurus. Epicurus seems to have been a saintly person, but his philosophy of life was rather homely and matter-of-fact, prosaic and unimaginative. The classical Epicurean appears to have been neither an "epicure" nor an exquisite. At the same time the Epicurean conception of intelligence suggests a mechanical and calculating intelligence such as the intelligence conceived by modern utilitarians; an intelligence *about* life, occupied in sorting and ordering the sensations forming the opaque material

---

[1] As expressions of the Epicurean *motif*, without the Epicurean pessimism, I know of nothing better than Milton's two graceful sonnets, " To Mr. Lawrence " and " To Cyriack Skinner ".

THE ENJOYMENT OF LIFE 179

of life, but hardly an intelligence *within* life, within the sensations themselves. It is the attempt to make the sensations themselves intelligent that marks, I should say, the distinctive quality of the Epicureanism of to-day and constitutes its aesthetic *motif*.

The philosophy of this *motif*, very properly called a philosophy, is contained in the writings of Walter Pater, whose version of "humanism" I have quoted in Chapter VIII. According to Pater the good life consists in the enjoyment of exquisite sensations. By moralists of the sober sort this philosophy of life is condemned with a vehemence almost vindictive as representing what Carlyle calls the "pig-philosophy" in only its most insidious and seductive form. On behalf of this criticism they can doubtless fairly quote chapter and verse. For my own part, however, I prefer to class Pater among the most suggestive of the greater moralists. Personally I do not wholly enjoy him. I seem to be in the presence of an obstructed mind—obstructed possibly by a too exquisite honesty; which, by the way, is the "lesson" of Pater's essay on style. And young Marius the Epicurean strikes me as not a very stimulating companion. The picture of him somewhere in a room furnished solely with a vase containing one rare flower—for concentrated contemplation —tempts me to irreverence. Moreover, I am sometimes tempted to wonder for a moment how much meaning lies behind Pater's words, and how far they may not be— words. And yet as I dwell upon them further I am impressed by their suggestiveness and they seem to work together into a significant if somewhat vaguely imaginative philosophy of life.

This I look for in the later "Marius" rather than in "The Renaissance". I have just noted that Epicurus' conception of intelligence suggests an intelligence about sensations and not within them; as if life were a game of playing with pictures. I think that, in spite of certain very suggestive counteracting motives, much the same may be said for the Epicureanism (or Cyrenaicism) of Pater's

"Conclusion" to the volume on "The Renaissance". To think only of giving "the highest quality to your moments as they pass, and simply for those moments' sake"; "to burn always with this hard gemlike flame, to maintain this ecstasy" of the concentrated moment; in the presence of which "we shall hardly have time to make theories (*i.e.*, to exercise any imagination) about the things we see and touch"—this especial kind of worship of "art for art's sake", of impression for impression's sake, seems to leave little room for any quality of soul, of humanity, even of experience, within the impressions themselves. It is not properly *sensations* that Pater is dealing with here, but simply the counters or poker-chips which function as "entities" for Mr. Bertrand Russell and the mathematical logicians, only now agreably coloured and illuminated. Thus far the aesthetic Epicureanism differs not essentially from the prosaic.

In a footnote to this "Conclusion" in a later edition Pater says, "I have dealt more fully in ' Marius the Epicurean ' with the thoughts suggested by it." To the reader of "Marius" it seems rather that he has arrived at a new point of view; or at least at a view not quite foreseen in "The Renaissance". And now we may see why Marius' contemplation of the lone flower was a religious exercise, and what is meant by "art for art's sake". The point of the aesthetic philosophy is now that it will put meaning into that great region of life, represented by sense-perception, which for the dull mind is merely opaque fact. It will put intelligence within the sensation. An impression is now no longer a fact, a thing, even a "flame", but a vision—"vision" is Pater's favourite word. And the enjoyment of impressions is an exercise of *imagination*. And what is more, it seems that imagination may possibly reach the dimensions of religious insight and become an intuition of life eternal. Of one of the episodes in the spiritual development of Marius we read that "He seemed to lie readier than was his wont to the imaginative influence of the philosophic reason—to the suggestions of a possible open country, commencing just where all actual experience leaves off, but which experience, one's own experience and not another's, may some day occupy."[1]

And so it seems now that the key-word of Epicureanism is not "sensation" but "imagination"; not sensation as an opaque fact but sensation as vision. And it is in this sense that I call myself an Epicurean; as one who looks for the realities of life in the exercise of imagination.

§ 51

This brings me to the point of the question that I have in mind. Upon what I have called its positive side, Epicureanism stands for the enjoyment of life. On its negative side, however, Epicureanism is marked—traditionally, at least—by an insistence that life is a determinately limited natural fact. Sensation is thus a fact; value (*i.e.* pleasure—or pain) is in like manner a fact. In general the world is simply a fact; and to call it a fact means that it is simply *this* world, which may be fully defined and apprehended without any implication of a world beyond. And thus life is a fact. My question is, Can life be thus taken by any reflective mind? Can it thus be taken consciously and critically? Or—is it possible to *enjoy* life while taking life as a matter of fact?

Epicureanism stands for the enjoyment of life. Every one, however, is committed to the enjoyment of life, somewhere, at some time, in heaven if not on earth. For enjoyment is an indispensable condition of value. Enjoyment stands for the *realization* of value. Vulgarly it is "cash-value"; and a value which can never be a cash-value is no value whatever. But now, what is the meaning of such "realization" as a conscious or spiritual fact? Here it seems to me, as nearly everywhere else, our ideas of things spiritual are encumbered by vulgar metaphors.

[1] *Marius the Epicurean*, 1910, Vol. II, p. 36.

We enjoy, and what we enjoy is blankly called "pleasure". Now, to enjoy is indeed to realize, to appropriate; and to appropriate most securely is, it seems then, to consume. On the other hand, what is enjoyed must be a realizable something; and thus, it seems, a quantum, something solid and substantial which is capable of appropriation. Hence the type of all enjoyment, the distinctively "solid" enjoyment, becomes the enjoyment of food; and the typical food-enjoyment the enjoyment of the animal.

But suppose we reflect. By "enjoyment" we are meaning all the while a mental fact, namely, *conscious* appropriation. Observe with this in mind and you will note that the dog, for instance, does not enjoy his food, he simply bolts it. For a clearer realization of values we should turn to the child, say five years old, who, innocent of table-manners but with fine instinct, turns over his piece of bread and jam so that the jammy side may be in direct contact with the taste-organs on the tongue; and then probably licks off the jam before he consumes the bread. Or, better, to the connoisseur who, with due respect, slowly sips his glass of port and holds each sip for a moment on the tongue lest any of its fineness escape him. Here it should readily be seen that enjoyment is not a bare fact. The wine indeed is a fact. The enjoyment, however, is a process of discriminating intelligence—a spiritual even a dialectical process. And a process without a determinate end. A realization of value indeed, yet never a completed realization. Even the enjoyment of wine is sustained by an unappeased curiosity, a quest for nuances of taste foreshadowed but not quite grasped. When the wine ceases thus to stimulate it becomes insipid.

And so of the enjoyment of life. It is doubtless a trifle suspicious when a more than middle-aged college professor undertakes to expose the mere pomp and vanity of a thoughtless world. And a trifle humorous—for what does *he* know about enjoyment? But this is to raise a question. For my own part, although I cannot for long enjoy the society of youth, I find at times a keen pleasure in observing the enjoyment of a group of healthy and happy children at play, or perhaps of a set of youths and maidens having the time of their life at a dance. And with the other elders I may sigh for the lost capacity thus to enjoy life. But not for long. If I were asked to change places with the youth I should hesitate. For there is something lacking to the completion of their enjoyment which, let us hope, has been won, if sadly, by the elders around the wall : namely, a thoughtful sense of life. It is delightful to contemplate the young ones. But the reflection comes, What a pity that they cannot know—as we seem to know—what a good time they are having ! Which means, whatever difficulties the thought may suggest, that only as they are conscious of enjoying are they really enjoying. And only thus far do we really sympathize with their enjoyment. After all it is the deeply earnest little ones who most stir us to sympathetic affection, those whose play is not in their own eyes mere play. And these, it seems, come nearest to realizing our idea of healthy, happy children. The utterly thoughtless, the silly, giggling little children, the dissipated youth— these represent not so much enjoyment as benumbed sensibility.

Accordingly there would seem to be no enjoyment of life apart from a reflective attitude towards life. And this though the reflective attitude come only with a diminished vitality, making enjoyment seem sombre and subdued. When I seek to illustrate the attitude from literature, in the person of one who seems most to enjoy the life that he presents, I find that, paradoxical though it seems, my thought turns to Tourgenieff, albeit that so many of his pictures of Russian life are grave and sad. Yet the attitude of absorbed contemplation, at once questioning, discerning, sympathetic, which lies in the background of all of Tourgenieff's realism ; a certain sustained gravity which, in the "Sportsman's Annals", for example, imports the whole problem of life into a series of ostensibly descriptive sketches ; this "divinest melancholy", as Milton calls it, marks an element indispensable to any true enjoyment, to any satisfying taste of life.[1] Any enjoyment of life implies a sense of the mystery of life. No fool can enjoy life.

To some readers this will seem a Pickwickian, perhaps a casuistic, version of enjoyment. They have thought of enjoyment as light-hearted; and heavy-hearted enjoyment appears to be a contradiction in terms. I will not pretend that my analysis is free from difficulty. It seems that any analysis of the critical life is bound to raise as many questions as it answers. But this only means that the crowning mystery of life is not so much the mystery of the universe as the mystery of ourselves. What after all is the object of the heart's desire? If one could answer this—if, for example, "L'Allegro" and "Il Penseroso" could be put into a single poem—doubtless all else would be clear. Meanwhile the fact remains that if we enjoy pleasure we also enjoy pain; tragedy no less than comedy. Pain, it seems, becomes our pleasure. And you and I at least would not care to subscribe to an enjoyment solely of comedy. This would mean that we were fit only to be persons in a comedy. Nor does it help matters to suggest that true enjoyment is to be found in a "properly proportioned mixture" of pleasure and pain, of happiness and disappointment, after the fashion of a well-seasoned dish. The figure is too crude. It suggests once more the consumption of physical goods. As a fact of consciousness enjoyment is not a consumption of goods but an experience of life. From this point of view a tragic experience of life may yet be an enjoyment of life, as giving an assured sense of the reality of life. I may feel perhaps that a less intensive consciousness of life would be easier but this only marks the limits of what I have the strength to enjoy.

On the other hand it means that for the deeper experience life is more than ever an unsatisfied aspiration. The merely physical consumption of goods is a fact, completed when the goods are consumed. If the desire for

---

[1] After writing the above I am not sure that George Eliot would not furnish an even better illustration.

goods were only a fact parallel to the process of consumption, enjoyment would be similarly a *fait accompli*. Desire, however, involves consciousness—the consciousness of desire; and the conscious satisfaction of desire only reveals the further implications of the desire yet to be satisfied.

§ 52

The point may be illustrated in the matter of friendship. For the disciple of Epicurus, we remember, friendship was the most available and likewise the most fruitful sort of happiness. In "Harriet Frean" Miss May Sinclair presents a characteristic episode in which two boarding school girls exchange pledges of "eternal friendship", each of course promising the other not to marry. This naïve confidence in oneself marks the youth of both sexes. Mature persons smile at these eternal friendships as Jove is said to smile at lover's vows. Experience of the conditions of life reveals the difficulty of maintaining a friendship; and self-experience reveals, alas! how quickly we forget. The Epicurean would therefore be careful not to demand too much. *Carpe diem*, he would advise. Remember that human nature is frail. Jones who dined with you yesterday was delightful, interesting, appreciative. To-morrow he will dine with your enemy, Brown, who will say unpleasant things about you. Jones will not only not resent them, he may even assent to them. But what difference does it make? You found him well disposed towards you yesterday. Clearly he enjoyed your company and you found him a good companion. *That* fact is your assured possession. As a person of sophisticated intelligence you will then take what the gods give and ask no questions.

But will this mark an exercise of sophistication or, rather, a repression of sophistication? I am well aware that the question may be answered in different ways. For my own part I can answer it only as follows. I think that an Epicurean tolerance for the weaknesses and difficulties of other men is a mark of superior intelligence and also of a fine morality. At this point the Epicurean attitude approaches the Christian forgiveness of sins. And it seems to me that the moral excellence of each consists in insight into human nature. But this insight, so far from confirming the substantiality of the enjoyment that you get from the friendship of a not very loyal friend, only reveals how little you actually do get; even less, it would seem, than the disciple of Epicurus, never optimistic, has reckoned upon. I will not deny that it is possible in a loose sense to enjoy the society of Jones though you know that he will laugh at you to-morrow. I deny that this is possible, however, in the stricter and the only true sense, in which you put the thought of Jones's frailty and your enjoyment of his friendship into the same moment of consciousness and combine them into one act of thought. The one will then dissipate the other. To enjoy the society of Jones you will have to forget for the time being what kind of a person he is. You must cease to be sophisticated for the moment, create an illusion, and assume an artificial naïveté. You may indeed preserve your self-consciousness in a cynical enjoyment of Jones's weakness; but this is hardly an enjoyment of friendship.

The point is not one of sentiment merely, but of logic. It is along the same line, for example, that J. S. Mill denies that a round square is inconceivable; for how may we say in advance of the fact that objects may not be found which will be both round and square? Or both enjoyable and worthless? To my mind the reply is simple. Nobody denies that we can *say* "round square". But if our utterance is to be more than mere sound, it must mean something. It will then appear that "round" means nothing if it does not mean "not-square", and that likewise "square" can mean only "not-round". The effect of asserting the possibility of a round square is then not merely that you "contradict yourself", or that you are "inconsistent"—this seems possible enough until you see that what it really comes to is that you say nothing whatever, you are merely talking. In like fashion I shall not deny that you may extend to Jones all of the forms of courtesy and appreciation, but with the consciousness of his worthlessness in mind you will not be enjoying his friendship.

The Epicurean advises: in the matter of friendship take what you've got and ask no questions. My reply, then, is that if you ask no questions you've "got" nothing. For to ask questions is only to exercise your imagination (*i.e.* your intelligence). Without imagination there is no enjoyment; and when imagination raises a question the enjoyment must depend upon the answer. The *enjoyment* of friendship inevitably raises the question of loyalty; and then it appears that the seemingly sentimental consideration of "eternal friendship" is implied in the very logic of friendship. All of our expressions of friendship betray this implication. We speed the parting guest with *Au revoir* or *Auf Wiedersehen* and the desire for another visit. In all matters of personal relations the intensity of the present enjoyment is measured precisely by the longing for further intimacy. We may know that the conditions of time and place, the cares of family and business, and the limitations of our courage and our strength, will all conspire to defeat this longing; but these considerations we banish to the background in order that we may now enjoy. Their presence in the background, however, moderates our enjoyment. And if by chance they get into the foreground the effect is chilling. If I am asked to meet a rare and delightful person, one who is certain to attract me, with the understanding that we are to meet only once, I shall probably say, No, it is not worth while; you might as well offer to lend me a single chapter of a novel. The pain will not merely outweigh the pleasure, it will paralyse the pleasure. The Epicurean sage may then urge me to forget the temporary side of it. His advice will only sustain my contention that no temporary friendship can be enjoyed except as you forget its temporary character.

The motive of friendship is very deeply involved with the motive of immortality, of religion, and of life itself.

Just as the thought of the finitude of friendship chills the ardour of friendship so does the thought of death dissipate the zest for life. Therefore death is not mentioned in polite society. James points out that no one can think steadily of his own death. Suppose you approach a parent delighting in the contemplation of the vitality and promise of his children and then remind him that after not many years as the world goes they will have run their span of life; their bodies, which had already grown old and withered, will then lie mouldering in the ground; and the world will go on comfortably without them. The effect of this cruel experiment will be to show how deeply, even in less imaginative men, the zest for life is bound up with implications of indefinite duration. If this is what it comes to, one will feel, then what is the use of it all? It were just as well at least that the children had not been born. It was the aim of Epicurus, and especially of Lucretius, to give a positive value to life by showing that death is nothing: the finitude of life is therefore not an evil. It would be a strange person, however, who should be stimulated to a delight in life by reading Lucretius on death.

The logic of the situation may be illustrated once more by considering the possibility of an Epicurean enjoyment of religion. Epicurus indeed wished to banish religion. Modern Epicureanism of the aesthetic sort sees no reason why religion should not be enjoyed as well as art (which indeed raises the same sort of issue) by treating religion, not as a belief in what we may call transcendental realities, but as a pleasing dream or picture. Surely the *picture* may be enjoyed for itself, as something that we experience, without regard to its cognitive significance. This conception of the value of religion, it is worth noting, is also proposed to-day by many who are hardly to be called Epicureans; by all of those indeed who, though treating religion as a merely natural, *i.e.* psychological, fact, yet recommend the cultivation of religion on behalf of the comfort of the individual, or of the welfare of the nation, or

THE ENJOYMENT OF LIFE

of the unity of humanity, or, it may be, of the perpetuation of the species.

As a carefully premeditated expression of the Epicurean view I quote the following from Mr. Santayana:

"In my adolescence I thought this earthly life (not unintelligibly considering what I had then seen and heard of it) a most hideous thing, and I was not disinclined to dismiss it as an illusion for which perhaps the Catholic epic might be substituted to advantage, as conforming better to the impulses of the soul; and later I liked to regard all systems as alternative illusions for the solipsist; but neither solipsism nor Catholicism were ever anything to me but theoretic poses or possibilities; vistas for the imagination, never convictions. I was well aware, as I am still, that any such vista *may* be taken for true, because all dreams are persuasive while they last; and I have not lost, nor do I wish to lose, a certain facility and pleasure in taking these points of view at will, and speaking those philosophical languages. But though as a child I regretted the fact and now I hugely enjoy it, I have never been able to elude the recurring, invincible, and ironic conviction that whenever I or any other person feign to be living in any of those non-natural worlds, we are simply dreaming awake."[1]

"And now I hugely enjoy it." After what has been said, I need do little more than put the question. What does Mr. Santayana enjoy? The dreams as dreams (*i.e.* as sensuous images) or the freedom of taking them critically? I can conceive that either may be enjoyed by itself; or both alternately, according to mood. Can both, however, be enjoyed by the same person in one moment of consciousness? The trouble with the dreams seems to be that they "are persuasive while they last". This means that they are not mere pictures, or merely ornamental arrangements of colour on the wall, but that they suggest a reference to reality. And thus to the critical mind they have the power of raising questions. The questions may conceivably leave the enjoyment untroubled—so long as they are only half-indolent questions and do not force the issue, whether the

[1] From the essay, "On My Friendly Critics".

dream is only a dream. Little as I am fitted temperamentally to enjoy "the Catholic epic" there are times when I find it impressive—because I suspect that nothing so catholic could be quite without significance. On the other hand one may banish the questions; but not, I should say, in the same breath in which one claims to be sophisticated. One may indeed be too resolutely sophisticated for the traditionally Epicurean repose of mind; but this will mean only that he who makes sophistication his profession should not expect repose. He should not expect to enjoy facts as facts or sensations as sensations.

§ 53

Accordingly for one who professes sophistication I can see no escape from a certain participation in what is called a "serious view" of life ("earnest" is Mr. Santayana's deprecatory word). The only escape, if that be possible, is to profess nothing whatever; that is, to stop thinking. And "serious" I mean in the sense in which Thackeray speaks, half jestingly, half sympathetically, of "a person of serious views", and tells us that the worldly Major Pendennis became "very serious" in his last days. Hence I am not interested in denying, but I would rather affirm—simply as a derivation from the Epicurean demand for the enjoyment of life—that a certain preoccupation with "eternal life" (Socratic, if we remember) is a positive mark of intelligence. After all I wonder what can be more characteristic of the critical life than wonder about the eternal significance of the life that is in us. It may be likewise intelligent to foresee that the wonder will not be satisfied; it will be no less true that to cease to wonder is to cease to think and thus to place an artificial limit, or to accept the limit of mental weariness, upon the exercise of sophistication.

The popular mind is likely to mistake a "stern and austere" dogmatism for a serious view of life. To the really serious view dogmatism is abhorrent. And thus of any ostensibly "serious" person I would ask always how far his seriousness stands for imagination and critical intelligence; and if not for a cultivated intelligence, yet for a native sympathy and understanding; how far, in short, it stands for an Epicurean sense of the variety and richness of life and of what each man's life means for himself. I seem to find none of this in the dull and stern dogmatism so often exhibited by "persons of serious views", or in the type of "seriousness" exemplified by many of Carlyle's "heroes". To me they are less serious than primitive. Without a critical appreciation of life I can conceive of no true seriousness, no real stirring of soul within the man; and any critical appreciation of life contains within itself the issues of "earnestness" and conscientiousness". No person destitute of imagination is entitled to be called either "serious" or "moral".

And this in spite of the obvious tendency of the critical attitude towards the sceptical and even towards the cynical. I will not pretend to understand the connection of motive here. It is one of the deeper perplexities of human life that the self-consciousness which begets the search for truth is no less the parent of that scepticism which despairs of truth or scoffs at truth. But the two are by no means divergent. There is a scepticism which is mainly indolence or helplessness and a scepticism which is responsible and intelligent. I suspect that, in Freudian fashion, all religious scepticism of the worthier sort is based upon positive religious feeling. Religious scepticism may thus easily stand for a juster sense of the meaning of religion than that religious pragmatism which so readily changes the character of God to suit the needs of the times. A man may say that "there is no God", not at all because he is a "fool", but because, precisely in his "heart", he knows too certainly what he is seeking.

Likewise of the relation between the serious attitude and the sense of humour. Here again there is a difficulty. Theories of humour constitute the least enlightening chapters of psychology, though nothing, it seems, is more intimately connected with the function of intelligence. But here again the distinction is to be drawn between a vulgar and an intelligent sense of humour. Not every sense of humour is equally a mark of intelligence. It depends upon what you find humorous—perhaps upon the breadth of view revealed in the sense of humour. Yet I should say that apart from a fine sense of humour there can be no deep sense of truth. The most deeply religious soul I have ever known, a scholar of world-wide reputation, was at the same time, of all men whom I have known personally and intimately, the most brilliant and the wittiest. And if this seems paradoxical let us remember that by common agreement (how properly I will not say) the critical life finds its type and spokesman in the person of Socrates. It seems to me not too much to say that Socrates is presented to us as the subtlest of Greek humorists, finer indeed, to my sense, than either Aristophanes or Lucian. Yet for Plato Socrates is at the same time the embodiment of religious seriousness, while in Xenophon he seems rather oppressively "Victorian". And it is likewise interesting to note that Augustine in his "Confessions", perhaps the classical expression of reverential devotion, attributes a sense of humour to God.

CHAPTER XIV

THE SUBSTANCE OF LIFE

§ 54. The particular nature of man. § 55. Biological evolution and the experience of thinking. § 56. Thinking and imagination. § 57. Imagination and human life. § 58. Imagination, morality, religion. § 59. Imagination and the metaphysical problem.

§ 54

AMONG the deservedly classical documents of moral philosophy are Bishop Butler's "Fifteen Sermons upon Human Nature", written in reply to Shaftesbury. Shaftesbury had derived morality from "human nature". True, is Butler's reply, but what, then, is *human nature*? What is "the particular nature of man"? His answer to this question was given in terms of "reflection or conscience". Butler's question will be the question of the present chapter, and the answer to be given I conceive to be substantially in accord with the answer that Butler gave.

The question may take various forms; among others the form of question implied in the distinction of the natural and the spiritual. Now the moral life I have defined in its various aspects as the critical, the thoughtful, the self-conscious life; and again as the spiritual life. But here a question may be raised. It may be objected that "the spiritual life" conveys an implication not to be found in any of these other terms. For none of these other terms— "critical", "thoughtful", "self-conscious"—implies more than what is known as a temporal and worldly point of view restricted to the contemplation of natural fact, or a mental process which is more than the operation of a natural human faculty. The spiritual life, however, implies a preoccupation with a Platonic or Christian "other" world of "eternal" realities, and a kind of supernatural insight.

Well, then, the general meaning of my reply will be, so in the last analysis, as it seems to me, do all of the other terms. For myself it seems impossible to fix the conception of a thoughtful existence, or of an existence in any proper sense conscious, upon a basis strictly "human" and "natural". Thought, or consciousness, finds no comfortable abiding place in a natural world; nor is she very warmly welcomed by natural scientists. And psychology, which would give us the natural science of thought, is neither good science nor good poetry. In moral terms the humane which is neither the beastly nor the divine is in unstable equilibrium; and the merely human refuses in the end to be distinguished from the merely animal.

The question may also be stated in terms of the conception of "life". What is "life"? In other words, what is it that in the last analysis distinguishes human from animal life; and which of the two is then more distinctively representative of "life"? It is from this point of view that I find the most convenient approach to the question; and in particular through a consideration of the relation of human and animal life suggested by biological views of evolution—which in two generations past have revolutionized our thinking about human life and human nature.

§ 55

Before evolution, to put it simply, man was distinguished from all of the other animals by having an immortal soul. This was inferred from the fact that man differs from the other animals in his power of thought. Among the animals, therefore, man was *sui generis*. And this distinction assumed such an importance that the similarities between man and the other animals passed relatively without notice. Evolution, however, has changed all of that. Evolution, we learn, has made it clear that man is only one animal among others. And as for the power of thought—thought is only one of the innumerable varieties of biological function, or organ; only one of those matters of detail that enable this or that species to survive in the competition for existence. As a biological function indeed thought is a unique success. Essentially, however, it belongs in the same category with the speed of the deer, the strength of the elephant, the horns of the bull, and the quills of the porcupine. Thought is a natural fact, one among others; it has no special meaning.

Now I have no wish to contest the theory of evolution; and certainly none to reinstate the idea of special creation. Yet as I study the "social" sciences of to-day and note the dominance of the biological point of view in all of their conceptions of human life, it seems to me that this seemingly naïve pre-evolutionary view was after all curiously right. In our preoccupation with man as an animal we seem to have overlooked the characteristic feature of human life. We have been so deeply absorbed in the "phenomena" of life that we have forgotten the *experience* of life. Observers of life, we fail to remember that we ourselves are agents of life. In a word, we have been so strongly fascinated by the biological effects of thinking that we have forgotten what it means to sit down "in a cool hour" (Butler's phrase) and have the experience of thought.

Let me try to paint a picture; a more or less fanciful picture of course, but it must be in the first person. I am sitting before my study fire in the darkening hours of an early December afternoon before the lamps are lighted, and my cocker spaniel is on the rug before me, also contemplating the fire. I have been spending the day in a task of writing, and as my mind slowly frees itself from this, I see other problems ahead; letters to be answered, purchases to be made, courses to be arranged, the beginning of plans for next summer; but meanwhile (dreadful thought!) Christmas presents to select. And then I think of my Christmases in other places where I have lived, in Germany in my student days, in New England, in the South and West, and on the Pacific Coast; and of the good companions and friends that I have had, here and there, whom I have in the past known so well, and whom now, to my shame, I rarely even remember. And then, strangely, there comes before me the picture of the little Irish newsboy, my admiration and my fear, who delivered our morning paper when I was a very small boy, and of the day when I saw him carried to the hospital, run over by a street-car, to die two days later; and then the picture of a college friend, one of the dearest fellows I have known, who sat on the side of my bed, as I was recovering from a slight illness, on the evening before our graduation, while we mapped out together our plans for the future. He was drowned a few days later. And it strikes me as somehow strange and uncanny that, in the many years since, the world should have gone on without my college friend and the little newsboy—just as if they had never lived—while it has carried me along with it. And then I reflect that in a few years more or less it will drop me too; and the world which, though I may not like it overmuch, I can hardly in thought separate from myself, will forget me as completely as though I had never been.

But this seemingly obvious reflection strikes a note of strangeness. And I am suddenly reminded that here is a point of view which for the most part is quietly left out of my world of daily life—of the practical and real world. And viewed in the light of it—viewing time in the light of eternity—this practical and real world becomes rather strangely unsubstantial and illusory. Practical life, I discover now, is sustained by a monstrous forgetting. And it is rather in the reflections of the cool hour—when, indeed, I should seem to others to be withdrawn from the world —it is here that I touch reality.

And now in this moment of meditation, when with a kind of blessed relief I seem to be for a time all myself, it becomes suddenly clear to me that even in the broadest daylight of common sense, when spiritual vision is most dazed and blinded, I never do accept as real this world of common objects—stupid, "inert", "unthinking" things with no "speculation" in their eyes. What is real, I know certainly, is of a different sort, something living and significant. And this array of seemingly opaque "phenomena" I can see now, certainly if vaguely, to be in itself the living expression of some sort of art, human if not also divine. Yet as I try to pursue reality further and get a sure vision of it, I seem to find the task overpowering and my mind appears to stagger under the burden.

And then I begin to fear that I am getting "abnormal". My neighbours, if they only knew, would suggest a sanitorium. And so—I will walk down the street and smoke a pipe and exchange a little scandal with a friend before dinner.

Meanwhile the dog is surveying the fire with a countenance suggesting to an observer hardly less reflection than my own. What is he thinking about? Not indeed about the Disarmament Conference, the unrest in India, or the future of the German mark. (I am writing in the year 1922.) Does he recall his gambols with the neighbour's dog of last summer in Maine and wonder if they will meet next summer? Or coming nearer home, does he say to himself that in three weeks the children will be home for their Christmas holidays, and then there will be life in the household? I would not venture to say just what the dog thinks, and for my purpose it is sufficient to take him as I find him. But if he knows anything about the approach of Christmas, about last summer and next summer, or possibly even about to-morrow, if he knows that the children are now "away" at school, and have not simply ceased to exist; if he can even conceive this distinction; then he must have sources of enlightenment wholly unknown to us. Doubtless he knows that he had his daily meal a few hours ago, because the sense of repletion is still present. It is probable that he will not begin to anticipate another meal, or even to think of the future in terms of food, until it is again suggested by the pangs of hunger or by the attendant household activities. Shall we say, then, that the dog's imagination is confined rather closely to the temporal and spatial present while our own ranges broadly? Even this would be hardly accurate. It would miss the most important point of difference. For I am living, say in this town and state of the United States of America, on a planet called the earth, in the year of the Lord 1922—all because I have been instructed in history and geography and because in this instruction I have been compelled to reflect, to order, to discriminate, and to form for myself a conception of the world in which I live. My temporal and spatial "present" is the expression of that conception. What the dog's present may be I am at a loss to say.

What, then, is he thinking about? From any human point of view we seem compelled to say, Almost nothing. In what kind and how much of a world, then, is he living? To me it seems, In almost no world. Does he even know that he is a dog? That I doubt most of all. Certainly not as I know that he is a dog, or as I know that I am a man. For this again is the fruit of some knowledge of biology; which, in presenting me with a certain system of distinctions and relations in the living world, enables me —like the sciences of history and geography—to locate myself in the world.

Man, it seems, then, is the only animal who knows that he is an animal. He is the only self-conscious animal, let us say; which, so far as it be true, means to me that he is the only really conscious animal. He is a conscious animal just so far as he is a thinking animal.

§ 56

And thus to be a thinking animal is to have *imagination*. In this use of "imagination" I am deliberately disregarding the definitions of scientific psychology in favour of the more popular usage of poetry and literary criticism which makes imagination equivalent to intelligence and uses "lack of imagination" to suggest stupidity. "Imagination" describes to my mind the experience of thinking for one who thinks. To one who merely observes the thinking being, thinking may easily appear to be nothing more than a photographic reproduction of the physical environment (as in the older but still popular associational psychology) or than a biological adjustment to the conditions of that environment (in the newer fashion of psychologizing). Neither of these expresses the *experience* of thinking.

Nor do I find this experience suggested in the traditionally rationalistic description of thought as "reason". If "reason" denotes only an operation performed upon symbols, or abstractions (to my mind the same thing)—if reason is only a sorting of cards or poker chips the term hardly suggests the experience of one who thinks. And likewise if reason or thinking be described in terms of "analysis"; when "analysis", like chemical analysis, is an operation performed upon a given material which adds nothing to the material. To think of a given object, I would point out, is always to think beyond it; and therefore to think of possible other, and possibly preferable, objects in place of it. And thus to think is inevitably to question; and the depth and significance of the question is measured by its range of imagination.

The traditional psychology, whether rationalistic or associational, marks off "imagination" as a consciousness of the fanciful (peculiar it seems to man, since the beasts are not granted imagination), from sense, or sense-perception, as a consciousness of present and solid reality common to man and beast. But where the boundary lies between the two no one has yet been able to show. I suggest that there is no boundary. To perceive the present clearly, or to be aware of it in any sense whatever, is just so far to view it in the light of what is not present—that is, of imagination. To be conscious of the temporal is to view it under the form of the eternal. When the present ceases to be illuminated by what is not present there is no *consciousness* even of the present. When in my meditations I become aware only of the fire before me, I am aware of nothing —I am asleep. Consciousness of any kind implies imagination. All consciousness means that you are looking beyond and around the present object.

§ 57

The modern scientific point of view tends to assume, with prosaic common sense, that as a matter of course, the "content" of mind must consist exclusively, or almost exclusively, of impressions derived from the existing objects of sense, and at each moment mainly of the impressions given by the objects then present. The soul, in a word, is a mirror of physical facts. These at any rate will be the content of every "normal" mind—which alone is respected by the scientific imagination or by prosaic common sense—of every mind enjoying a normal experience of life. What is then at any moment left to "imagination" will consist of impressions of the past reproduced according to the laws of association, or of anticipations of the future automatically initiated by the operation of the same laws; all of which is prefigured in the photographic conception of mind. "Free imagination", if such be conceivable, imagination indifferent to fact, present, past or future, or imagination critical of fact, will play the part only of an occasional indulgence like an after-dinner nap. From this point of view imagination is a waste product which the normal mind reduces to a minimum.

I wish now to suggest that as a picture of actual life this view is grotesquely false; and gigantically false if it purports to give us the spiritual history of the race. Perhaps indeed tragically false—for I will face the possibility that the outcome of the suggestion may be only a sense of the vanity of life. Yet even so a sense of the meaning of "life". The reader may perhaps recall the closing chapter in "Don Quixote" in which the dying gentleman, come as it seems tragically to himself, betrays in his parting words to Sancho the shock and blankness of disillusion. In this impressive conclusion one feels that the hero has turned upon his creator, revealing himself, in pathetic greatness, no longer as the tilter of windmills, but as the type, inevitably absurd from any standpoint of fact, of all who seek to give worth and dignity to life.[1] But I think that one can hardly grasp this scene without turning with a certain suspicious insight to self. One begins to wonder whether, after all, the Quixotic world was much further from prosaic fact than the world of many another of us; whose illusions have not yet been revealed to the world, nor possibly to himself. I wonder of how many men it is not true—at least of those whose practical life is punctuated by moments of critical reflection—that they find themselves living in a world, and will insist upon living in it, which they suspect at times to be non-existent from the standpoint of fact. I myself have lived for thirty-odd years past amidst an academic tradition, somewhat faint-hearted indeed, of the dignity of scholarship and culture. When the tradition conflicts with the fact academic men, professional *laudatores temporis acti* and believers in a Golden Age, turn as a rule to the past, as a sort of evidence that the academic tradition is grounded in fact. One may be permitted to doubt whether the dignity of scholarship has ever been or will ever be a fact.

There are men breathing to-day who are living, however,

[1] The reader who is reminded here of the " Quixotic " philosophy of the contemporary Spanish writer, Miguel de Unamuno, may be interested to learn that this and the following chapters were completed, nearly as they now stand, before I had heard of Unamuno. Since then I have read nearly all of Unamuno with immense appreciation and delight. Besides *Del Sentimiento Tragico de la Vida* and *Vida de Don Quijote y Sancho*, he has published several volumes of essays, also novels, short stories, poems, memoirs of travel in Portugal and Spain, and of his childhood and youth in the Basque provinces. To the English reader who would make the acquaintance of this remarkable man—a " passionate " writer who never loses his critical sense—I recommend the two volumes of admirable translation by Mr. J. E. Crawford Flitch, *The Tragic Sense of Life* (N. Y., Macmillan, 1921) and *Essays and Soliloquies* (N. Y., Knopf, 1925).

in the Victorian age. And for myself, when I seek refreshment of soul, I turn ever again to the literature, particularly to the novels, of the Victorian age, to Thackeray or Dickens, to George Eliot or Mrs. Gaskell, or even to Trollope or to Mrs. Oliphant, finding there, as I think, something homelike and familiar, civilized and intelligible, and in the fact of the Victorian age a kind of guarantee of the essential dignity of human life. Yet at times I suspect that the Victorian age never existed outside of books; and that present-day lovers of the Victorian age, permitted to re-visit that world as it existed in fact, would be mainly bored and disgusted. Yet I am not quite prepared to condemn the Victorian age as a fiction—not more at least than, with Vaihinger and Poincaré, I would stamp the entities of science as fictions.

It may seem that this is true mainly of bookish men. Certainly I take it to be characteristically true of reflective men. But I suspect that every man who lives at all has a hidden imaginary world carefully guarded from public ridicule where he really spends his life; and if we could discover that world we should know the man. Anthropology tells us that the primitive man lives mostly in an imaginary world. And the little working-girl seated opposite me in the subway is reading (so I am told) Laura Jean Libbey—surely an imaginary world! Thus pathetically will she escape the facts of life. Yet where shall we find those who live in the fact? In the business world it seems that the "live" man is defined by a taste for adventure and speculation. And the big business man is likely to disclaim the sober purpose of making a necessary living in favour of a pure delight in the game. This is the man's way of escaping the facts of life; the wife is probably seeking forgetfulness in afternoon bridge, and dreading nothing so much as a day without engagements. All of which suggests a perplexing question, a question I should like to put to Epicurus or Lucretius: why do men dread death and yet shun the facts of life? Why do they cling to life and yet find it a task to pass the time?

Let no one accuse me, however, of desultory moralizing. I am trying to arrive at a sober psychological actuality. Lévy-Bruhl tells us, with some exaggeration indeed, that the primitive man fails to distinguish fact from imagination. Modern science tells us that the civilized man, having achieved this distinction, has properly banished imagination. What I would suggest is that the world of the civilized man is no less a world of imagination, only (let us hope) of a more reflective imagination. Take the Victorian imagination once more. This is the world in which all of us have been educated who, lettered or relatively unlettered, represent in the United States the newly emphasized Anglo-Saxon tradition. This world of our imagination underlies our sense of values, but no less our view of fact. It is a *world* unknown to the immigrant from Continental Europe; and hardly less, I fear, to our undergraduate sons; who tell us coolly that Thackeray or George Eliot may be good enough for the older generation but not for them. But what shall we do about it? Shall we see that the younger generation is educated in a world of sober fact, and thus spared the intellectual weakness of a mind burdened with tradition and imagination? Alas! Only the lower animals have no tradition; and they, as I have suggested, live in no world whatever.

And if it then be our task only to separate imagination from fact, I think we shall be surprised by the magnitude of the task. Every moderately educated person carries with him as a part of his mental furniture some sort of history of mankind. I wonder how much of this has come from a study of sober history. How much of the *history* of the Victorian period has not come to us through the Victorian novels? And what else do most persons in this country know about the English people? Yet they do not doubt—and it is a question why they should—that the people whom they thus know are those who live in England; as little as those of us who have met the Russians only in the pages of Tolstoi or Tourgenieff or Dostoievsky doubt that we have some real knowledge of the Russians. We all think that we have a knowledge of the history of the race; and this knowledge is history and not poetry; yet which of us in his conception of the life of the race can distinguish the history from the poetry?

Yet in this kind of historical and geographical world we have a comfortable sense of reality. The question whether Hamlet was really insane is a genuine question though referring only to the Hamlet of Shakespeare. Maggie Tulliver seems as real a person as George Eliot—Hamlet is certainly more real than Shakespeare. By the side of Major Pendennis, Napoleon seems, to me at least, rather legendary; and the Major seems to have more certainly the attribute of existence than half the people I read about in the daily paper.

It is only the academic historian who appears to have any real interest in separating imagination from fact. And of him we may ask, when imagination is finally excluded, what is left of the fact? Reading "The City of God" lately it seemed to me curious that Augustine, preaching the one and only true God, and explaining how the pagan gods were creatures of human imagination, still takes them naïvely as solemn realities; only not as gods indeed but as devils. But I remembered that in my schoolboy reading of Homer and Virgil the gods were certainly real even though my background was that of the Augustinian theology. The pagan gods had been superseded by Jehovah and Christ, but they were of the same order. And this leads me to ask what kind of mental activity it would be possible to sustain within the world of Homer and Virgil and the Greek tragedians, or within the Greek civilization generally, while retaining a clear consciousness of the fact that the gods were only—names. One thinks again of the world of mediaeval Europe as a world governed and ordered in a peculiarly intimate fashion by the Christian God. I wonder whether any scientific historian studying this period can fail to think of God as real for the time being; and how he could then cancel God from his reality and leave the rest of his story a story of the real world.

If I follow the suggestion of the natural scientist that he, rather than the historian, is the purveyor of solid facts (which are to be found in their most solid state in the sciences of physics and chemistry) I seem only to be confronted more than ever with—imagination. I have been looking lately into a text-book of physical chemistry, which science, I believe, claims above all others to reveal the nature of the hard and solid fact. What I found there was some very beautiful patterns of the arrangement of electrons, or ions, or what not, in the atoms of such substances as common salt. I could find nothing salty in these patterns. And indeed I should say that they differ somewhat more from what is presented to me as common salt or the like than the Paradise of Milton or the Delectable City of Bunyan or the Utopia of Sir Thomas More differs from what is presented to me as human life. I do not doubt that these physico-chemical patterns are fine products of thought and capable in a real sense of "verification". But then I have to wonder whether they alone among the products of human thought are capable of verification, and whether as products of imagination they are to be distinguished uniquely from its other products.

Such, then, if you please, is the substance of life. For if there be no experience apart from imagination, must we not say that there can likewise be no life, in men or in beasts, apart from imagination? Certainly, it seems, if the term "life" is to denote any experience of living. If we are then to think of the lower animals as living creatures it seems that we must after all grant them imagination of some kind or degree. For the presence of imagination will then mark the only difference between being alive and not being alive; and this means that it will mark the ultimate difference between life and matter.[1] If, on the

[1] Note the significance in common speech of "being alive" to a fact or an implication; and note also the ground of one's more instinctive appreciation of the presence of "life", say in a meadow occupied by horses and cattle through which you are passing. The fact that (and the degree in which) the animals manifest curiosity towards an intruder seems more conclusively an evidence of life than the fact that they reproduce their kind.

other hand, there may be life without experience of living, in the form of merely "organic" life, it seems that we are left with no essential difference between an organism and a mere mechanism. It would be very interesting indeed to examine this conception of organic life, which, based upon the triple classification of matter, life, and mind, would offer us a "life" which is neither matter nor mind, and an "animal" which is not "spiritual" and yet not "material". But since I am interested mainly in the "particular nature of man" and its implications, I will return to the difference between man and the lower animals.

§ 58

And once more let us remember that among the vast multitude of animal species man is the only animal who knows that he is an animal; he is the only animal who is also a biologist.[1] This statement has a wide range of implication. Man is the only animal that can be said to have a *history;* that is to say, the only animal that lives to-day in the light of accumulated racial experience. He is the only animal who has a *science;* the only animal who can survey the present fact in the light of facts that are temporally and spatially remote. He is the only animal who may properly be said to have a *society;* that is, the only animal who can be conceived to act here and now in the light of recognized relations to his absent fellows.

He is also the only animal who can be conceived to have any clear consciousness of *family relations.* Think of what the consciousness of family means in human life! Yet if it be a wise child that knows its own father it must surely be a wiser dog. The Australian blacks are said, by Spencer and Gillen, to be ignorant of this relation—though the claim is disputed by Andrew Lang. It may easily be seen, however, that the apprehension

---

[1] Some of what follows here is from my article on "Birth-Control and Biological Ethics" in *The International Journal of Ethics*, Oct., 1916.

THE SUBSTANCE OF LIFE

of this causal connection, between two events separated by a considerable interval of time, and under conditions of more or less promiscuity, calls for a fairly developed scientific imagination. One may wonder how soon, if the knowledge were lost, it would be rediscovered. And some degree of imagination must be attributed to the bitch who recognizes her pup as her own after the period of infancy is past. Hence it is much to be doubted if she does so.

In all of these relations it is the presence of imagination that determines what they are for us; and that determines the meaning of the words used to refer to them. To speak therefore of "animal marriage" or of "animal society", after the fashion of biological psychologists, is to leave Hamlet out of the play. "Marriage", for example, denotes indeed a sex-relation; but a sex-relation between two persons who have deliberately avowed a preference for one another; who expect their association to be permanent; who have purposely given their friends ground for the same expectation; who know that the sex-relation is to include a common household and a common social life; who doubtless expect to be common parents of children; who at any rate know that this is the natural outcome. It is precisely this *consciousness* of the situation that invests marriage with moral responsibility and gives significance to the word. To apply the term indifferently to the sex-relations of men and of animals suggests to me not so much a significant scientific generalization as an indulgence in rather naïve sentimentality.

In a word, then, as distinguished from the lower animals man is not merely more "developed", or more "efficient", or simply *more* of anything. He differs from all other species by the fact that he has a *culture;* which means that he offers the only case in the animal kingdom where the processes of life are surveyed and criticized from the standpoint of those in whom they are taking place. And this is to say once more that he is the only animal to whom we may in any significant sense apply the term "moral".

But then, just because he is the only moral being, man is the only animal who can be conceived to have a religion. Much mystery has been made of the origin of religion by those who find nothing mysterious in the presence of consciousness in the world. And if the mind be conceived as a photographic reproduction of the natural world, then surely the ideas of God, heaven, and immortality; or of a Platonic supersensible, or metaphysical world; of Kantian things-in-themselves underlying their appearances, or phenomena—in brief, all ideas of a realm transcending the realm of sense will constitute a mystery. How shall we account for the idea of the supernatural in a world purely natural? It seems that the mystery can only be explained —according to one's logic of explanation—by recourse to special revelation on the one hand; or on the other to such counterfeit sense-impressions (from the naturalistic point of view—though naturalistically explicable) as dreams and visions of ghosts.

For one who reflects upon "the particular nature of man" it seems to me that neither explanation is necessary; and there is no mystery—no mystery beyond the mystery of consciousness itself. For imagination, as I suggested above, is not an automatic anticipation of fact; as when, by association, I expect the sun to rise to-morrow or rain to follow thunder. Imagination means that we not only anticipate the fact but criticize the fact; and therefore that we can look for a more satisfactory substitute for the fact. Accordingly, to explain the presence in human thought of the idea of another world and another life we have only to fix our attention upon the fact that man alone among the animals knows that he is to die. I do not deny that animals have experience of dead bodies. Like ourselves they eat them. Yet how many persons entering a butcher's shop feel themselves in the presence of death? Nor do I deny that animals shrink from death—at least from situations which we know to be fatal to them. This does not mean that they know what they are shrinking from. It calls for a somewhat extended reflection to know that death is the end of life ; and especially to realize that this applies to you and me. The primitive man, it seems, does not know this. He has not grasped the fact of *natural* death. When his friend dies, he asks, Who did it ? Who cast a spell upon him ? It is one of the seemingly ironical products of culture that in so far as we advance in the examined life, we live our lives in a shadow of certain death of which the unimaginative creatures can know nothing. The social device of banning death as a topic of polite conversation only reveals the shadow in the background.

And therefore as between the pre-evolutionary view which distinguished man as having an immortal soul and the evolutionary view which translates his soul into a competitive biological organ, or function, like the horns of the bull or the speed of the deer, I would point out that the older is after all the truer view for any insight into human nature—whatever be suggested by the external study of man as a biological species. Man is the only animal who can form an idea of a life beyond this, of a spiritual world beyond the world of nature. Not only can he form this idea, logically he must form it if he forms an idea of nature herself.[1] And by a logic no less inevitable he must protest against death. It seems to me therefore strictly true to say—precisely from the standpoint of "human nature"—that *man is by nature immortal*, even though we say that he is mortal as a matter of fact. Religious belief is no accident of sense-experience, due to ghosts or dreams. It is the inevitable suggestion of any reflective life.

[1] I have in mind here the argument by which T. H. Green shows, in his *Prolegomena to Ethics*, that the idea of a natural world is possible only for a consciousness—for a person—who distinguishes himself from nature and therefore himself transcends nature.

§ 59

It is this intrinsic connection of religion with the life of a conscious being which (as I venture to conceive the situation) sets for us the central and ultimate problem of all being ; the problem of the genuineness of morality, the problem of the meaning of life, the problem of religion, and the major problem of philosophy. For let us remember that if consciousness were not essentially imaginative, at once creative and critical, if mind were indeed only a matter of photographic reproduction, extended by a process of association, then the problem of life would be solely a technical problem. It would be a problem of adjustment among *given* values and *given* facts—a problem of finding among the past experiences that which has been shown to fit the present fact—and not any problem of giving a meaning to life. And the problem of comprehending the world as a whole, which is one way of stating the problem of philosophy, would be the distinctively scientific problem of ordering facts under laws, with never a suggestion of any ulterior reality underlying the fact.

But to grasp the full meaning of the problem we need a larger background than the contrast between human and animal life, larger again than the world of animate nature. For in this world of animate nature we are still relatively at home, within the relatively familiar and intelligible ; and we may easily forget how insignificant, from any external view, is this world in the universe at large. The full scope of the problem is suggested in that widely quoted saying of Kant that the two things most sublime within our imagination are "the starry firmament above us" and "the moral law within us". I wonder how many persons pause to ask what it means to put these two things within a single sentence.

A few years ago I listened to a distinguished astronomer while for two hours, to an unwearied audience, he explained what had been revealed by the latest developments of the reflecting telescope. As he unfolded step by step the vastness beyond all previous imagination of that silent universe, apparently lifeless, mindless, godless, the picture became ever more fascinating, but to me ever more oppressive and horrible. I admired the courage which enabled one to be an astronomer. At the close of his lecture he paused for an impressive moment, and then, to the astonishment of all, he recited, with the eloquence of a perfect sincerity, the psalm beginning with, "The heavens declare the glory of God and the firmament showeth his handiwork." If I could convey the effect of this to my reader I should have given him the problem in all of its dramatic significance. How can one—I will not say that one cannot—but how does one face modern astronomy and yet believe in God?

For it is in the contemplation of the astronomical universe that we face the deeper mystery of our existence; and of this universe, not as displayed in the calm beauty of a star-lit night, but as unfolded by the science of astronomy. Here we are bidden to remember that the earth, which is to us so vast, is but one of the minor planets in one of countless systems; that only very recently, geologically and astronomically speaking, has the earth supported life, and yet that the human race has existed for hundred thousands, possibly millions, of years. But only for a few thousand years does the race seem to have been very human or to have had any clear consciousness of itself as a race; and of the millions upon millions of souls who have lived during this historic period, for each of whom doubtless, as for you and me, his own life and the fate of his own soul has seemed to be the central and important fact of the universe, the names of only a few survive. What, then, does the world know about you or me? What indeed is the whole realm of life but a fortuitous concourse of atoms at one point in an infinity of space and time?

Man, as I have said above, is the only animal who knows that he is an animal; and this to him means that he is the only important animal. Yet I have sometimes wondered whether this self-consciousness might not mean only that of all animals man is the most ridiculous and contemptible.

And one may imagine—though whether one may, is precisely the question—an ironical snail or oyster who, accepting the starry heavens above him, thanks God that he at least has no illusions of importance and has been spared the temptation to think of himself as other than he is.

And yet again "the moral law within us". My one purpose in this volume has been to present to the reader's imagination, and to get into my own, all that is implied in "the moral law"—so vastly more, I believe, than is suspected in any of the common talk about "sound morality". As I see it the moral law means nothing less than the supreme and exclusive importance of the conscious life—of the person. Nothing is good, it asserts with Kant, but the good will. And with this assertion the moral law faces the starry heavens above and rejects all compromise—all of those utilitarian compromises which would reconcile life to fact by a renunciation of the meaning of life, all those which would make the consciousness of life an instrument of "life". "The moral law" asserts the supreme value of the conscious life for its own sake; and therefore the supreme value of each person for his own sake. With Kant once more, each is to be regarded always as an end in himself, never as a means. This implies a truly "social" world; and what is much more, a social universe, a universe in which we may in some sense expect to find God. But this only means again that in the social universe each person is all-important.

How can this assertion be made in the presence of the starry heavens above us—as the nature of the heavens is revealed by astronomical science? How can the starry heavens and the moral law both be sublime? For if anything be sublime it must at least be real. Yet if the firmament of science be sublime—which for science can mean only that it is big—the moral law looks like an accident; nay less, an illusion. And if the moral law be sublime the firmament of science seems similarly an illusion.

Or may we say that the scientific firmament is a peculiar and limited version of a universe which in the end, understood as we understand the life of our human fellows, is the expression of the same moral law that we find in ourselves ? This, I suspect, was in Kant's mind when he declared the moral law and the starry heavens to be both sublime.

And thus among the many problems set by the presence of the moral law is the problem of truth and reality, the problem of knowledge. Life is an activity of imagination ; the world in which we live is a world of imagination ; is it therefore an imaginary world ?

CHAPTER XV

THE EXPERIENCE OF TRUTH

§ 60. The man of science and the man of culture. § 61. " Mere ideas " and the picture-psychology. § 62. " Mere feelings." § 63. Science and anthropomorphic prejudice. § 64. Truth and satisfied imagination. § 65. Error and lack of imagination. § 66. Experience of reality *vs.* coherence and correspondence.

IMPORTANT among the moral questions as here conceived is the question, What is truth ? In the answers commonly given it seems that truth is an impersonal *relation*: a relation of coherence among our ideas, for one view ; for the other a relation of correspondence between ideas and facts. For these views it seems that truth is not a moral question—rather perhaps an "intellectual" question. I may then distinguish the moral question by asking, What is the *experience* of truth ?

But this will compel us to ask, What is the experience of "ideas"? And of "feelings"? And for the purpose of stating all of these questions I will suggest the following situation.

§ 60

Let us suppose that we have before us, in a college catalogue, the long list of courses constituting a modern curriculum. Half of the courses bear titles that are more or less unintelligible, each of them is to be identified in the end only by its number. The catalogue does not thus far seem to be very lively reading or at first glance very significant. Yet a moment's reflection will tell us that what lies here listed before us is the greater part of the many and various developments or expressions of the human spirit.

And what the curriculum would represent if it could, is a *tout ensemble* of reflective human life.

If we now go a step further we shall find that by common consent these studies are divided roughly into two classes, known respectively as the sciences and the humanities; or as scientific studies and culture studies. Typical scientific studies are physics, chemistry, and biology. Typical culture studies are languages with their literatures—in a word, literary criticism; but also art and art criticism; and properly also (though not often found in the college curriculum) music and musical criticism. But to these we should add the study of philosophy, so far at least as philosophy includes moral philosophy, the philosophy of beauty, or the philosophy of religion. And thus we find on the one side science; on the other literature and poetry, art, music, morality, religion. On the one side (let us say for the moment) knowledge; on the other, taste, feeling, and insight. It seems, then, that in the distinction of science and culture we have two worlds of discourse. By Royce they are named the world of description and the world of appreciation. By others the world of facts and the world of values. Having in mind the foregoing chapter I prefer to call them here the world of fact and the world of imagination.

What, then, is the difference? Putting this question to a professor of science, he will probably answer as follows. All of these studies, he may admit, stand for operations of the human spirit. Science no less than the other studies has a human history. But in science—and in science alone—the spirit does more than operate; it operates *upon* something. It grasps something which is other than itself. In other words, science is knowledge of reality. In these other fields of the spirit all that happens is a movement of the spirit within itself; a movement which at best yields pleasing images, ideas, or feelings—objectively, fiction. The not too developed scientific conscience may tolerate these diversions of the spirit as a kind of justifiable relief from the strain of scientific thought. The more resolute scientist condemns them in his heart as a sinful waste of time, and if unrestrained by the academic amenities he would probably explain that the proper place for a professor of literature is not in a university but in a sanatorium.[1]

In a word, then, the world of science is a revelation of truth and reality; the world of imagination (as I prefer to call the other world) is a world of *mere* ideas and *mere* feelings.

The attitude of the professor of literature towards the professor of science is probably no less supercilious (in his heart—for he too is restrained by the academic amenities), though in these days less confident. For him, however, I suspect that the scientist is no better than a carpenter or a clever machinist. The professor of literature feels that he himself has a grasp of something which the scientist has missed, and the scientist is then set down as "lacking in finer spiritual insight". Insight into what? Well, at any rate, insight into human nature. In other words, science is not the only knowledge; criticism is also knowledge, knowledge indeed of human nature and human life. There is nothing in the whole range of literature, poetry, art, religion, which is not such knowledge. But it seems that more than this is involved. It is hardly a satisfying theory of poetry to say that poets are occupied in describing to one another their personal states of mind. Rather, it would be said, their insight; insight into a reality which may be variously described as a realm of ideas, a world of imagination, a spiritual world including and also transcending the human world. The professor of literature, I say, is somewhat less confident to-day than the professor of science, but at bottom we may suppose him to be cherishing the conviction (vital, it would seem, for any critical justification of his profession) that his world of imagination is somehow not less objectively real—rather it is more truly real than

[1] To those who suspect me of exaggeration I will say that such is precisely the kind of recommendation made by a philosopher, an unbending exponent of the scientific point of view, for the benefit of those who differed with him, at a meeting of the American Philosophical Association not half a dozen years ago.

the scientist's world of fact. If so there are no "mere ideas"

And so, Are there "mere ideas"? Such, it seems to me, is the deeper question involved in any issue of knowledge and truth. And the question includes the other question, Are there "mere feelings"? I shall meet the question by proposing the following disjunction: either the ideas (or feelings) in question are an insight into reality—into a reality which, like the reality which science claims to reveal, is other than ourselves—or they are no "ideas" whatever, but bare words or other vehicles of expression.

§ 61

No one, I will venture to say, has ever experienced a mere idea. Modern philosophy, following Descartes' *Cogito, ergo sum*, has been full of the notion that, while we may doubt the existence of the things to which our ideas refer, we can never doubt the existence of the ideas themselves; and its ever-recurring scepticism has been, How can we assert the existence of anything except mere ideas? And yet if I ask you what is a chair you will easily tell me, but if I ask you what is an idea of a chair, and how it differs from a chair, you will be at a loss to reply. It seems that these most certain entities are the hardest to locate or describe.

Regarded as an entity, an idea is no more to be found in human experience than the atom of physical science. As a matter of experience we may say that the idea of a tree is one among the other aspects of our experience of the tree. It is that aspect which is suggested by such adjectives as "clearness", "distinctness", "familiarity". The physical or "real "tree is of course neither more nor less "distinct", neither more nor less "familiar". When, however, I speak of an idea of a tree as a duplicate of the real tree I am resorting to a metaphor for the purpose of adjusting certain difficulties presented by a comparison of your experience of the tree with mine. When I myself see a tree what I see is just a tree ; not any idea of a tree. But when I observe your seeing a tree—and most of what I observe is that you look at it—then I have to wonder how you can see the tree, at least the tree that I see. For that tree is thirty feet high, and how it can get through your eye, and your smaller optic nerve, and so on, is more than I can understand. Moreover, you sometimes claim to see a tree when for me there is no tree there. To settle these difficulties (rather than to explain them), I find it convenient to assume that what you directly perceive is not the tree but a symbol, or representative, of the tree—something like a picture, a banknote, a baggage-check, or a poker-chip, the function of which is to represent. Upon this assumption rest the theory of representative perception and the correspondence-theory, or copy-theory, of truth.

Among the possible representative metaphors the picture is the nearly universal choice. It is hardly too much to say that for common sense and for science alike the idea is just a picture—qualified, however, as a "mental picture" or a "mental image". Upon this metaphorical basis is built most of the traditional psychology, especially that which makes a special claim to be "empirical", to communicate the facts of mind just as they are. This view, which makes of human life a gallery of pictures exhibited in succession, has been stigmatized by Bergson as the "cinematograph-psychology"; a comparison so apt in detail that we might almost conceive the cinema to have been invented for the purpose of objectifying the traditional view of mind. The synthesis of a succession of instantaneous pictures into an experience of motion illustrates precisely, when the process is reversed, the method by which for two centuries past psychologists have "analysed" all of the life of the soul into coexistences and successions of atomic "mental states". As an explanatory metaphor, however, even the simple picture has a unique advantage. For it seems to us that pictures represent their object necessarily and inevitably. Their representative function is not a matter of convention as in the case of a poker-chip or baggage-check.

At the same time there may be a picture to which no reality corresponds; it will then be a "mere picture". Accordingly, by furnishing the soul with pictures we seem to explain, not only how our ideas always seem to be significant (as they might not seem if they were thought of as poker-chips), but how we may have significant ideas which are yet only "mere ideas". "Mere ideas", of course, are "mere pictures".

What I will say, then, is that in our human experience there are, and can be, no mere ideas, mere pictures, or mere symbols. The purpose of the picture-psychology is to offer a "scientific" theory of mind which will dispense with the person, that is, with the activity of "apperception", or of imagination. But apart from the activity of imagination a symbol is not a symbol, a picture is not a picture; and it "represents" nothing. As a brute fact a picture of course knows nothing; it is the person looking at it who knows. The plausibility of the picture-psychology, with its apparatus of mental "images suggesting one another", all rests upon the idea that pictures are somehow natural conveyors of knowledge. Yet a little reflection must show that the idea is the fruit of sheer innocence; of an innocence comparable only with that of an unlettered person who wonders at the stupidity of a man, though he be born French or German, who derives no intelligence from plain English; or of the innocence (of one of us perhaps) who, surveying a page of Chinese, doubts gravely whether true intelligence could ever be expressed in anything of that kind. I think many persons must have noted that a very young child—say, a child between one and two years old, and thus quite old enough to distinguish many of the objects about him—derives nothing from a picture. Show him a picture of his mother, and he smiles wonderingly in reply. The late Carl Lumholtz tells us that the Australian blacks saw nothing in a photograph of himself. And what, then, of ourselves? I think we are all inclined to wonder how the cave-man, or the child of four or five, could suppose his crude sketches of animals to be representative of reality. And in looking at a Japanese print I can only wonder what idea or scheme of representation the artist had in mind. It does not easily occur to me that, unconscious of any scheme of representation, he might regard this as only the natural way of presenting the object. And yet why should he not? In brief a picture or an image is one kind of symbol—one kind of language—among others. It has no more meaning *per se*, and no more self-evident cognitive power, than the Morse Code. For it is only imagination that knows.

And this means that so far as imagination is awake and active we no longer merely "have a picture"; we face reality. This is true even when in the physical sense we are facing a picture. I hold, for example, in my hand a photograph of Westminster Abbey upon which my eyes are resting. From a physical point of view the facts are simple. But now when I reproduce the photograph in a *mental* picture (so to speak) and say that I have also a picture of the Abbey *in my mind*, the whole situation is dissolved. For so far as the picture I am assumed to have fulfils its functions as a picture I no longer "have" anything. I *see* Westminster Abbey. Or better, I *am in the presence of the Abbey;* and thus far the Abbey is not *re*presented but presented. On the other hand so far as the picture is in evidence—so far as I only "have a picture" of the Abbey—I have not even a picture. To say, in other words, that I am not in the presence of the Abbey but only in the presence of the picture is to reduce that picture to the meaningless thing it would be if I could view it with what the draftsman calls "the innocence of the eye", and see it, no longer as a picture, in perspective, but only as a certain distribution of light and shade.

There are certain ingenious stereoscopic pictures which illustrate the point nicely. Viewing them with the naked eye all that I can make out as an uninitiated observer is a rather complicated tangle of straight lines, all now in one

THE EXPERIENCE OF TRUTH

plane—not a picture of anything. I shall be told, however, that this tangle is a picture in perspective of a rather simple arrangement of lines, or threads, in three dimension. And when I survey the card through the stereoscope (but only then if imagination gives the cue) suddenly the perspective meaning of the picture is revealed. I use the word "revealed" because this word alone is just to the dramatic contrast between the two experiences. But now in this second experience it is quite false to say that I "have a picture". A picture, let us remember, is all in one plane. But what I now see is in three dimensions and in several planes, nearer or more remote with reference to myself. In brief, I *am* in the midst of an objective situation.

The printed page is another illustration. I am reading Doughty's "Arabia Deserta" in the quiet of the midnight hour before going to bed. If I chance to grow dull and sleepy, then what I find before me is just a printed page. But while imagination remains awake I *am* in the Arabian desert even though I am also in my easy chair.

And therefore my thesis : there are no mere ideas. All experience of mind is insight ; and thus, as experience, an apprehension of a reality other than myself. The possibility so often suggested in modern philosophy that our whole world may be nothing but "mere idea" and all consciousness illusion, is meaningless for mental experience. It presupposes that mental life is life in a picture gallery. This view of mind, as I have pointed out, is the fruit, not of experience of mind, but of observation of mind, rather of observation of behaviour, of other persons. It is thus not more nearly related to the experienced realities of mind than the observation of toothache is related to having a toothache, or the observation of love to being in love. The question as I am thinking of it is not how it looks to have a mind but (if you please) how it feels—what it is to *be* conscious. For one who is conscious there are no subjective "mental states" waiting to be attached, on the one hand to a knowing person, on the other hand to a thing known. In any degree whatever in which you are conscious you are aware, however vaguely, of a distinction and a relation between yourself, a knowing person, and a known which is other than yourself. Any one who thinks is just so far a person confronted with reality.

This means that consciousness, or spirit, is not in any sense a "state" as digestion is a state; or if a state, consciousness is a state of knowing something other than myself. Nor is consciousness an "effect", the effect of an external object stamping itself upon a *tabula rasa ;* or if an effect, it is an effect which, as a consciousness of effect, somehow knows not only itself but the system of things constituting its cause. Nor is consciousness a "reaction" (to speak with the vulgar). If a reaction, consciousness is at any rate a reaction which knows why and to what it reacts. As against these banalities of popular psychology, I turn rather to Walter Pater's characterization of the mind as essentially "vision". Yet this too may be misleading. It may be that vision, as the best developed of our senses, is highly significant for the nature and meaning of all. But mere vision seems to me too cool, too dry, too possibly superficial and disconnected from all of the other functions that make up our spiritual being—through which also we apprehend the various natures of objects—to stand alone as the mark of the spirit. And therefore I prefer the term "insight"—imaginative insight.

§ 62

Just as there are no mere ideas, so likewise are there no mere feelings. And not even for the earth-worm—who for popular thought stands close to the boundary between mere physiology and the least possible psychology, and is said to have a vague sort of feeling, but no cognition. Put yourself, then, in the place of such a worm crawling up, after the rain, between the bricks, and just over the edge of a brick, of an old-fashioned sidewalk. Now of course he does not know the brick as we know it, as the product of a brickyard. But what does he feel? If he feels the brick then it seems that thus far he knows that a brick, or something, is there determining for him his scene of action. Or does he feel, not the brick, but only the worm? If so, he is gifted with remarkable powers of abstraction. Or does he feel no difference between the brick and the worm? In that case he feels nothing; and there is no feeling, but only (say) digestion.

Pain again is insight; indeed a most illuminating insight. Those who keep personal feeling and knowledge of fact in separate psychological compartments should tell us what could be known of the world by a creature which had never suffered pain. The crudest bodily pain is an apprehension of a fact; of a disturbance located somewhere, and never indifferently in tooth or toe. Any pain contains indefinite possibilities of vision. In my own very slight experience of pain I recall an instance, not very tragic as a matter of pain, which amounted to a kind of conversion. At the climax of a splitting headache, just before pain yielded to the sleep of exhaustion, and just as I began to wonder, somewhat impersonally, how a head that throbbed like mine could much longer hold together, my mind seemed suddenly opened to the terrific possibilities of sentience in all organic matter; to sentience indeed as essentially inherent in all matter whatsoever; suggesting, not very cheerfully at that moment, that our human sentience is but the tiniest drop in a world of sentient experience. In the same moment I seemed to see before me the tragic experience lying behind the daily record of accident, suicide, murder, even of divorces and of strikes; and for the first time it occurred to me that a pessimistic philosophy of life might have something to say for itself; at any rate that one who had reached the pessimistic conclusion need not be merely a fool. I dare say I am here only recording the experience of many another. The next morning we forget. Does this mean that the vision was wholly false?

But this is to suggest once more that all distinctions

between sane and morbid vision, between normal and abnormal views of life, are mainly conventional. And if I were writing a theory of knowledge it would be my chief purpose to show that standards of truth and reality have the same utilitarian status as standards of morality. It is needless of course to deny the comfortableness for all ordinary moods of the society of sane persons—if they are not too obstinately sane. And I suppose that as a worldly-wise parent I should counsel my son to prefer as his wife a sane and sensible woman to a spiritual genius. But this only shows in the end that by sanity we mean a convenient similarity or communicableness of temperament and point of view. In the last analysis there are at least as many types of sanity in the world as there are languages; of which your type of sanity or mine is only one. No Anglo-Saxon, I will repeat, can think of a Frenchman as either quite sane or quite moral; and in French literature the Englishman is treated always as a creature strangely, if also splendidly, barbaric. Yet it is certainly a contradiction in terms, a *reductio ad absurdum*, to condemn a whole people—for example, the Russian people—as "morbid". But why, then, visit this condemnation upon any single sentient soul just because he happens to be different? That may mean that he can see what the rest of us fail to see. Surely this has happened often enough in the history of the race.

Hence I am disposed to think of each individual organism, of each peculiarity of personal temperament, and of each individual fate as a special opportunity for insight into reality. This applies not alone to "morbid" temperaments, but no less to exceptionally glad and happy natures, and perhaps conspicuously to such exceptionally "vital" personalities as Shakespeare and Goethe. If poverty and disease are revealing, leisure and vital abundance may be no less so. Yet the morbid temperaments are possibly the more instructive because theirs are the deliverances which are most likely to be questioned. It is therefore well to remember that if a man is blind, or crippled, or otherwise

THE EXPERIENCE OF TRUTH 225

debarred from participation in common social activities, this may mean only that some of his senses are exceptionally acute, or that he is exceptionally placed for reflection upon life, and possibly even for stimulating his fellows to a sense of the meaning of their own lives. In a curious book of some thirty years ago, J. F. Nisbet[1] sought to prove from a comprehensive survey of men of genius that all men of genius are potentially insane, at least in the sense that genius is inseparable from a morbid excitability. So much, however, was suspected before. Genius, we might say (after Croce), is only a peculiarly intensified consciousness of life. We may therefore reasonably ask whether an absolutely sane person would be quite a human being.

A highly interesting study in this connection is the Russian novelist Dostoievsky. Dostoievsky was an epileptic. The epileptic fits, I have read somewhere, began, or began to be periodic, after an exceptionally racking experience. Dostoievsky was stationed, blindfolded, with three others, to be shot as a political criminal, and the word to fire had almost been given when the reprieve came and he was sent to Siberia. It is significant that one of his companions went mad on the spot. Dostoievsky's novels, all written after that date, are morbid, I suppose, if anything is morbid; though I think that their morbidity may be exaggerated by a too impressionistic reading. Read carefully, they reveal not only marvellous powers of perception but shrewd judgment. It is recorded by Merejkowsky[2] that each epileptic fit was the climax of an intensely impetuous mental activity, accompanied by an exceptional clarity of vision. Now I have never enjoyed the experience of an epileptic fit, but in former days it was a frequent experience to discover that an exhilarating sense of mental power was the forerunner of a prostrating nervous headache. But what of it ? I suppose that few of us

[1] *The Insanity of Genius.*
[2] *Tolstoi as Man and Artist; with an Essay on Dostoievsky.* English translation, N.Y., 1902.

would care to purchase intensity of vision at the cost of epilepsy. But granting that intensity of vision is a morbid "effect", does it follow that the vision is any the less true? Does it not rather follow that epilepsy is exceptionally revealing?

If indeed we are to speak of cause and effect in this connection, then we must note that normal experience is the effect of normal conditions and every experience an effect of something. The solution of a mathematical problem may be the effect of a night's rest or a cup of tea; the solution is not therefore to be suspected. Intellectual clarity after days of dull and hopeless perplexity may be the effect of a cathartic; the clearness will be none the less objective. And thoughts of love are none the less of true love because they are induced by the moonlight. When persons forget themselves they may reveal themselves— even to themselves. Nor is it a final condemnation to say that this or that judgment is the effect of a prejudice. If prejudices are blinding, they are none the less revealing. A man's enemies are at least well equipped to detect his weaknesses. And on the other hand the mother, who in the daily round of getting the child up and putting him to bed sees him in his most intimate moments, is better situated than others to grasp the uniqueness of his individual personality—which need not, however, be imposed as an article of faith upon visiting bachelors.

§ 63

For the scientific or matter-of-fact point of view the participation of temperament or feeling in cognition means that reality is viewed "through a medium"; and every medium is *per se* a distortion. Or it suggests the taint of "anthropomorphism"; man creates nature, the world, God, in his own image. But in whose image, I am obliged to ask, can God be made intelligible to man? In whose image can he speak to man? Shall we say, in no image? In no language? In terms purely impersonal? One could better comprehend the possibility of impersonal, unmotived and "mediumless" thinking if science would furnish an example. For myself, I am impressed rather by the very palpable presence of human motive—of the soberly practical and business-like sort, however, or else of the engineering sort—mechanicomorphic rather than anthropomorphic—in all scientific thinking. And it seems to me that Bergson's suggestion—that the mechanical theory of life, which construes organic development as a series of distinct operations, like a factory-system, is a reflection of man the machinist—amounts virtually to a demonstration. Yet I would not deny that the mechanical theory may in the end embody one of the possible ways of describing the process of life.

As for the unwearied delight of scientific men in simplicity of formulation, and in the "law of parsimony", which implies that the simplest statement is the truest—well, I would not deny the (to me tautological) statement that truth must be in some sense "simple" to be intelligible; but it strikes me as a huge anthropomorphism to suppose that simple statements are distinctively statements of reality. This assumes that nature has kindly shaped herself to the measure of our understanding. One might rather suppose that simple statements would be suspicious.

Whatever else science may be, it remains, I should say, a medium, a method, a convention, a point of view, no less humanly motived in its own way than other points of view, but one among others and no less potentially distorting. And when science makes the exclusive claim to be authenticated by facts it is well to remember that only those facts authenticate which are communicated and put together, and that if an age be sufficiently dominated by the scientific convention none will be communicated (if even perceived) which fails to authenticate. In the Middle Ages I fancy that most of the facts authenticated the biblical tradition. And though I have no lively faith in "psychic phenomena", yet when I find so many men in their more confidential moments (when encouraged by a similarly confidential attitude in others) avowing experiences of the "psychic" sort, I am compelled to wonder whether there may not be here an immense field of experience which is not communicated. At any rate it seems clear that science like any other convention may play the part of a Freudian "repression".

This, I will beg the reader to note, is not to reinstate the crude anthropomorphism of primitive man. There is all the difference in the world between thinking that knows that it is anthropomorphic and thinking that does not know, between thinking that knows that it is prejudiced and thinking that is blissfully unaware of prejudice. The primitive man does not know that his thinking is anthropomorphic—it is we who know that. And I fear that the man of science very often does not know; at least he commonly refuses to admit that the presuppositions of science have logically the status of human prejudices. It is through the consciousness of prejudice that we escape the bondage of prejudice, through the consciousness of temperament that temperament reveals. As Socrates taught long ago, it is precisely our knowledge of self that opens our eyes to an objective reality. We can never possibly view the world from other than a human or a temperamental point of view, but we may perhaps discover what our point of view is; and then we shall know what our temperament discovers in the world. This I conceive to be the true meaning of the critical process, so far as it has gone, whereby science has freed us from primitive superstition. Yet howsoever sophisticated, our thinking remains human thinking; and when our thinking ceases to be human it will cease to be thinking.

§ 64

To say that all consciousness is insight does not mean that all thought and feeling are indifferently true—not any more at least than to say that all conscious action is moral action means that all conscious action is indifferently moral. For the distinction between truth and error I may then remind the reader of Chapter XII, wherein it was shown that all moral distinctions are distinctions in the degree of self-consciousness. In like fashion is the distinction of truth and error a distinction of self-consciousness. That want is good which after criticism, challenge, trial and error if you please, knows what it wants; and that insight is true which after a similar ordeal knows what it means. It is true, in other words, *so far as* it knows what it means. From this relativity (if it be such) there is no escape within human life. The distinction between error and truth is then a distinction between before and after a given process of criticism. And just as there is no standard of morality, so is there no standard of truth. The final question about a want is, Do I still want it after knowing what it is I want? And the final question about a meaning is, Do I still mean it after knowing what I mean? And just as a want that admits defeat by criticism is shown really to have wanted nothing—not indeed to have been a want, but only some kind of bodily reaction—so is a similarly defeated meaning shown to have meant nothing. And then I was not thinking but only talking.

Not *thinking*, I say. In the sense to be attached to this word lies the point of the whole matter. For "thinking" seems to suggest "ideas". And the term "idea", very convenient for marking off a subject of discourse, has a doubtful connotation. Almost inevitably it suggests "abstract ideas", "mathematical thinking", thought divorced from imagination; and thought divorced from imagination is for me simply words. Any *experience* of thinking is concrete thinking. "Thinking in images", it is sometimes called, but for me thinking *about something*, thinking directed upon some more or less definite subject-matter—or object-matter. And with Berkeley I am obliged to say that whenever I think about a man, it is about some definite man, or men, each with definite qualities.

To think is then to imagine. But this is not to imagine anything you please. And therefore I dispute that statement of Berkeley in which he says that "I can imagine a man with two heads, or the upper parts of a man joined to the body of a horse". The latter, for example, I can easily enough *say*. But when I come to imagine how the insides of the man are joined to the insides of the horse I find myself in trouble and confusion. And then I discover that I am not at all imagining a real man and a real horse but a stone man and a stone horse which I have seen joined in some gallery of sculpture.

Accordingly, I will answer the question about truth by saying that *experience of truth is the experience of a satisfied critical imagination.* Or I might say that truth lies in *fullness* of *critical* imagination. If imagination is full it is bound to be critical—try to join the insides of the man and of the horse and you will have questions in plenty. And imagination can hardly be critical unless it be full. When Mill tells us that he can conceive of a round square, he offers plenty of opportunity for assertion and counter-assertion but little to think about.

This means that the experience of truth is neither the logician's experience of truth nor the scientist's experience; neither of which I can recognize as a personal experience. It comes nearer to the conception of artistic truth, or poetic truth; or, if you please, of moral truth. And this truth I hold to be an insight into reality.

Hence truth is, once more, a matter of criticism, just as (as shown in Chapter XII) morality is a matter of criticism. And criticism, in morality, in art, in logic, is a search for thought, vision, inspiration, behind or in the form of expression. A year or two ago it occurred to me to look again at Poe's "Raven", which had thrilled me as a boy, and which I had not read in many years, to see if I could find any meaning in it. Perhaps it was because the hour was late and I was sleepy, but I found little. But the illustration will enable me to put the truth-situation

THE EXPERIENCE OF TRUTH

simply, if baldly. Does the croaking of the raven, viewed critically, convey to you the vision of a dim, mysterious, unearthly realm? Is there any meaning in his "Nevermore"? If so, I suggest, that realm is objectively real. And if it be not real there is no meaning and the raven is only croaking.

§ 65

If this is truth, then what is error? Many a theory of truth has been shattered by this mischievous question. But the question is so important that, although I am not offering here a systematic theory of knowledge, I turn aside for a moment to suggest the answer—by means of a single illustration. The answer is that (if truth is a matter of imagination) error is a lack of imagination.

And as an illustration I will take the classical puzzle of the bent stick—the stick half immersed in water which appears broken. We may distinguish several stages of sophistication. At what we may call the lowest stage (to which some present philosophers would have us return) a man may say simply that the stick *is* broken by the water—and makes itself straight again in coming out of the water. But this view would be quickly dissipated by the suggestion, among others, that under the same circumstances one's leg does not feel broken. The view is too unsophisticated for modern reflection.

At a higher stage of sophistication, the stage reached, let us say, by common intelligence of to-day—also, I suspect, the stage at which many of our standard "illusions" are defined as such—at this stage the bent stick is described as an illusion. By this it is meant that I do not see the stick as it really is or as I ought to see it. But a little further reflection should show that this view is itself an illusion, in the sense that it marks an imperfect imagination. If I see the stick other than bent, or broken, it seems there must be something amiss with my eyes. The view is unconscious and lacking in imagination in two respects. First, it takes no account of the circumstance that half of the stick has passed from air to water. In other words, it takes no account of refraction; and this because the difference of medium, easily perceptible as fact, has somehow failed to suggest any questions. Secondly, it assumes naïvely that the stick in air is the real or standard stick—as if in a world where perception occurs under such a variety of conditions a standardized way of seeing things could be anything but a useful convention. When these considerations are introduced the "illusion" disappears. I ought, it seems, to see the stick broken when it is half immersed.

But there is a conceivably higher stage of sophistication at which this now asserted "ought" will itself prove doubtful. Suppose that a man had worked the experiences of refraction so completely into his imagination as to be immediately conscious under all circumstances of the nature of the medium of vision and of its precise effect upon the image of the object. This would mean that with equal immediacy he could see the precise effect of substituting any other medium. He would then have reached the stage of sophistication of the skilled musician who plays in one key what is written in another and finds it unnecessary to transpose the score in writing. At this stage one key is as good as another, one medium as true as another. Yet there remains the distinction of truth and error—you must not mix the keys. And this distinction is solid and real so far as unsophistication is solid and real. Error is thus real. Its reality is none the less resolvable into a lack of imagination; into a failure to reflect that all vision is mediumed vision, standard vision with the rest, and a corresponding failure to note what your standard medium is.

But all of this is to suggest that the current scientific and every-day view of things, which lives by the habit of standards, is of necessity highly conventional and thus far very incompletely sophisticated.

§ 66

The picture-theory of mind, as I pointed out above, implies the correspondence-theory of truth as opposed to the coherence-theory. In this opposition we have the traditional antithesis of fact and idea, of induction and deduction, of verification by fact as a criterion of truth *versus* consistency of idea. Truth as fullness of critical imagination I conceive to be committed to neither theory, though partaking of the motives of both. Consistency? Yes by all means. With Berkeley I should say that "it is a hard thing to suppose that right deductions from true principles should ever end in consequences which cannot be maintained or made consistent. We should believe that God has dealt more bountifully with the sons of men." But "consistency of idea" or of "principles" suggests a bareness, a mere-wordiness, which amply justifies those who deny that "ideas" can grasp realities.

On the other hand nothing is verified by brute fact. Indeed I do not know whether we might not translate the antithesis of idea *vs.* fact into a case of words *vs.* blows. Neither gives truth. The facts must satisfy imagination. Suppose that twelve honest and intelligent men swear to you that, having carefully measured a small triangular piece of ground, they have found the sides to be three, four, and five yards long respectively, yet all the angles acute angles. Will you believe them? Or, better, take the experience of the inventor—which in the interest of science I have shared in a small way. He draws his plan; it must work. He constructs a model; it doesn't work. Does this mean that his plan is wrong? Not yet. He must first examine his design and discover where it is inconsistent—where his imagination was defective. If critical imagination still justifies the plan, then, facts or no facts, it *must* work; the trouble must lie in the model. And he does not arrive at truth (although he may be overborne by "facts") until imagination is satisfied. He may easily discover that his imagination was defective. It is very likely to be so. And herein lies the value of laboratory experiment; it helps the imagination. But this only means that imagination may more or less anticipate fact; more in some men, less in others. So far, then, as imagination is in good working order it gets further into reality, on the basis of the reality already grasped, and needs not to wait passively for the deliverance of fact.[1]

This union of consistency and fact, or of consistency and experience, is well described by Professor A. E. Taylor in his "Elements of Metaphysics" as "immediate experience", though it is not brought out to my own satisfaction that immediate experience implies imagination. What I would drive home, then, if I can, is that this immediate experience is no "mere experience" but an experience *of* reality. And therefore another illustration. A few years ago the newspapers were for some time full of a case in which a man and a woman had been found in a lonely spot, clearly murdered. There were several clues of more or less significance, but the case has remained a "mystery". I need give no details. I will simply point out that if your imagination is working on such a case it is working really towards a certain goal: namely, the immediate experience of the murderer. His experience (let us say—it need not be true absolutely) would give us the reality. But how would you get at that experience? There are no rules. It would be a "moral" rather than a logical process, a matter of insight and intuition based upon the situation, including the human situation, as thus far presented. Yet the successful intuition would be a

[1] For those who insist upon the ritual of verification I will relate the following, told me by a salesman in a department-store. A woman came to his counter and asked for a pencil and piece of paper upon which to do some calculation. After a few minutes she returned the pencil and departed, leaving her calculation upon the counter. It was found to be this: $1.00
.75
———
$1.75
I wonder if any reader of mine could conceive that by such his mental arithmetic had received an added shade of " verification ".

grasp of the whole reality. You would then see the situation as the man himself saw it; and in that seeing there would be a fullness and a coherence of detail which would be—not, as I was about to write, its own authentication of reality, but reality itself.

And it matters not for our conception that you never quite get that finally full and critical grasp, and that fact is therefore almost invariably illuminating. For though you get it not before the fact, neither have you got it completely after the fact, and certainly not from the "dead weight" of fact. Truth is relative, and relative to sophistication; and its nature is apprehended if we can see the difference between the earlier and the later stage of sophistication.

As a final illustration—very significant for any moral conception of truth—I will instance the resurrection of Jesus Christ. I do not believe in the resurrection of Christ, and it is unlikely that I shall believe in it—not, however, as I conceive, upon any *a priori* grounds, logical or scientific, but because I do not expect to find the satisfying evidence. What would that evidence be? Well, in reading the accounts given in the gospels, which tell us that Jesus met several persons after his resurrection and conversed with them, one's feeling is, I think, if only those conversations had been recorded! If only those meetings had been presented so vividly and fully that in reading the accounts we could measurably find ourselves there! Then we should know whether Christ had risen or not. And we should know it through a critical appropriation of the experience then offered us. Suppose that a dead friend of yours appeared to you—say in your sleep. Suppose that you then had an old-time heart to heart talk with him. A real conversation; not a Platonic or Berkeleian "dialogue" in which it is the chief function of one person to say "Very true" to the other, but a conversation in which each response stands for fresh thought. Suppose that he communicated and made intelligible to you some of the experience of death and resurrection. Could any logician ever convince you that it was not your friend, and that he had not returned from the dead? And then why is it that the spirit-manifestations of psychical research remain so unconvincing? Not, I should say, because of any defect in scientific method, but because the spirits when they return have so little to tell us.

CHAPTER XVI

THE PRESENCE OF THE DIVINE

§ 67. Knowledge and " communion with the divine ". § 68. The motive of knowledge and the motive of love. § 69. The idea of God and the presence of God.

THE purpose of this essay on the critical life has been to develop the *motif* of self-consciousness ; to follow it, I might say, to the end. But to this pursuit, it should now be clear, there can be none but a temporal end. There can be no logical conclusion : the critical process reduced to a conclusion would be a *reductio ad absurdum*. And therefore the intention of these two concluding chapters (which are to form a continuous discourse) is not to arrive at a conclusion but to suggest the deeper and more comprehensive question ; which will yet express the realities of human nature and of human life so far as it be a significant question. In the end what is being presented is a point of view ; and the last term in a point of view is not the top-story of a house, its security guaranteed by the solidity of the under-structure, but a horizon, where vision is dimmest and least certain and thought is more than ever of the nature of opinion.

Truth, it has just been said, is the expression, not of theoretical consistency, nor of verifying fact, but of satisfied imagination ; and a satisfied imagination (to the degree that imagination is ever satisfied) is an immediate experience of reality, an awareness of the presence of reality. But to speak of a satisfied imagination is at once to ask what will satisfy the imagination deeply and if possible finally: what are the desires, the yearnings, of an unsatisfied imagination? This is to raise the question of religion; its meaning, its reality as something more than a form of words; and then to ask about the significance of religion for human experience in general, and especially for the experience expressed in poetry and art.

§ 67

For what I would say of religion I find a convenient text and introduction in the following from Burnet's "Greek Philosophy": "Greek philosophy is based on the faith that reality is divine, and that the one thing needful is for the soul, which is akin to the divine, to enter into communion with it. It was in truth an effort to satisfy what we call the religious instinct". In modern terms this means, as he explains, that Greek philosophy was more akin to religion than to science. The Greek philosophers were not "intellectualists."

Yet the motive fundamental to the Greek imagination was the desire to know. And it is in connection with this motive that I would consider the faith that reality is divine. That reality is divine—what does this mean more than that reality is real? What is meant by "the divine"? To me this can mean only that reality is personal—it surely does not mean that reality is merely big, or that it is merely mysterious—and therefore it means that impersonal reality is a false or merely conventional appearance.

I should put the matter simply, by saying that reality is God, if this were not to suggest an appeal, not as I intend, to the religious imagination, but to the current system of theology (the science of God!) for which "God" is *a* person if not indeed the only person. Now in the logic of the religious instinct it may very well be that for you or for me God is just one person—and for each a different person. The system of theology, however, in which God is conceived as "the Lord and Proprietor of the Universe" (in Butler's phrase), the absolute monarch, the sole creator of moral distinctions and the sole arbiter of the worth of men—this "system" is to me less suggestive of the religious instinct than of the logic of authority. Its appeal, I should say, is not to the soul of man but to the conveniences of social order, and in particular to the supreme convenience of conceiving the human social order as continuous with the order of the universe, thus bringing the fear of God into the government of men. It is in this sense only that I can understand why a faith definitely monotheistic must be the religion of civilization. This means, however, that the conception of God as one and only is the expression of the same administrative convenience as that which prescribes one President for the United States or for the Pennsylvania Railroad. Hence as against this systematic view I prefer to speak generally, if vaguely, of "the divine", and of the presence of the divine as in another connection one might speak of the presence of the human.

For a concrete sense of the divine presence and an obvious expression of the religious instinct one is likely to turn not to the wise and cultivated but, say, to the Russian peasant, to whom it seems that God is ever vaguely present, or to the desert Mohammedans in whom religion, "the factious passion of their Semitic souls", as Doughty puts it, suggests "the Lord's hand working in all about them", and "they call upon God in every mouthful of words". For them it seems, in the words of Thales, that "all things are full of gods". But in thus appealing to the mujik or to the Bedouin we seem to be clearly turning our backs upon the critical life. And this is to state the question forming my first topic, namely, whether "God" or "the divine" is a term of significance for any critical imagination. Does "God" express an idea or is it only a word—a verbal expression which sophisticated reflection has shown to be without meaning? This I believe to be the form which the question tends finally to take. He to whom "God" conveys an intelligible meaning will, I suspect, ever hesitate before a final disbelief The conclusive disbelief expresses itself by saying that, whatever the word may mean to others, it means nothing to me.

My suggestion will be, then, that critical reflection, so far from dissolving the conception of the divine, only makes the conception truly significant—if under critical reflection we include the consciousness of self. For it seems true enough that reflection upon "the world"—the world presented by the sciences, notably by astronomy and geology, a world extended in an infinity of space and time in which you and I are nowhere—tends to dissipate the meaning of divinity. But this is not the world in which we live, and reflection confined to such a world is not reflective human experience. Any least reflective human experience involves a consciousness—an even painful consciousness—of self; the presence in me of an activity of intelligence which "naturalistic" explanations of human life persistently overlook. When, for example, naturalism ascribes religion to fear it is usually upon the assumption that fear is a *blind* "impulse". It makes a difference when (with Marett in his "Threshold of Religion") we ascribe religion to awe; for "awe" suggests a reaching out of the mind, at least a curious wonder. And when religion is ascribed to an infantile sense of dependence it is well to remember that the child's sense of dependence upon his mother is not his "sense of dependence" upon the floor that supports him. In his mother he is seeking a responsive intelligence.

In the ninth chapter, in which I said that for me the motive fundamental to life is to know, I distinguished two all-the-world different versions of knowing, namely, impersonal, scientific knowing which yields as its realities "things" and personal knowing, or insight, which yields persons. Now it may help to clarify my present meaning (if also to reveal the peculiar weakness of my mind) if I say that my vocation to philosophy came, all at once, in my last year at college from reading Martineau's "Types

THE PRESENCE OF THE DIVINE

of Ethical Theory"; and that some fifteen years later when I had been several years a teacher of philosophy, and was now utterly weary of it and ready to escape, my vocation was renewed, permanently it has seemed, by reading Royce's "The World and the Individual". To the non-academic reader I may explain that among English-speaking philosophers of half a century past these two are possibly the clearest representatives of a "dangerously unsound" "imaginative style" which tends to personify its realities. I am not committed to the doctrines of either writer. But it will state my point of view to say that it has become my most assured conviction that the logic of this "style" is the only true logic of knowing.

This is to say that in the last analysis the only intelligible experience of knowing is a person's knowing of another person; namely, personal insight; and on the other hand that impersonal, scientific knowledge, so called, is not knowledge but the negation of knowledge. To me it seems that, as Kant suggested a century and a half ago, science is not so much knowledge as a method of prediction; and a method of prediction which latter-day pragmatism has shown to be dictated by practical purposes. A marvellously successful method indeed—for me this constitutes the perplexing problem. And when I reflect upon science's power of elaborating its predictions I seem compelled to admit that the conceptions of science, even the most purely mechanical (which means the most distinctly scientific), must stand for some sort of knowledge. But this is still to say that science is not simple truth but only one point of view, one way of taking the world, among others; and it is likewise still to say that in science as elsewhere *truth*—as distinguished from so-called "verification"—is satisfied imagination. And it seems to me that so far as science is more than bare prediction, so far as its conceptions are more than mere methods, so far as its facts have meaning, it is by the presence and operation of that "anthropomorphic" sort of thinking which modern scientists so unsparingly condemn. To me the more purely "scientific" the form or language in which a subject-matter is presented the blanker it seems, the more meaningless and unreal; and I can begin to believe that (in accordance with Newton's first law) a body in motion must move until stopped and a body at rest must rest until moved when I reflect that I myself do not feel it necessary to move or to stop moving until I have a reason for doing so.

And if you ask me whether I do not know when I am up against facts—alas! when my money is all spent, or when I knock my head in the dark against the edge of an open door, I know as well as the next man that I am "up against" something. But to be "up against" is, I should say, not yet to know; it is rather (to borrow for my own purpose a word from Professor Dewey) to undergo. I do not begin to know the fact, or object, until it is grasped in imagination and made intelligible; I do not know it finally until imagination is satisfied.

And it may illustrate the point of view to repeat what I have suggested elsewhere, namely, that in my opinion two centuries of modern philosophy devoted mainly to the problem of knowledge have never really touched the point of knowing. And this because the discussion has been conducted wholly in terms of the so-called knowing of inanimate things, supposed to offer a "simple" and typical case of knowing. Berkeley, for example, begins with "the table I write upon" as his example of knowing. Presently he is reminded of his fellows; and then, with a shameless inconsistency but a no less significant insight, he makes it clear that he knows them far more certainly than he knows "the table I write upon". But the table remains for him and for all subsequent discussion the typical case of knowing; and what course the philosophy of knowledge would have taken had our fellow been made the type, remains an interesting speculation.

This, I hope, will give a human meaning to the thesis that to live is to know. When Aristotle begins his "Metaphysics" by saying that all men desire by nature to know, suggesting indeed that in human nature knowing is funda-

THE PRESENCE OF THE DIVINE 243

mental, he surely does not mean that the soul of man is exhaustively defined by the desire for the successful prediction of fact. Aristotle was not a scientist in the orthodox modern sense, restricted by the rules of his profession to statements of temporal coexistence and succession of "phenomena", but what might better be called a naturalist; exercising an imagination more or less animistic in an outreaching curiosity about the inner nature of things, and seeking an insight into Nature of the same sort, ultimately, that we seem to have into our fellow men. This naturalistic curiosity is the most distinctive sign of "life" in men or, as I have suggested above, in the beasts of the field. When the cow raises her head from the grass and slowly looks at you, then you know for certain that she is a living being. It is therefore not properly to be described as "animal curiosity", rather as "a lively curiosity", a lively intelligence seeking insight. Every pulse of life is such a thirst for insight. The old lady, who, relieved of life's heavier burdens, now keeps herself alive by playing solitaire—she too is seeking insight. In a certain unsatisfied curiosity, it might be said, lies all the difference between being alive and being dead.

Of this we have a depressing realization when to the struggling self-consciousness it seems that being dead, or being torpid, is the more pervasive aspect of experience; when we note how small the circle of light in most moments of vision, how immense the surrounding dimness, and how helpless our attempts to penetrate it. Royce has pointed to the logical significance of the "sluggishness" of our minds. To me it seems that the chiefly striking fact about human experience, surely most significant for any theory of human life, yet mainly overlooked both in logic and in psychology, is the evanescent quality of all actual experience, the rapid fading of impressions as they pass, and the resulting concentration of our mental activity upon the task of reinstating the experience in its living reality. The symphony of César Franck which I heard a few weeks ago—I talk about it to-day with enthusiasm and with conviction, yet all the while I know that what I now have before me is mainly an echo, an abstraction, a ghost of the living experience.

In this sluggishness of the mind I am tempted to formulate the whole problem of life. To me it seems that the chief "burden" of living, be it great or small, and all the weariness of life, resolves itself into confusion of mind; and all weakness of will amounts in the end to simple uncertainty. The task is never too heavy when we know what we have to do—at least we are resigned. In modern life especially, in which the diminishing necessity for physical effort is overbalanced by a multiplied responsibility, the indulgence we crave from our neighbours is that they should not add to our problems, and their helpfulness in time of stress consists in doing our thinking for us. And thus it seems that all moral weakness and disloyalty and estrangement must mean that men forget—imagination is dull. When one sees a man and wife facing one another in the divorce court with a venomous bitterness, one's first impulse is to wonder whether either now recalls what the other was for him twenty years ago. Could we remember, could we only preserve the personal meaning and vividness of the experience of life once actually our own, we might be spared the baser humiliations. Let our experience be as limited as you please, we should still enjoy a fair measure of free and honorable living, true to ourselves and masters of ourselves. The problem of living is the problem of knowing, and the desire to live is the desire to know.

Hence the character, as I conceive it, of the unsatisfied imagination: its search for reality in the form of an eternal life in which, simply as the fulfilment of life, all shall be known. "For now we see through a glass darkly," but then we shall know, even as we are known. It will suggest the universality of this appeal to the imagination, its presence as a motive in the religious instinct in whatever form that instinct may take, if by the side of the biblical quotation I put the following from Joseph Conrad:

"A heavy atmosphere of oppressive quietude pervaded the ship. . . . The problem of life seemed too voluminous for the narrow limits of human speech and by common consent it was abandoned to the great sea that had from the beginning enfolded it in its immense grip; to the sea that knew all, and would in time infallibly unveil to each the wisdom hidden in all the errors, the certitude that lurks in doubts, the realm of safety and peace beyond the frontiers of sorrow and fear."

§ 68

But, as I have suggested, for a more intimate realization of the quality of knowing—and thus of living—we must turn to our relations with our fellows. Now we may be told that in these relations living is not so much a matter of knowing as it is of loving. And therefore, I reply, of knowing. For to me the very meaning of love, and all the charm and delight of loving, lies in understanding. I might then state the motive both of loving and of knowing in terms of the motive of *intimacy*. In some such motive must we look for that union of feeling and intelligence, of love and knowledge, which is implied in Plato's conception of love as the inspiration for philosophy and Spinoza's "intellectual love of God". Even curiosity about nature seems to imply a desire of personal intimacy; in the words of Burnet, we desire to "enter into communion" with her. In human relations this is the pervasive motive—even in the midst of hate. Suppose that in old-fashioned terms we compare the pleasures of life in the quest for the *summum bonum*: shall we not say that the sensuous value of things is in the end of little consequence compared with their "social" value? What, for example, is the meaning of "wealth"? Here is a man setting up an establishment: without the apparatus of hospitality the establishment would be commonly of little use; and perhaps also apart from the impression—involving a recognition—to be made upon those who are to be excluded. It is hard to conceive of any seriously considered action which will not in some fashion be an invitation to one's neighbours or of any apparatus of life which will not turn into a vehicle of expression. And in the development of institutions it is very interesting, and not seldom curious, to see the social motive displacing the useful. "College spirit" is commonly a stupid affair; yet even so it means that the human relationships consequent upon meeting for a common purpose tend to make themselves the chief meaning of the purpose.

But human rather than "social". For the term "social", implying to-day a public rather than a private and personal relation, conveys only a diluted suggestion of what I mean, And therefore I prefer the term "intimacy" as recalling us to the self-consciousness of the critical life. If from any introspective standpoint (from which we measure the value of things for the critical life) we ask which of the goods of life are of real value *for you and for me*—rejecting now all of those intrusive "social" and "public" considerations —for myself I seem to find but one answer : the only deeply satisfying things are the personal intimacies. All of the casual "social" goods are of value only as they retain the flavour of the personal (which, curiously, they always make a pretence of doing). And all of the ostensibly impersonal interests, such as an interest in books, in scientific investigation, in social reform or commercial enterprise—which, it seems, are necessary to give breadth and substance to life—these again take on the quality of life just so far as they furnish the subject-matter of intimate intercourse. To my own imagination indeed the greatest pleasure in life is a quiet talk by the fireside or a stroll in the country with a congenial soul when, business and convention both forgotten, each is for the time being his unembarrassed self, and there is a mutual unburdening of the spirit, a mutual enlargement of mind. The scholar's delight in a book is a pleasure of this kind; though he misses the immediate response, he is probably enjoying his author at the author's best. And it seems to me that he who in this human sense is at home in the world, who in the circle of family and kin

THE PRESENCE OF THE DIVINE

finds an ever satisfying affection and understanding, and in his friends an intelligence ever responsive to his tastes, has the best that life has to offer; and that he who lacks these lacks everything. No impersonal breadth of interest can replace this quality of intimacy.

But this is once more to think of life as a problem. Of how many persons can it be said that they are thus at home in the world? Unimaginative persons recommend love as the easy cure for human ills as if love, the crown of the virtues, were also the simplest; and they think it simple for a man just to be himself. It is simple, I suspect, for a simple person, just as it is easy for an easy-going person to make friends. Of personal intimacy he knows correspondingly little. To be oneself sincerely and to take one's personal relations seriously is at once to appreciate the difficulties of understanding, along with the special delights of understanding between natures highly individuated, and at the same time to become aware of the complications presented by repressions, suspicions, defensive reactions, or what not; of all those contradictions which the Freudian psychology has uncovered in the impulses of sex, making them inarticulate and ashamed by their very intensity, but which, it seems to me, are characteristic of all self-conscious human nature. It is rather notorious that culture, which refines the sympathies and quickens the thirst for them, does not therefore make brotherly love easier. Among persons of good breeding it seems to be agreed that the most distinctive mark of a refined consideration is that we shall not touch one another—which means, somewhat paradoxically, that nothing is so repulsive to our sense of touch as our human fellow. Simplicity and frankness attained in and through these complexities of human nature mark a rarely assured self-consciousness. So remote from the intercourse of every-day life is the natural enjoyment of sympathic intelligence that in the poetic imagination such enjoyment becomes the special mark of a "Golden Age".

This enjoyment "the religious instinct" then seeks in the

experience of "communion with God". Communion with God is to be an intimacy more deeply satisfying than any possible human intimacy. To the imagination of the mystic it is the final experience both of love and of knowledge. But to speak of "intimacy" in this connection is inevitably to be reminded of the current theory which explains religion as only one of the phenomena of unsatisfied sexual desire—at first glance the least edifying among theories of religion; yet at the same time a theory which anthropological research makes it difficult to ignore. Primitive religious ceremonies are often sexual orgies, and even in modern religion the language of impassioned devotion is full of erotic metaphor. Yet coolly considered I do not see why this association should be especially depressing; or why it should be more depressing at least than the more general consideration, forced upon us by biological evolution, that all of human life, all that is finest in human imagination, has its roots in our animal nature. Or why, in reverse fashion, the association of sex and religion may not be taken to point to the *meaning*—the personal and spiritual meaning—of the relation of sex. To the modern imagination this relation stands for the most intimate of personal relations; it is the personal relation *par excellence*. In modern literature it is connected with most of the poignancy of life, and by the side of it the enjoyment of "friendship", which appears to be the ideal personal relation of classical literature, seems thin and uninspiring. Marriage, says Jeremy Taylor, is "the queen of the friendships".

Now it is not necessary to say that sex is all of life or all that is personal in life. In the logic of personal relations there are perhaps no *a priori* necessities. Yet the sex-motive in literature is no mere modern convention, but a revelation—of tragic depths of human nature to which the imagination of classical times was simply obtuse. If (as Plato seems to imagine) the sex-appetite were indeed only a physical appetite, like the appetite for food, there would be no "sex-problem". The sex-problem would then be a simple economic problem, one among the other problems involving an exchange of services. It is because the relation draws into itself so much of ourselves that there is a special "problem" ; it is because marriage embodies so much of personal aspiration that we discuss its "failure". But this failure of marriage—so often precisely where marriage means most—may then be viewed as simply a crucial illustration of a universal spiritual problem; the problem, namely, of satisfying our imagination in intercourse with our fellows—even such a problem as the common sense of social life betrays by substituting the game of bridge for the inadequacies of conversation. The more intensive self-consciousness (always abnormal from any common-sense point of view) serves only to suggest a certain inevitable inadequacy in every form of social intercourse. The final result of the culture of the spirit is then what a recent writer describes as "the awful incommunicability of souls", expressed in a mutual recognition of the loneliness of any more thoughtful form of life.

And therefore, as I have suggested, the quest of the unsatisfied imagination for communion with God. But here once more we are confronted with doubts and questions regarding the nature of the motive. Since God is so often the refuge of broken lives, of disappointed love or personal bereavement, we face the suggestions of a theory of "compensation"; or once more the suggestion that any intense desire for communion with God, such as marks the mystic or the devotee, is the fruit of a morbid imagination. Yet I wonder why the idea of God should not be a "compensation". This would mean only that the thought of God is suggested like any other thought, by the presence of a need. How should men think of God as long as human intimacies satisfy? And then I need only repeat what was said above, that a morbid imagination may be (even must be, I should rather say) a special source of insight. When I hear men speak of the religion of a sane and normal mind I am tempted always to ask why a sane and normal mind should be interested in religion; or in anything beyond the football games and the market reports. Thoughts of religion are suggested commonly—one might almost say, normally—by the presence of death. Thought itself in any graver sense comes from the tragedy of life. One may conceivably deny (as I suppose Professor Dewey would deny) that there is any "tragedy of life." But this is only to say that when we speak of the "tragedy" of life we locate the quality of "life" in the poignantly personal—not in the impersonally rational and practical. There is nothing properly tragic in losses by fire and flood considered in themselves, or in any losses of a merely "worldly" kind. The tragic loss is the personal loss, typified by personal bereavement, and the tragic unfulfilment is the unfulfilment of those deeper personal longings of which the sex-longing is illustrative—but only illustrative.

Illustrative, however, of any of the deeper, *i.e.* of the religious stirrings of life, whether in the form of personal love or of reflective thought or of aesthetic taste. Let us recall the faith which for Burnet satisfied "the religious instinct"; "the faith", namely, "that reality is divine, and that the one thing needful is for the soul, which is akin to the divine, to enter into communion with it". It has been my purpose here to suggest that every impulse of the mind is an attempt to "enter into communion"—with a reality such as to respond. "For at the bottom of much of our desire for great poetry," writes Vernon Lee, "is our desire for the greater life, the deeper temperament, for the more powerful mind, the great man"—and there is something similar, I suspect, at the bottom of our desire for scientific knowledge. But the desire for the great man inevitably leads the imagination beyond man. The conception of the divine will then be as variously personal, the person of God will be (and in logic must be) as variously temperamental as the many who seek him; but for each the search for the divine will be a desire for personal communion. "Thou hast made us for thyself and our hearts are restless until they find rest in thee." This classical expression of Christian piety is, it seems to me, a true revelation of the religious motive. We find the same personal motive, however, in a total difference of tone, in the hymn of praise to Zeus of the Stoic Cleanthes, beginning with "O God most glorious":

> "We are thy children, we alone, of all
> On earth's broad ways that wander to and fro,
> Bearing thine image wheresoe'er we go."

And again the same motive, strange to say, now clearly unsatisfied and defeated, in Bertrand Russell's picture, in the peroration of his essay on "A Free Man's Worship", of the free man hurling defiance at an insensitive universe. The significant revelation of this striking passage,[1] it seems to me, is "the heart of man"—for there is surely no logic in defying an insensitive universe. Russell's free man, supposed to represent the ultra-sophisticated man, may then be regarded as almost a perfect expression of the unsatisfied imagination, an eloquent testimony to the loneliness of a universe in which there is no divine presence, and once more an evidence that God—the divine—is the inevitable imagination of the human consciousness of self.

§ 69

And yet it may seem that all of this is only to demonstrate a difference between the imagination of the divine and any sense of the presence of the divine, between the idea of God and the presence of God. Hence I will carry the theme further by asking what it means to have an idea of God.

[1] The passage is as follows: "Brief and powerless is Man's life; on him and all his race the slow, sure doom falls pitiless and dark. Blind to good and evil, reckless of destruction, omnipotent matter rolls on its relentless way; for Man, condemned to-day to lose his dearest, to-morrow himself to pass through the gate of darkness, it remains only to cherish, ere the blow falls, the lofty thoughts that ennoble his little day; disdaining the coward terrors of the slave of Fate to worship at the shrine that his own hands have built; undismayed by the empire of chance, to preserve a mind free from the wanton tyranny that rules his outward life; proudly defiant of the irresistible forces that tolerate, for a moment, his knowledge and his condemnation, to sustain alone, a weary but unyielding Atlas, the world that his own ideals have fashioned despite the trampling march of unconscious power."

Here we are reminded of the traditional "ontological argument" for the existence of God, which, in substance, derives the existence of God from the existence of the idea : I have an idea of God, therefore God exists. Now the questionable feature of this argument, to my mind, is not the "logic" of it. Really to have an idea of God, I will suggest, is to know that God does exist. The question is what might roughly be called the question of fact : Have we an idea of God ? And what does this mean ?

Now in the traditionally "logical" sense of idea—as implying a consistently systematic view, complete and free from all internal contradiction—I should say that we have clearly no idea of God. The conception of God as one person, eternally living yet eternally satisfied, omnipotent yet permitting freedom, benevolent yet tolerating evil, beyond all moral weakness yet sympathetic with weakness—this if anything is a mass of problems and contradictions. And yet if this means that we have no idea of God it seems also to mean that we have no idea of our fellow-men. For any of them, subjected to a sufficiently careful scrutiny, appears to be similarly a mass of contradictions. Not only, then, have we no idea, say of Plato ; we have possibly least of all an idea of those who are nearest to us. Yet of them it seems that we have certainly a personal experience, and an assurance of their presence.

But when I turn to the personal experience as constituting the idea, I am reminded of those words of Christ : "He that loveth not his brother whom he hath seen, how shall he love God whom he hath not seen ?" When we remember that "loveth" must include "knoweth" this seems to suggest that the experience of God may be for any human capacity of imagination almost impossibly difficult ; and thus in the end any real belief in God. And this leads me to ask, What survives of belief in our human fellows (not to speak of love) when they have ceased to be present to the senses—when they have been long absent ? What remains of our belief in those who are long ago dead ?

As I was pondering this question in the middle of a summer vacation and seeking a way of stating what it means to me, I happened to be reading again George Eliot's "Scenes of Clerical Life" and it occurred to me that "Mr. Gilfil's Love Story" would help me to state the point.

The story begins with the death of Mr. Gilfil. Mr. Gilfil was an elderly Church of England clergyman of the kind that George Eliot loved to draw—"who smoked long pipes and preached short sermons"; a shrewd, matter-of-fact, and rather sceptical old gentleman, more distinctly "sound" than "spiritually-minded". Also a rather reserved man who lived much to himself, an aristocrat and a gentleman, yet popular in his parish because of a benevolence which duly respected the animal want; and welcome at every farmhouse because, himself a man of a little property and a breeder of cattle, he could discuss breeds of cattle and the like in the farmer's dialect as man to man. Mr. Gilfil, in short, was an unromantic old gentleman, and as a clergyman probably a fit subject for evangelical suspicion.

Forty years before, however, Mr. Gilfil had buried the wife who had been the pet and playmate of his boyhood and youth. She is pictured as a rarely lovely child (one thinks of her as a child), the orphaned daughter of a penniless Italian painter, bred from infancy in the quiet manners and sober traditions of an English country house, yet inheriting the dangerous southern passions which after an experience of treachery and deceit—when for the time her imagination had wandered from Maynard Gilfil—had all but issued in bloodshed. Mr. Gilfil's brief year of wedded happiness was the sadly peaceful end of a troubled story.

The memory of Caterina had then become Mr. Gilfil's religion. Her room, carefully preserved as she had left it, his sanctuary. Her name was rarely spoken. Few persons remembered her existence. This, however, was Mr. Gilfil's love story.

A very sentimental story, it will be said to-day—"very old-fashioned", was the comment of one of my friends, an anti-Victorian. But to suggest that the story is sentimental is precisely to put my question. For as one reads the story one hardly grieves for Mr. Gilfil. It seems indeed that he enjoyed the greatest gift of life, a supreme and satisfying devotion. But as I lay the story down disturbing questions arise. As Mr. Gilfil sat night after night before his fire with his pipe and his book (or his newspaper) and his glass of gin and water, did the vision of Caterina never waver ? Did her presence after the lapse of years never forsake him, leaving him to wonder whether after all she had been real, whether his love had been more than a youthful infatuation, whether his loyalty had not now become a formal gesture ? For myself I prefer not to think so.

But the question will serve to mark the issue between sentimentalism and realism. For to call Mr. Gilfil's story sentimental means simply that we charge his author with claiming for him a depth of experience, a power of imagination, beyond the human capacity. We mean that his worship of Caterina was not a genuine experience, animated by a steady sense of her presence, but a gesture, a form of words. But this is only to put the logic of the issue—the logic of the experience of God, as I have it in mind—in line with the logic of morality as explained in Chapter XII ; where it was said that the morality of an action is a question simply of the intelligence, of the genuineness of the experience lying behind it. And in line with the logic of beauty, the beauty of an object being similarly a question of how far the object is merely an object or an "expression"— of a genuine experience.

In all of such matters the logic is neither the logic of mathematics (or of abstract metaphysics) in which truth is determined by the law of contradiction ; nor the logic of science, in which truth is determined by the power of fact ; but the less determinate logic of interpretation, of appreciation, of *criticism ;* the logic of divination, one might almost say, yet the logic of all extra-scientific human intercourse, of all in which it is a question, from your neighbour's action and his words, not of deducing their consequences, but of realizing the experience of which they are the expression. Such is distinctively the logic of literary and artistic criticism. When the critic tells you briefly that some of William Blake's verses are poems, others are only verses, you will be raising the question of logic when you wonder (as I often wonder) how he knows. And such also is the logic of the "inspiration" of any sacred scriptures, Christian, Mohammedan, Mormon, and of their status as a revelation of the divine. Their truth is not a question of historical authenticity, much as this may help to show what they mean; still less of miraculous attestation. Let their origin be what you please, they would be just as true or just as false as they are now. The question is a question of content and significance, of what they have to reveal; the logic of their inspiration is the logic of poetic inspiration.

In the logic of criticism, the reader will perceive, the judgment of significance is the affirmation of a "presence", of the reality somewhere in the spiritual world, if not in the world of space and time, of a personal existence. It was this aspect of the matter that led me to link Mr. Gilfil's story with the presence of the divine. For what is involved in the story is somewhat more than the preservation of a memory of sense-experience (though one may ask how the perfect preservation of a memory can differ from a present experience). A thoroughly cynical critic may ask whether Maynard Gilfil had ever really known Caterina, whether indeed her loveliness was more than a simple illusion of sex. And this will remind us that, even in the case of those who are most distinctly with us in the flesh, our grasp of themselves is a work of insight, of imagination. Do we not know that the prophet may be least recognized in his own country and his own house, and that husband and wife, father and son, may be least fitted to know one another?

And it may help to link the logic of our neighbour's presence with that of the divine presence if I refer once more to what it means to be a "lover of books". Among undergraduate students it seems, strangely, that the presence of the writer is the last thing to be grasped: yet to me it is the one important reality. Take such a work as T. H. Green's lectures on "Political Obligation", a deservedly classical work in political philosophy, yet assuredly drab and unadorned; brief and compact, yet exasperatingly—conscientiously—repetitious. Green is profoundly convinced that the cause of authority is the cause of God—and of Man. But he is too sensitively honorable not to explain where the cause seems weak, too innately respectful of his fellows not to give their opposing views a sympathetic consideration, and too much a lover of liberty to preach authority except in its name. To grasp these several motives is to find in a sober academic treatise a dramatic conflict, no less dramatic because quietly serious, within a human soul. It is to feel Green thinking; to experience the "presence" of the man even more immediately than if your hand held his pulse. He who expects to find in the book only a system of facts and arguments will miss the point entirely, and it will not be strange if he shall say that, in the mutual destruction of argument by argument, in the sum total he finds nothing there.

Of such sort, as I take it, is the logic of any sense of the presence of the divine; of such sort precisely though implying an exercise of imagination of vastly greater range and import; yet still natural as our knowledge of our fellows is natural, and drawn from life as any inspiration of poetry or intuition of beauty is drawn from life.

Hence—just as a matter of sophistication, if you please —I feel that I must treat any ostensible experience of the presence of God with a certain reverent, though never undiscriminating, expectancy. In his introduction to the Everyman Spinoza, Santayana concludes Spinoza's message by saying: "It counsels us to say to those little gnostics, those circumnavigators of being [*i.e.* those who have ventured to claim for themselves an experience of God]; I do not believe you: God is great." This is hardly to credit Spinoza with the humility appropriate to a philosopher. And it seems to me that both a juster and a subtler warning is conveyed in the words, "He who loveth not his brother whom he hath seen, how shall he love God whom he hath not seen?" For myself, I will not resent my neighbour's experience of God until he insists upon making this experience the major premise of a "system" of theology or of metaphysics. Then perhaps I may protest that "God is great." Meanwhile, having in mind the logic of human experience, and the arbitrary nature of any limit placed even upon *human* experience, I feel compelled (at the least) to agree with William James when he says, "I firmly disbelieve, myself, that our human experience is the highest form of experience extant in the universe."[1]

In all of this I am speaking mainly from the external standpoint, from the standpoint of the other person who is the critic of religious experience. For myself it often seems as if all of my own religious experience could be summed up in a wonder, curious and critical, yet not irreverent, not unbelieving, and even at times envious, about the religious experience of others. And yet I am not quite certain. When I try to state a fact (in answer perhaps to a questtionnaire) about any very personal experience of my own, it seems that the word "fact" becomes strangely inapplicable, and I seem to find here, in this most intimately personal part of life, a curious lack of distinction between stating a fact and creating it. And then I wonder what would be a minimum of religious experience. To me so much at least seems certain, that to seek the presence of God in one's own life is only fundamentally rational; and it may illustrate my sense of the rationality of this if I point to those two seemingly very simple novels of William Hale White, "Mark Rutherford's Autobiography" and his "Deliverance", in which an evangelical sense of the presence of God seems somehow to survive a Spinozistic conviction of the bigness and hardness of the world, as literature which I have read and re-read with an absorbing interest and which appeals to me as a dramatically faithful presentation of religious experience. And then I must wonder whether even Bertrand Russell's "free man", anathematizing the in-

[1] *Pragmatism*, p. 299.

sensitive universe, is not the expression of a religious experience—whether even this attitude, supposed to represent the merest of mere ideas, can fail to imply some sense of a divine presence. Certainly if we found a lower animal, a dog or a monkey, thus expressing himself, we should find it hard to dissociate such an accession of self-consciousness from the idea of a divine revelation.

Accordingly, in the "logic" of the situation, it seems to me that we must take any expression of religious experience, as we would take any piece of poetry, both sceptically and expectantly, for what it will reveal of the possibilities of experience and of insight. In such judgments we are not merely expressing a taste, we are analysing realities. The Gospel of Jesus Christ, the Koran, the Book of Mormon—one need not, I think, be committed to any Christian theology to grasp a real difference between the Gospel of Christ and the Koran, and a possibly greater difference between either and the dull inanities of the Book of Mormon. And yet one might hesitate before pronouncing even the last to be absolutely meaningless, before declaring that there was no vision whatever in the mind of the prophet Joseph Smith. And this measure of criticism I would also apply to any individual religious experience. I will not reject it as simply strange. Take the following from Henry Ward Beecher (quoted by Leuba and James): "In an instant there rose up in me such a sense of God's taking care of those who put their trust in Him that for an hour all the world was crystalline, the heavens were lucid, and I sprang to my feet and began to cry and laugh." I cannot conceive of any such exaltation of my own spirit as would make this view of the world presently real to me; yet it does not pass my comprehension. At the worst I cannot make it mere words. And if real as an experience it was an experience of reality; of reality as apprehended by one temperament, one form of receptivity. And what would be reality apart from any form of receptivity, I do not know; to me this is unreality.

If, then, it be objected that the forms of receptivity are

possibly infinite, and if I am then asked how are all to be included in a systematic unity of reality, the unity of God the Absolute, the reply must be (as suggested above) that to my view the conception of the Absolute is a derivation from the needs of business administration. For the needs of business I have a wholesome respect, but I will not make them a criterion of divine truth.

CHAPTER XVII

POETIC ILLUSION AND POETIC TRUTH

§ 70. Poetry and religious experience. § 71. Experience as experience of the real. § 72. Man as an animal and man as a human being.

§ 70

"AND so religion is merely poetry and piety is but one form of aestheticism among others"! Such, I fear, may be the summarizing response of many a reader to what has just been said in the last chapter. But to speak of "merely poetry" would indicate that I have failed to convey my meaning—for me *mere* poetry is mere words. And in thus identifying the logic of religious experience with the logic of poetry it has been my purpose not to "reduce" religion to the level of poetry but, if you please, to raise poetry to the level of religion; and thus not to simplify the problem of truth but to make it more portentous. Religious inspiration, I say, is of the same order as poetic inspiration. True, but genuine poetry as then conceived will be the expression of an *experience* of the same order as religious experience. And as such it will be a revelation of reality, of the presence of the divine.

On the other hand, any truly religious experience will then be the expression of a poetic nature. I have said above that no person is entitled to be called moral who is lacking in imagination; I will now add that no such person is entitled to be called religious. The language of personal piety may very well be that of an unschooled mind (not therefore of an unreflective mind) whose experience of the great world is small, whose experience of literature and the arts is little or nothing. It is not impossible that one may thus enjoy a deeper realization of the meaning of life. Perhaps we may say that piety is only the poetry of such a mind—it is at least that ; on the other hand, since poetry is at home only in a more or less personal or personified world, it may be that in the language of personal piety we have the most characteristic, even though the less developed, expression of the poetic motive. Be this as it may, to me it is quite inconceivable that a genuine piety may be conjoined with a positive insensitiveness in other matters There must be some pervasive tenderness in the nature of the man and some fineness of perception, or I cannot grasp the attitude as religious. A religion of finally hard logic, a religion of pure authority, is to me finally brutal and meaningless.

For any proper development of this theme I have had unfortunately too little "experience" of poetry. It may amuse some readers to be told that, though "acquainted with the poets" all my life like any other not illiterate person, I have only rather lately begun to be interested—only after philosophical reflection had assured me that poetry ought to be significant. But it may contribute to my question to explain in part why this has been so. First, because poetry has been commonly represented, even by lovers of poetry, in terms of "the poetic illusion". This means that poetry is a source of polite amusement and entertainment for cultivated persons. And—I do not know whether it is an excess of sophistication or a defect of imagination, but I am not amused by illusions. Nothing interests me very much except as it promises illumination. Nothing is really amusing except as it is also serious. There is for me no humor in a jest, a pun, an epigram, except as it be subtly just ; otherwise it is merely tasteless. And I seem to have noted that the smile of a child indicates that he has grasped something, that the conventional smile of greeting is supposed to express recognition ; and that the old gentleman sitting opposite me in the library who has been reading for an hour past with a facial expression of mingled perplexity, irritation, and disgust—when he breaks out into a broad smile I know that he has got the point.

More deterrent, however, than the conventions of poets and critics of poetry have been (for a professional teacher of philosophy) the conventions of philosophers, and in particular those of the philosophical tradition in which I have lived. Philosophy, I suppose we may say, is a criticism of life; of all life; a criticism of art and poetry and religion no less than of science. Philosophy is human experience and human life becoming conscious of itself. But not even may philosophers be expected "to see life steadily and see it whole", and philosophical traditions show selective variations. In the rather slender Italian tradition, for example, it seems that philosophy is mainly a criticism of history, of history conceived as an *Erlebniss*, as something lived though. And thus in the style of Croce and Gentile, and even perhaps of Varisco, there is a suggestion of the dramatic and the poetic which may very well strike our own philosophers as scandalously sentimental. For in our own tradition, inherited chiefly from Britain and Germany, and concentrated in the issue between Hume and Kant, philosophy is mainly a criticism of natural science. Kant's great critique, the "Critique of Pure Reason", could be justly entitled "What is Science"? His critiques of "Practical Reason" (morality) and of "Judgment" (taste) are minor critiques.

Accordingly in framing a formal definition of philosophy almost invariably do we define philosophy in the single relation to science, usually in accord with the traditional conception that philosophy is the "science of sciences". Or if we think of philosophy as criticism we then define it as a criticism of the presuppositions of science—as if there were in human life and human thought no other presuppositions worth criticizing. In much of contemporary philosophy science has ceased merely to supply the material for criticism, she now provides also the standards of criticism. When also it is our purpose to defend or to justify philosophy we do so to, or against, science. And if we

POETIC ILLUSION AND POETIC TRUTH 263

wish to distinguish serious philosophy from dilettantism, serious philosophy from popular philosophy, it seems that we must distinguish it as "scientific" philosophy. Our whole conception of philosophy is the expression of what I have elsewhere described as "the scientific prepossession".

From this point of view the term precisely antithetical to philosophy is—poetry. A private person may then excusably divert his idle hours by the reading of poetry; or even a natural scientist (if he cares to do so), since poetry is so uncompromisingly remote from science and the scientist's strength of mind is already guaranteed. For the professional philosopher the enjoyment of poetry even as recreation is a reflection upon his intellectual chastity. And should he aspire to be himself a poet—or (by way of parallel) a novelist—I may quote for his benefit the most devastating criticism of a philosopher within the range of my personal experience, a remark referring to Royce: "Yes, he has written several books of philosophy—*and a novel*"!

And yet it may also help to give shape to the general question that I have in mind if I confess that, though reading little verse, I have not been totally insensitive to poetic impressions, at least of the more vulgar and commonplace sort. I have in mind a charming illustration of a passage in Kingsley's "Water Babies" in which Tom, the Water Baby, "looked up at the broad yellow moon . . . and he thought that she looked at him". This is a simple expression of what the philosopher or the sophisticated critic calls "the pathetic fallacy". But I suspect that this fallacy, this illusion, this *Schein*, as the Germans call it, is of the order of what Kant calls necessary, at least empirically necessary. For in the solemn stillness of a moonlit night, with a broad expanse of nature lying before me, it seems that the moon also "looks" at me, and to me also she seems to speak with an overpowering directness; not now indeed of thoughts of love, nor precisely of thoughts of death, but of thoughts of eternity; of the immeasurable generations of men whom (as I recall Hans Andersen's story) she has "seen", and whose monuments lie now extended before her in a view the significance of which no human imagination, even no historian's imagination, can adequately conceive. Only in such moments do I seem quite to realize that being in time I am also in eternity, and that this experience of present life which seems to vanish towards a horizon of misty vagueness must yet be continuous with an infinite experience beyond.

In the stuffiness of one's study, in the sober bareness of the scientific laboratory, the notion of a "communication" from nature seems an empty conceit; a poetic convention indeed, but a silly convention. It is different, I think, for even the less imaginative of men in the presence of nature herself. To me it seems that the mere escape into the open after the confinement of work brings a certain mental expansion. A relief to the nerves, it will be said. But why, I wonder, this postulate of "nerves"? Why not an illumination, a new field of vision? What strikes me most forcibly in any absorbing experience of nature is the strangeness, in this view, of the other world of common life. It seems now that it is science that has become the convention, and the scientific description of nature now seems nearly as remote from the immediate experience as the poetic impression is remote from the experience of the laboratory. To confine the realities of the moonlight scene to those of mathematical physics is only a less strain upon the imagination than to conceive one's best beloved in terms of physical chemistry.

And most remote and roundabout seems then the scientific description of the poetic impression, of this my immediate experience, which, to avoid the implication of a "communication" suggested by the experience itself, will convert the poetic impression into an "association of ideas", a play of pictures within the gallery of the mind. This explanation, obliged at the outset to limit the stimuli of association to what can be put through sense-organs and brain-paths, must then complete its story by a chain of reminiscences extending indefinitely backward to the uncertain experiences of primitive man or to the equally uncertain instincts of our animal nature. And the result, it seems to me, in thus

POETIC ILLUSION AND POETIC TRUTH 265

disposing of communications from nature, is to render equally remote any communications from our fellow men.

Meanwhile it seems that something has been communicated. Let it be nothing more, if you please, than a vague communication of the reality of eternity. Yet in this intuition of reality, and in a mass of other communications similarly poetic, lies all of the material of philosophical questioning, all that stimulates philosophy to think about a world; and in such also lies all that sense of living in a world (and not in a picture-gallery) which fills the background of consciousness in daily life. Among the other poetic impressions is the conception of a scientific universe. Kant showed us long ago that while scientific method may indefinitely link fact to fact it can never grasp a universe. Without the capacity for poetic impressions where should we be? And if these are not communications where are we? And therefore I have to wonder whether Tom, the Water Baby, was guilty of a "fallacy", pathetic or otherwise, when he "looked up at the broad yellow moon . . . and he thought that she looked at him"

The question, it will be perceived, is once more the question of "mere ideas". The theory of the poetic illusion means that poetry is a mere idea; and a mere idea is an activity of the soul, yet without illumination. To me this is unintelligible. And therefore, whatever the difficulties of the conception, I seem compelled to think of poetry either as somehow a grasp of reality or as having no mental quality whatever.

And then my question; which I may put—very seriously —by asking what is implied in a sophisticated sense of humour. For to many persons it marks an undeveloped sense of humour to find no enjoyment in illusions when they are known to be illusions. Let us recall, then, the picture presented above of the professor of science and the professor of poetry in the academic faculty. By the logic of his profession it would seem that the professor of science is obliged to despise the professor of poetry as a teacher of falsehoods; as a parasite, at best a trifler. To the professor

*

of poetry, on the other hand, the professor of science is a person lacking in insight. Yet the two get along very well together on the basis of "the poetic illusion". The professor of poetry takes his illusions very seriously, yet he hardly ventures to teach poetry as sober knowledge. On the other hand, the professor of science is not indisposed to adorn a scientific discourse with a bit of verse at the end ; and he may even recommend the courses in poetry to his son as a part of the education of a gentleman ; conceiving (strangely) that a taste for what is true should be supplemented by a taste for what is false, and that illusions are somehow good for the soul. The question that troubles me is this : whether this unanimity of interest in illusions, known to be illusions, is the mark of a sophisticated sense of humour or a subject for it.

I will then close the topic by pointing to a poem of George Herbert which seems to me very nicely to suggest the question of the logic of the experience both of poetry and of religion. "When God at first made Man", after bestowing upon him all of the other riches of life, he hesitated and thought best to withhold the gift of mental repose.

> "For if I should (said He)
> Bestow this jewel also on My creature,
> He would adore My gifts instead of Me,
> And rest in Nature, not the God of Nature,
>   So both should losers be.
>
> "Yet let him keep the rest,
> But keep them with repining restlessness :
> Let him be rich and weary, that at least,
> If goodness lead him not, yet weariness
>   May toss him to My breast."

In these graceful lines the poet of "The Church Porch", from whom we expect only a serene and even a childlike confidence, has sounded the whole "tragedy" of life. At the same time he has suggested, in terms very intelligible from the point of view of recent psychology, that in this "repining restlessness", in this experience of conflict and dissatisfaction with things as they are, lies the only road to a sense of spiritual realities. The poem might then be described as a poetic-religious version of a philosophical truth, at least of a philosophical problem. But (and this is the question) why a "version"? Let us assume, if you please, that you or I would find other terms more immediately intelligible. Yet if we have here only a version, in what terms shall we state the original? What, in other words, is God's language, the language of truth, which describes things as they really are? It is too naïve to suppose to-day that the divine language was Hebrew, and it is too cheap to smile at the suggestion; but are we now to say that the language of absolute knowledge is that of mathematical notation and symbolic logic? And if it then be objected that we cannot describe or conceive of reality itself except in one version, finally objective and authoritative (and for practical purposes it may be that we cannot), then the question will be whether this is not our limitation, perhaps our misfortune.

§ 71

It will be evident, however, that the question is not confined to the significance of expression in the form of verse—or in the form of words. The poetic marks only what is typical of all imaginative experience; and in the last analysis it becomes the mark of all experience so far as this is personal *experience* and not a "registration" (one thinks here of a human adding machine) of abstract fact. And thus I go on to suggest that the quality of objective illumination which has just been claimed for the experience of poetry is a quality of all genuine experience; and that it is therefore especially to be looked for in those regions in which experience has become relatively articulate in the several forms of artistic expression.

The several arts may be taken to represent so many differences in the native quality of imagination; and interest in poetry rather than in music, or in music rather than in painting, may then be taken to mark the direction in which, for this man or for that, things become most intelligible ; to mark, in other words, the peculiar direction of his personal logic. This personal logic is never indeed wholly to be described as a preference for one form of art to another ; nor may it be finally stated, in psychological terms, as a distinction between (*e.g.*) a "visual" and an "auditory" type of memory or of imagination. Yet it is instructive to be told, for example, by a critic of Walter Pater, that Pater was not so much in love with youth as with "pictures" of youth. True or false of Pater, it may at once occur to us that this "picturesque", or predominately visual, quality of imagination helps to explain the peculiarity of the point of view which we take to be distinctively "French"; its marvellous lucidity and (to our sense) corresponding "superficiality"; its desperate regard for appearances, whatever else be lost, its sensitiveness to ridicule and preference for ridicule as a weapon of offence. But such differences of imagination may be found, I suspect, at the roots of abstract science. Enriques, the Italian historian of science, traces two lines of development in modern physics corresponding to national and racial differences in thinking ; a French, Cartesian physics, based upon vision, which states its conceptions in the form of mathematical equations, and an English, Newtonian physics, based upon the senses of touch and movement, which thinks in terms of working models. And it seems to have been at bottom an issue between a visual and a muscular imagination when Leibnitz contradicted Descartes by saying that it is not the quantity of motion that remains unchanged in the universe but the quantity of force, or energy.

It is then his quality of imagination that determines for each of us, like a Kantian form of thought, what is to be for him intelligible. For most persons it seems that a proposition is best made intelligible by presenting it, in the form of graphs or diagrams, to the eye. And the visual form of presentation has at any rate the "objective" advantage of being easily communicable. But there must be many others to whom, like myself, an important avenue of intelligence is the ear. To me as to most persons my neighbour's face is an indication of his character and intelligence, yet I seem to be more attentive to what is communicated in the quality of his voice. The face is appearance—it may be true or false; but the voice reverberates directly the intelligence of the soul. And this preference for the sound of things goes so far that for me the drama is utterly false while the opera is relatively true to nature. I find that I am not believed in this; yet it seems that I have never witnessed the presentation of a tragedy which did not—and then only in the best moments of such artists as Edwin Booth and Duse—give me that irritating sense of make-believe which we have when some one off the stage is "playing a part"; on the other hand, when Isolde *sings* her lament by the side of the prostrate Tristan it is to me all most natural, most logical, most real.

Hence, granting the deficiency of imagination that may be urged against me, I seem for my own part obliged to believe that the experience which appeals to the ear, so far from from being a sign or symbol of some other kind of experience supposed to be intelligible in itself (which is probably the more common view), has a logic of its own and a message of its own. And I suspect that the logic of musical harmonies and relationships enters far more deeply into our criticism of literature and even of philosophy than we are commonly aware. For my own part it does not occur to me to attempt the conventionally logical "demonstration of a proposition" in the case of anything which cannot, like my balance at the bank, be reduced to figures. In all other matters it seems that I must be content to convey an impression. In the effort to do this I seem to discover that "ideas" (so called) refuse to abide by formally logical definitions and insist upon developing infinitely various though characteristic suggestions, like Wagnerian *motifs*. It is this refusal of ideas to conform to the rules laid down in the logic and grammar of words, that seems to constitute all the difficulties both of thought and of expression in their subtler aspects. The statements may be formally correct and logically coherent, yet the assemblage of words full of discordant suggestions, of "false notes", which reveal themselves only to something like a musical ear; the effect of which is to convince me that what I am trying to convey is not so much a proposition as an impression. And when I then ask myself what would be satisfying as a form of expression ideally and completely logical, I find that I am not thinking of anything resembling a syllogism, but of such a balance of emphasis in the development of a theme, such a suggestion of harmonies among considerations and ideas, as we look for in a symphony or a symphonic poem.

Devoted believers in the significance of music find in a great experience of music "a revelation of the divine". To the scientific critic, interested mainly in the historical development of harmonic relations, of the symphony, or of "the sonata form", the conception of musical appreciation as insight is a phenomenon of adolescence. And lovers of the plastic and pictorial arts, conceiving that their own taste is more intelligent (or more "intellectual") because it is more visual, are disposed to treat the lover of music as a sentimentalist, not to say a sensualist. The student of physiological acoustics explains, moreover (following Helmholtz), that the difference between tone and noise is reducible to simple auditory comfort. To my mind, all of these considerations, important and interesting in themselves, and relevant to the special analysis of musical meaning, are irrelevant to the purpose of showing that music has no meaning. If Beethoven was an incident in the development of the sonata form, equally incidental must have been Shakespeare in the development of the sonnet form; and if consonance and harmony stand for ease in the process of audition what shall we say of the mechanics—the rhyme and the rhythm—of verse; or for the matter of that of the mechanics of prose? Let it be remembered that human audition is a process, not of "registration", but of consciousness; animated, therefore, by the impulse to grasp and to understand. To say that a certain relation of tones is easier to grasp is then only another way of saying that it is more intelligible. Some sort of physical fitness and physiological adjustment must be postulated for every vehicle of expression. To point to such conditions in relation to the life of a conscious being is then only more pressingly to raise the question of meaning.

And thus we may ask why the greater and more inspired music should not be conceived as a revelation of the divine. What I have tried to suggest is that in the interpretation of human experience "communion with the divine", in however slight a sense, offers the only alternative to a merely animal existence. Every genuine creation in the realm of experience is thus in some measure a revelation of the divine—every vision of things that transcends, or breaks in upon, the commonplace experience of fact, as a creation and not a copy. And if this idea is suggested oftener in connection with music, it is probably only because music by its very nature is less obviously exposed than some of the other arts (painting in particular) to the vulgar interpretation that art is an imitation of fact.

In any case I seem to share the adolescent experience—and still after many years in which just this experience has been for me a constantly interesting question. Not indeed that the hearing of great music brings with it necessarily the sense of transcendental insight; but only that this is what I seem to get on the rarer occasions, not of emotional exaltation, but rather when I am capable of the soberest and clearest attention and can grasp, not again all the significance that is there, but the presence of so much beyond that I do not grasp. At any rate, if the words in which we speak of "a divine revelation" stand for anything in human experience, for me it is this experience. Some time ago I heard unexpectedly—having accepted an invitation on the spur of the moment with no prevision of programme—an orchestral rendering of Bach's "Passacaglia", a new and glorious addition to my realm of experience. My mind had been full of a perplexing pedagogical and philosophical problem which called for practical solution in a day or two to come, namely, how to explain to a few hundred immature students the meaning of Plato's theory of transcendent and supersensible ideas—how, I mean, to make this conception of transcendence intelligible from the point of view of human experience. As I listen to Bach it became suddenly clear to me that if I could convey that experience they would see what Plato meant, and that without some such experience the theory of ideas could never be for them more than a form of words.

I will then for convenience put my general suggestion (or question) into the form of a thesis : the thesis, namely, that all human experience, so far as it is experience, and not mere words or the like, is an insight into reality—into an "other" and a "beyond" in reference to any mere "presentation"—and that all experience has thus a logical quality, or a quality of intelligence.

So much, then, for the remoter suggestions of the critical life. To many readers this may seem a strangely romantic version of critical intelligence ; quite fantastic also from the standpoint of fact and common sense. And there may be some to discover in these suggestions of the critical view of life the philosophy of that ingenious gentleman, Don Quixote de la Mancha. I will not venture to dispute the comparison ; it is sufficient to indicate that I have it in mind. But if this be taken to mean that "the critical view of life" is indifferent to fact and experience (words commonly conjoined), my reply will be that far as I have indeed strayed from the world of fact I have not wandered so far from the world of human experience. Fact is one thing, experience is quite another. The world of fact, as I have suggested in Chapter XI, is, whatever else it be, one creation of imagination among others ; and precisely what is meant by "fact" in our world of experience, is a nice question. As "point-event" items in the stream of thought it seems that facts have ever been the smallest part of human experience ; they are the smallest part of what comes and goes in the mind of any living man. But any resolute pursuit of the question of fact would call, not for another chapter, but for another volume.

§ 72

Meanwhile it is human experience that I have had in mind, and human nature. And the point of view of "humanism". For humanism as I conceive it the issue lies—the moral issue and no less the issue of truth and reality—between man as an animal and man as a human being. And for humanism human nature is not even human unless it be also divine. For animalism, *i.e.* for a view of life resolutely biological, truth and reality are restricted to animal fact, defined as "sensation". Sensations are the sole material of reality and test of truth. For humanism there is no aspect of human experience, no working of human imagination, which is not a revelation of reality—"nothing which has ever interested living men and women . . . no language they have spoken, no oracle beside which they have hushed their voices, no dream which has once been entertained by actual human minds, nothing about which they have expended time and zeal". And then the other words of Pater; "only be sure that it is a passion—that it does yield you the fruit of a quickened and multiplied consciousness". Be sure, that is to say, that your words and deeds are significant and not mere sound and gesture. Such I conceive to be the whole meaning of truth and of morality.

INDEX

Addams, Jane, 108.
Addison, 31.
Andersen, Hans, 263
Aristippus, 47.
Aristophanes, 192.
Aristotle, 3, 15, 22, 24, 25, 27, 30, 33, 61, 69, 113, 114, 117, 129, 242, 243.
Augustine, 192, 204.

Bach, 271
Balzac, 140.
Beecher, H. W., 134, 258.
Beethoven, 47, 122, 270.
Bentham, J., 26, 31.
Bergson, 115, 218, 227.
Berkeley, 151, 229, 230, 233, 242.
Blake, William, 255.
Bonaparte, Napoleon, 158, 204.
Bosanquet, Bernard, 66, 67, 77, 173.
Bradley, F. H., 68.
Burnet, Professor John, 238, 245, 250.
Butler, Bishop, 14, 16, 41, 53, 193, 195, 239.

Calvin (Calvinism), 173 (note).
Carlyle, 58 ff., 138, 158, 179, 191.
Cicero, 55.
Cleanthes, 251.
Conrad, Joseph, 244.
Croce, Benedetto, 3, 82 ff., 135, 137, *passim* in ch. xi, 153, 154, 225, 262.

Darwin, 76.
Daudet, Alphonse, 160, 162.
Descartes, 217, 268.
Dewey, John, 49, *passim* in ch. viii, 242, 250.
Dickens, 139, 202.
Dostoievsky, 23, 203, 225.
Doughty, Charles M., 221, 239.

Edison, 99, 132.
Eliot, George, 43, 174, 184 (note), 202, 204; " Mr. Gilfil's Love Story", 253 ff.
Enriques, F., 268.
Epicurus (Epicureans), 13, 31 ff., *passim* in ch. xiii, 202.

Freud (Freudians), 93, 247.
Friends (Quakers), 129.

Gaskell, Mrs., 80 (note), 202.
Gentile, Giovanni, 262.
Giorgione, 133.
Green, T. H., 25, 53, 67, 209 (note), 256.

Hammurabi, Code of, 13.
Helmholtz, 270.
Helvetius, 26.
Herbert, George, 266.
Hobbes, 124.
Homer, 204.
Hume, 262.

James, William, 84, 96, 113, 149, 174, 188, 257, 258.
Jesus Christ, 105, 149, 150, 204, 235, 252, 258.
Jevons, W. S., 119.
Jodl, F., 26 (note).
Jowett, B., 117.

Kant (Kantian), 10, 31, 32, 41, 49, 63, 82, 87, 128, 151, 160, 208, 210 ff., 241, 262, 263, 268.
Kingsley, Charles, 263.
Koran, The, 258.

Lang, Andrew, 206.
Lee, Vernon, 250.
Leibnitz, 268.
Leuba, J. H., 258.
Lévy-Bruhl, L., 203.

Lewes, G. H., 43.
Locke, 149.
Lucian, 192.
Lucretius, 54, 171, 188, 202.
Lumholtz, Carl, 219.

Macaulay, 175.
Macchiavelli (Macchiavellians), 109, 110.
Marett, R. R., 240.
Martineau, James, 64, 240.
Mather, Cotton, 57.
Maupassant, de, 140.
Merejkowsky, 225.
Meyer, Eduard, 158.
Michelangelo, 146.
Mill, James, 31.
Mill, John Stuart, 10, 31, 186, 230.
Milton, 163, 178 (note), 183, 205.
Mohammed, 158, 161.
Mormon, Book of, 258.

Nemirovitch-Dantschenko, 56.
Newton, 31, 242, 268.
Nisbet, J. F., 225.

Oliphant, Mrs., 202.

Paley, William, 79.
Pater, Walter, 99, 159, 179 ff., 222, 268, 273.
Pattison, Mark, 173.
Pepys, 46 (note).
Plato, 6, 22, 24, 30, 39, 67, 76, 114, 122, 123, 192, 194, 208, 245, 248, 251, 272.
Poe, 230.
Poincaré, H., 202.

Quixote, Don (Quixotism), 200, 272.

Royce, Josiah, 96, 131, 149, 150, 215, 241, 243, 263.
Russell, Bertrand, 116, 179 ff., 251, 257.

Santayana, George, 173, 189 ff., 256.
Schiller, F. C. S., 99.
Schopenhauer, 41.
Schweitzer, A., 149, 150.
Shaftesbury, 16, 193.
Shakespeare, 104, 204, 270.
Sinclair, May, 185.
Smith, Joseph, 158, 258.
Socrates, 3, 53, 114, 123, 133, 192, 228.
Sorel, Georges, 25, 26.
Spencer and Gillen, 206.
Spencer, Herbert, 58, 59, 61.
Spinoza, 15, 245, 256.
Stephen, J. F., 45, 58.
Stephen, Leslie, 11.
Stoics, 31, 178.
Strong, C. A., 134 (note).

Taylor, A. E., 234.
Taylor, Jeremy, 248.
Thackeray, 95, 139, 190, 202, 203.
Thales, 239.
Tolstoi, 23, 139, 155, 203.
Tourgenieff, 23, 140, 183, 203.
Trollope, Anthony, 79 (note), 202.
Tschaikowsky, 23.

Unamuno, Miguel de, 201 (note).

Vaihinger, H., 202.
Varisco, B., 262.
Villon, 139.
Virgil, 204.
Voltaire, 55.

White, William Hale, 257.
Wilde, Oscar, 132.
Wordsworth, 122.
Wundt, W., 10.

Xenophon, 192.

For Product Safety Concerns and Information please contact our EU
representative GPSR@taylorandfrancis.com
Taylor & Francis Verlag GmbH, Kaufingerstraße 24, 80331 München, Germany

www.ingramcontent.com/pod-product-compliance
Lightning Source LLC
Chambersburg PA
CBHW071809300426
44116CB00009B/1256